WOMEN and the ANCESTORS

WOMEN
and the
ANCESTORS

Black Carib Kinship and Ritual

VIRGINIA KERNS

UNIVERSITY OF ILLINOIS PRESS

Urbana   Chicago   London

© 1983 by the Board of Trustees of the University of Illinois
Manufactured in the United States of America

This book is printed on acid-free paper.

Library of Congress Cataloging in Publication Data

Kerns, Virginia, 1948–
    Women and the ancestors.

    Bibliography: p.
    Includes index.
    1. Black Carib Indians—Kinship.   2. Black
Carib Indians—Social life and customs.   3. Indians
of Central America—Belize—Kinship.   4. Indians
of Central America—Belize—Social life and customs.
5. Blacks—Belize—Social life and customs.
I. Title.
F1505.2.C3K47   305.4'896729   82–2601
ISBN O-252-00982-7   AACR2

To
Ruth and Liz
and other sisters who have helped

CONTENTS

LIST OF MAPS

LIST OF FIGURES

LIST OF TABLES

ILLUSTRATIONS

FOREWORD

This is a book about how mature Black Carib women manage the ceremonial component of their culture so as to preserve much of its unique flavor in spite of massive out-migration by males and younger women. Their special matriarchal status both reinforces and is enhanced by the solemnity of their activities, which are centered on the belief that Carib ancestors have influence over their descendants' life and death, health, and general fortune or "luck."

In order to do justice to this work, it is necessary that I speak both as a woman and as an ancestor (though one who is still very much alive!). Virginia Kerns herself uses this analogy when, speaking of "previous generations" in Caribbean research (1977), she places me among her elders—indeed, in the very generation about which she writes in this book. This results from my quarter-century of research and writing, much of which focused on women and the Black Caribs. Having achieved a certain maturity, it is therefore my obligation to help launch, nurture, and applaud those newcomers who advance the anthropological tradition. I do not take this task lightly, especially when it concerns those interested in the culture of the Black Caribs.

My first foray into the field, nicely given voice to by Kerns as both a "personal odyssey and an intellectual exercise," was in 1955, just after receiving my M.A. in anthropology from the University of Michigan. The Guatemalan highland Indian village in which I lived for two months offered a fascinating opportunity, and I might have returned there for my doctoral research but for the chance remark of a Guatemalan acquaintance who urged me to visit the north coast village of Livingston before I left the country. There I would find, I was told, an exotic African people who spoke a "mixture" of English, Spanish, and French, who sacrificed humans and animals in unspeakable rituals, and whose women did all the work while their men loafed in hammocks.

What budding anthropologist could resist such a temptation? I went, spent two days, and was conquered. The fact that the description was wrong in all respects neither surprised nor dismayed me. There was much else to write home about and eventually on which to write a dissertation. Ironically, in the early '50s, even though we knew hardly anything about the Caribbean and its peoples, it was not yet one of the preferred fieldwork sites — in my opinion because many anthropologists tended to think of its culture as being somehow impure, a hybrid of African-European origin, and not intrinsically interesting. The Herskovitses' cursory treatment of Trinidad and Haiti seemed more like "practice" exercises for Africa, which consumed their later years, than bona fide ethnographies. Bascom had similarly used Cuba as a stepping-stone to the African continent. Steward had not yet published the remarkable *People of Puerto Rico,* in which several of his best students broke new ground and set new styles and standards for anthropological research. Neither had we yet any of the seminal works of the two Caribbeanist Smiths — M. G. and R. T.

Therefore, in spite of the fact that at Michigan we were then being urged to become more problem-oriented, it was considered appropriate in my case that I plan a community study. It had not escaped me, even during my two-day stay, that women were more prominent in this village than they were in the highlands, and that undoubtedly had also figured in my decision, even though Women's Studies had not yet been born, and anthropologists generally tended to scorn what were then called "status of women" topics.

This book is dynamic evidence of how much our field has changed in twenty-five years. Kerns has herself traced and documented some of that herein. Our theoretical and analytical frameworks, and therefore the way in which we structure our problems and choose our questions, are new. Few can afford the luxury of being able to sally forth to study a community or a culture just because it is *there* and because little is known about it. But probably few would want to do that anyway. We now choose sites because they present characteristics which lend themselves to the unraveling of specific problems or to the understanding of particular juxtapositions of sociocultural elements.

The Caribbean today has become a standard — even popular — "culture area" and place to work. I can no longer keep up, on a personal basis, with all the students and senior scholars who have visited the Black Caribs. Some of this new interest in the area is the result of expediency — the Caribbean is close to home, relatively inexpensive, the people often speak English (either as a first or second language), and political tensions are neither so severe as to make prolonged residence unacceptable to the host country nor uncomfortable for the researcher. That is, the people and their governments are for the most part cooperative, even friendly to outsiders.

Still, I like to think that there are other, more profound reasons for us to study in the Caribbean area. There is a rich cultural heritage deriving from several ancestral roots that has developed into a variety of patterns which themselves are worthy of description, but which are also interesting to those curious about how traditions form, become established, and are maintained. The same can be said for the study of ethnicity, which finds many different expressions throughout the area.

In this century, many of the Caribbean population units, from villages to whole nations, have become dependent upon external labor migration, which has both eased population pressure and provided income from abroad to sustain those left behind. The ramifications of this phenomenon are legion; social scientists of various persuasions are only now delving into some of the subtler aspects of the process. What happens, for example, to the shape of the sociocultural tradition in the homeland? How do second-generation migrants relate to a society they know only through oral traditions, possibly books, and perhaps a vacation or two "at home," if they are lucky? At what point does wholesale adoption of a new culture give way to a re-examination of the old, and what are the differences between the responses of Caribbean twentieth-century migrants and those who flooded our cities from Europe in earlier times? What is the influence of the intellectual, probably trained at least in part in North America or Europe, who either returns or writes about the native land from abroad? There is a host of other questions about the effects of migration upon the receiving society and upon the continuing interrelations between the old and the new.

Anthropology seems more prepared and likely than other disciplines to broach such subjects. We have developed concepts such as networks, quasi-groups, matrifocality, cultural pluralism, ethnogenesis, symbolic transformations, cultural evolution and adaptation, and many others to help us interpret the data from both scientific and humanistic perspectives.

Women and the Ancestors is an important modern anthropological work on a Caribbean people. Although its writer decries definitions and descriptions based on what a work is *not,* I cannot help pointing out that this is not "just" ethnography, though it is brilliantly descriptive and attests to Kerns's observational powers and sensitivity to the field situation. Though no two observers "see" exactly the same things, much less produce identical ethnographies, repeated fieldwork in the same culture can and does serve as a checking and correcting mechanism, for those who become familiar with a set of "ways" will recognize whether the "feel" is right, or, as the Black Caribs say, whether a description is "true." In that sense, I find this work extremely impressive. Kerns has rightly pointed out that Taylor and I diverged in what we chose to write about, and probably also in terms of what we spent our time observing. So she has turned the kaleidoscope again to produce a new picture of Black Carib society, which certainly rings "true" to me, and which recombines the "pieces" which Taylor and I had earlier structured in different ways.

Thus, this work is not merely an extension of our previous knowledge of the Caribbean and of Black Carib society. It is a startling new synthesis which builds on past work, and at the same time brings fresh insight and modern sophisticated analytical tools to bear in interpreting a culture which, more than many, has survived the onslaughts of time and "modernization," including labor migration, for nearly 200 years.

As Kerns says, "For the past twenty-five years, household and family structure in the Afro-Caribbean have commonly been described as matrifocal." The significance of this, however, has not been fully appreciated or understood, except in terms of the periodic absence of men and the necessity to keep the domestic establishment intact in the face of ever-threatening poverty and pressures to acculturate and assimilate. As a woman who studied the role of women, I was certainly *aware* of the Carib woman's role in ritual affairs, but I was far more absorbed in more mundane daily household matters, and in the ways in which family members of both sexes interrelated at home and abroad. Neither did I focus precisely on age differences in the status and behavior of women, though my field notes and general familiarity with the culture again point to the accuracy of Kerns's perceptions.

It is significant that two changes in our own society over the last two decades have profoundly affected our sensibilities vis-à-vis field situations. It is not surprising that anthropologists, like everyone else, should increasingly turn their attention to the roles of women and to the aging process. After all, we are not now and never have been immune to the vagaries of intellectual and societal fashion, for as we should know better than others, we are creatures of our culture. The frontiers in our science lie not in exotica, but in more familiar things and events. What signals the new sophistication is the ability to perceive and to formulate responses to puzzles arising in our own and other contemporary cultures which are already fairly well known.

It is fitting that Kerns, as a representative member of a new generation of anthropologists, should have turned her attention to matters which are at once anthropologically and socially important. She has produced a study which is truly innovative — even a breakthrough in Black Carib studies — as well as one which should provide insights for feminists and gerontologists.

And it is also appropriate for me, as a senior member of our field who is both a Carib scholar and an applied anthropologist, to speed her on her way through the ritual of writing a foreword to her first book!

Nancie L. Gonzalez

ACKNOWLEDGMENTS

I thank the Wenner-Gren Foundation for Anthropological Research, the Fulbright-Hays Commission, and the National Institute of Mental Health for the funds that enabled me to spend a year and a half with the Black Carib. I am grateful as well to a number of people who helped me as I wrote this book. Norman E. Whitten, Jr., offered valuable guidance, both intellectual and practical, as I initially wrote and then revised the manuscript for publication. Nancie Gonzalez read various drafts of each chapter and gave me sound advice at every point. I owe them much for their unfailing encouragement and counsel. I also appreciate the comments of others who read the original or portions of the revised manuscript: Clark Cunningham, Robert Dirks, Joseph Palacio, David Plath, and John Stewart. Ruth Kerns provided bibliographic assistance as well as comfortable quarters in London while I did research at the British Library on the historical background. Debbie Rhea, Kasha Maxson, and Shirley Ahlgren patiently helped with final preparation of the manuscript, which Liz Dulany edited and ushered into production at the University of Illinois Press. My thanks also to Mary Rojas and Sheila Slaughter, who listened and encouraged.

Many men and women in Belize assisted me in the course of my research there, and always with such courtesy and good grace that I almost came to believe in national character. I especially want to thank Hon. David McKoy, Hon. C. B. Hyde, the staff of the National Library Service, and (again) Joseph Palacio, then Archaeological Commissioner of Belize. Richard Hadel, S.J., kindly shared his extensive knowledge of the Carib language, and the American Counsel provided information on emigration to the United States. It was through a fortuitous meeting with William V. Davidson in Belize that I made my initial contact with the Black Carib in 1973.

Fieldwork can be a lonely pursuit. That I experienced so few moments of loneliness is due to the many women and men who were not only teachers but friends. I remain deeply grateful for their always patient, often painstaking efforts to explain their language and their "ways" to me. Among them all my greatest debt is to Avelina and Nana, who taught me most about being Black Carib and female; and to Therese, who showed me her world as a child saw it.

Chapter 1

INTRODUCTION

When I met Black Carib women, one of the first questions that they routinely asked me was, "Do you have your mother?" And when I told them yes, that she was alive, they assured me, "Then everything is all right for you." But my reply to their next question never failed to cast doubt on that assertion. Did I have children, they inquired. When I said no, they could only shake their heads with sympathy and perhaps urge me to seek "medicine" that might remedy my affliction. "You are young now, but remember that someday you will be old," they would caution. Then, as if to reassure me, they might add, "Don't worry. There is still time."

I was to find that, no matter their age, women primarily identified themselves as mothers; and, young or old, they identified closely with their own mothers. Women (and men) consistently spoke of their mothers as supportive and strong figures, as protectors. They equated motherhood with strength. A fifty-two-year-old woman, speaking of the work that she had done throughout her life, summed up with these words: "I am like my mother. I am strong. I have borne fourteen children, six [still] living. And I still work."

Motherhood has more than this personal significance. Links with and between women as mothers provide the stable framework of social life. The mother-child bond — and particularly that between mothers and daughters — is the most enduring and strongly reciprocal of all relationships. Black Caribs allude to this in a proverbial saying that a man first mentioned to me. Musing about the differences between sons and daughters, he concluded ruefully: "A son gives [to people] outside, a daughter brings into the home" *(Wügüri iráhü íchiga baúgudin, hiñáru iráhü anüga múnadaun)*. As he and so many women were to explain this piece of conventional wisdom, daughters "remember" their mothers throughout life, show themselves more steadfast than sons in "helping" their mothers financially and otherwise. Nor do women forget their parents after death. Black Carib ritual centers on the remembrance of deceased lineal kin; and older women — mothers of the living and daughters of the dead — organize the requisite rituals, collect the funds needed to perform them, and take most prominent part in them. In doing so, they protect and represent their children, grandchildren, and other lineal kin to the ancestors.

Older women hold the central positions in kinship and ritual. Residential patterns, interhousehold exchange, and fosterage all attest to the special strength of bonds between female lineals. Women, as mothers and daughters, also form the stable core of households and extended families. These families are noncorporate groups, organized around and by older women, the mothers of grown children.[1] Men, as sons and spouses, link extended families; as wage laborers, they periodically leave their home communities to work in non-Carib locales. Women's lives have deeper roots in the intracultural domain of kinship and community, while men divide their lives between home and outer world.

Research Background

Although my specific interest lies in the system of kinship and ritual, and the central position of women within it, only four chapters (7-10) deal specifically with this topic. I discuss the historical background, contemporary setting, and various aspects of social life at some length — not in overzealous pursuit of holism but in order to clarify the nature of ties between female kin.

While the kinship system of the Black Carib has a strong female bias, this structural feature exists to varying degrees in some other bilateral kinship systems as well. Studies of several different ethnic groups and communities elsewhere in the world — for example, in Europe, the United States, and Southeast Asia — have shown that women maintain closer ties than men.[2] These closer ties manifest themselves variously: in residential patterns, mutual aid, frequent interaction, and strong emotional bonds between female kin. The degree of asymmetry varies, as does the emphasis on intergenerational or intragenerational ties, and the particular "social forms" associated with it (Yanagisako 1977: 208).

Studies in various areas of the Afro-Caribbean also offer evidence of a female bias in kinship, "an unconscious and a conscious bias towards the maternal." The emotional "primacy," the social "constancy" and solidarity of mother-child ties eclipse marital bonds, which tend to be brittle.[3] Ties between mothers and daughters are especially strong. Several ethnographers allude to groupings of female kin: "short matri-lines of mother, daughters, and daughters' children," "female solidarities," "linked generations of females," and "close-kin networks, centering on mother and daughters."[4] Others note that women help support their mothers and also turn to them in times of need, and that many older women foster daughters' children.[5] Ethnographers consistently emphasize the emotional aspects of these bonds, and their relation to household structure. Their cultural meaning, and structural expression outside households, remains obscure in nearly all accounts.[6]

For the past twenty-five years, household and family structure in the Afro-Caribbean have commonly been described as matrifocal.[7] (Elsewhere in the world, families and kin networks with a female bias have been labeled matrifocal, matricentric, matral, mother-centered, matrilateral, matri-centered, gynefocal, gynocentric, and woman-centered.)[8] The term "matrifocality" has been used very specifically, as R. T. Smith (1956: 223) originally employed it, to refer to domestic systems in which women, in their roles as mothers, are the focus of domestic relations and de facto heads of households. For the most part, however, it has functioned as a label, casually and impressionistically applied to "a certain kind of family built around females" (Slater 1977: 1). As Alexander (1977: 372) points out, the question posed is nearly always why "the father plays a less central role than the mother in the family." The usual explanation proposed directs attention to what men do not do: they do not support their families adequately; they are not regularly present in the home; they lack significant status in the larger society.[9] The implication is that men fail and women make do. They attain a central position in families by default, and sustain it by means of strong emotional ties with their children.

This conclusion inevitably follows, given a general script in social science that casts men and women in opposing roles and places them, respectively, at center stage and in the background. Their spheres, roles, and modes of action are polarized: public and domestic, instrumental and expressive, social and emotional — and the list goes on.[10] As Okley (1975: 73) observes, female conflict is very often dismissed as "jealousy" (emotional), while male conflict is analyzed in terms of status and competition (as a social phenomenon). The social takes analytical precedence over the emotional, as does the public over the domestic. Social process presumably works "from outside in," from the public world of men to the domestic world of women (Rosaldo 1980: 408). Whether or not women's roles and bonds between women are primary in the empirical sense, analytically they are secondary and derivative. Yanagisako (1977: 217) notes the marked tendency to treat close ties between female kin as "a psychologically mediated behavioral pattern." By most accounts, they have no apparent cultural meaning or social consequence outside family units, and simply emerge in "the absence of countervailing pressures such as status and property considerations."[11]

Gender-linked polarities, if preconceived, not only invite but assure a double standard in analysis. As Rosaldo (1980: 409) suggests, they "teach that women must be understood not in terms of relationship — with other women and with men — but of difference and apartness." In the case at hand, they also tend to conceal rather than to reveal either the cultural basis or social significance of women's bonds. Black Carib women are not lesser beings, confined to the home and subject to the authority of men. Indeed, her own research with the Black Carib has led Gonzalez (1970a: 231) to define matrifocality as "female role dominance in concrete social structures" — not only households and families, but also voluntary associations and communities.

Women's bonds and collective action by women have broad social significance and reveal an implicit cultural logic. The principle of female responsibility to lineal kin serves to structure relationships between Black Carib women, and also their ties with men. It underlies cooperation by female lineals as well as competition between female affines and sexual rivals. People commonly attribute conflict between women (and between men) to an emotional cause: jealousy, *emeídini*. But their jealousy and conflict usually spring from competition for a scarce resource (male support) in order to meet a cultural imperative (their responsibility for lineal kin, especially their children). Female consanguines cooperate to achieve the same end, as do the older women who take part in collective ritual.

Cultural expectations about men and women vary, and their means of fulfilling them also differ. The primary obligation of men, who work for the most part as manual laborers in non-Carib enterprise, is to support the women and children with whom they live (on a daily or occasional basis). The simplicity of stating this obligation contrasts sharply with the complexity of meeting it and, for women, of coping with the consequences of nonsupport. Because marital ties are brittle and employment unstable, even women with spouses cannot rely solely on them to provide for their own and their children's needs. Young women without spouses must seek employment in a labor market that allocates the lowest-paying menial work to females. Those who live in rural areas have little choice but to migrate to urban centers to look for paid work, leaving their children in the care of female kin. As for older women, few can find any employment since hiring policies give preference to young women. Under these conditions, which are discussed in detail in subsequent chapters, women routinely seek help from female kin, especially their mothers and daughters.

The economic aspects of these bonds have undeniable significance and deserve close scrutiny. But their strength does not derive solely from a quest for financial security during adulthood. From an early age, girls learn hard lessons about their responsibilities to lineal kin. A distinctive pattern of socialization, which instills in women a profound sense of identification as mothers and with their mothers, punishes female negligence swiftly and surely. Diverse cultural beliefs — about relations between parents and children, women and men, old and young — share an implicit premise: that women bear a comprehensive and lifelong duty to protect lineal kin, especially their children and other juniors. Men have responsibilities as well, but theirs are more specific, largely financial: an obligation to support spouses and lineal kin, primarily their dependent children (cf. Gonzalez 1969: 64).

The premise of female responsibility links specific beliefs, and belief with behavior toward kin. This premise is tacit, but tangibly shown in many of the actions that women take, both in daily life and in ritual. It is evidenced as well when they speak openly and critically about nearly any instance of female negligence. People do not clearly express this as a general principle. It finds explicit expression only in highly specific prescriptive statements: that a pregnant woman, for example, should observe certain dietary restrictions to protect her unborn child.

As the protectors of lineal kin, especially their children (both dependent and grown), women possess a dual strength, positive and negative. They have the capacity to create and sustain life or to harm or even destroy it through lack of restraint (especially in sexual conduct) and other forms of negligence. Women help each other to meet these responsibilities, to exercise this life-sustaining strength. But they also actively enforce a code of parental obligation and female restraint. According to this code, sexual misconduct by young women is regarded primarily as a form of maternal irresponsibility — not, as might be assumed, erroneously, a violation of male rights in women. In daily life and on ritual occasions, older women act together to sustain moral and social order. Its cornerstone is their lifelong responsibility to protect and care for their children and other lineal kin.

Maternal obligations are primary and absolute, while those to other lineals depend on a complex of factors: a woman's relative age, physical proximity, financial capacity, and position among next of kin. Responsibility for the care of other lineal relatives (living and dead) usually falls to the eldest proximate female among next of kin. Both collective rituals and episodes in daily life provide evidence of the complexity of obligations to lineal kin, and of the breadth and depth of female bonds. Women certainly use their relationships with each other to cope with a difficult set of life circumstances, but they do so in culturally patterned ways, in accordance with shared expectations about their responsibilities to children, to each other, and to other lineal kin. To explain their actions as merely a practical response to male "default" of some sort, or as largely a matter of emotional intimacy, reduces complexity to "a false simplicity" (Yanagisako 1977: 207). Worse, it obscures the cultural link between actions that women take in ritual and other domains.

Consider an older woman who is summoned to intervene in a dispute between her brother and another young man, before it erupts into physical violence; who organizes a ritual to cure a son's sickness, after other remedies have failed; who provides food and shelter for a daughter who has

left her spouse; who criticizes a young woman for neglecting certain pregnancy observances; who is advised by a neighbor to make private offerings
sought by an ancestor through dreams to her elderly father. Female responsibility for lineal kin, living and dead, links all of these episodes. It finds expression in a body of cultural beliefs about women as mothers and
daughters. It also receives wide recognition. Other people, by their words
and actions, acknowledge the woman's responsibility (and right) to protect
lineal kin: the man who runs to summon her to the site of the dispute; the
grown son and daughter who seek her help; the neighbor who encourages
her to comply with an ancestor's request for ritual attention. To overlook
this link imposes a degree of randomness on an ordered world.

Certain features of Black Carib life initially make it difficult to "see" its
order. Villages, as well as many households, have the appearance of an ongoing diaspora. People come and go so frequently that simply keeping track
of them can become a full-time task. And in this fluid social world many
boundaries overlap, while others are highly permeable.[12] (For example,
children readily change households within extended families, whose boundaries crosscut others'.) Perhaps the sharpest boundaries are local and cultural, drawn respectively among Black Carib communities and between
Black Caribs and non-Caribs.[13] People commonly visit other communities,
but rarely take up permanent residence in them. A man who leaves his
home to live with a woman from another town or village will always remain
a "stranger" in the eyes of the native-born there. These communities are not
linked by formal ties, political or economic. An entrenched localism shows
itself in stereotypes that the people of one community apply to those of
another, and in the importance of birthplace to social identity. Most men
gain their livelihood through wage work in external enterprises, working
for and with non-Caribs. They return home periodically, where they speak
a language and follow certain "ways" that distinguish them from "other
races," as they put it.

Wage labor, as well as several corporate groups — village council, school,
and church — provide the primary links between each village and the larger
non-Carib society. A few men hold most of the offices in these corporate
groups; and nearly all men work as wage laborers, at least on an occasional
basis. Women do not lead cloistered lives, confined to the home and
isolated from the world beyond. Most of them have worked for wages, and
villagers routinely elect one or two older women to the village council. Still,
men act as the primary mediators with the non-Carib world, which they
must meet on its own terms: filling offices and finding employment in non-
Carib organizations.

Women, in contrast, occupy the central positions in households, extended families, and ritual — in areas of the social system that, to borrow
Gonzalez's (1969: 10) words, "retain a degree of structural self-sufficiency."

They transmit a set of cultural beliefs and practices that hold great meaning in Black Carib communities but not in the non-Carib world beyond. In ritual, older women perpetuate the primary markers of Black Carib culture: music, dance, supernatural knowledge, and a system of morality and exchange that centers on obligations to lineal kin.[14] As spiritual mediators they protect their descendants by representing them in ritual. In daily life and in ritual, their actions serve to strengthen and sustain ties between lineal kin: male and female, young and old, living and dead.

The chapters that follow document these points. Chapter 2 deals with the historical antecedents of the Black Carib, from their origins as a maroon society on the island of St. Vincent. Evidence indicates that the Black Carib have always lived on the margins of colonial and national polities, dependent upon the market economy but never fully integrated into it or the larger society. From the beginning, men have acted as the primary mediators between Black Carib communities and the non-Carib world: first as chiefs and warriors, and as *compères* and allies of the French colonists and missionaries; later as wage laborers, soldiers, and local government officials. Women have never lived in complete isolation from the outer world. In the eighteenth century they marketed produce in the capital of St. Vincent, and in the nineteenth century some women worked for wages in Central America. The historical record offers little insight into other aspects of their lives, but it does document their long-standing part in ancestral ritual. An English visitor to a Black Carib settlement in Honduras in the first half of the nineteenth century noted that women "in great numbers" danced in the paramount ritual for the dead (Young 1847: 133).

Chapter 3 provides a summary description of Belize (formerly known as British Honduras), the national setting of this study, and identifies some salient differences in employment opportunities for men and women. Gonzalez (1969) has discussed the chronic insecurity of Black Carib men in the labor market. Young women face even greater obstacles when they search for paid work, and few older women can find any gainful employment at all. For women in the underdeveloped southern region of Belize, where employment opportunities are particularly scarce, these problems are acute. My fieldwork was based in one of the southern districts, the only area of the country where Black Caribs outnumber non-Caribs. As shown in Chapter 4, few village women in this district can locate even temporary work in the vicinity.

The three chapters (5–7) that follow address various aspects of social life, including property ownership and exchange, interpersonal conflict, age and gender, and the reckoning of kinship. Households and extended families, organized around and by women as mothers, are the subject of Chapter 8. Chapter 9 outlines the sequence of rituals for the dead, and the next chapter identifies the female organizers and workers, the sponsors, and the attendants. Rituals for the dead show a consistent pattern of organization. An older woman, nearly always one with grown children and usually the senior female among her lineal kin, collects the funds and recruits workers. Her extended family shoulders most of the expense, and other older women provide most of the labor. This pattern can be understood in terms of a complex of "predisposing" and "enabling" factors, cultural and material, that both incline and empower older women to take the central roles in rituals for the dead.

The final chapter, of course, contains conclusions. These include some "informed speculations" about the part women have played in perpetuating ritual and other conventions of kinship, and some comments about the relevance of my research findings to cross-cultural studies of female status. While the term "female status" is a conventional one, I use it here with a certain reluctance because its meaning, "measurement," and analytic value remain subjects of debate. Analytically, it implies that women as "a" uniform category have "a" social position, whether in a specific community or culture, or universally (cf. Bujra 1979: 17f.; Quinn 1977: 182). Black Carib women, however, vary in autonomy and power, both in specific domains and in relation to each other and to men. Their age, reproductive capacity and histories, relations of reciprocity and solidarity with other women, control of esoteric knowledge, positions of seniority among lineal kin, and other factors account for this variance in autonomy and power. Otherwise put, some women have more and some have less in Black Carib communities — and this despite the cultural emphasis on personal autonomy and a palpable dislike of hierarchy.

To the outsider, and perhaps to Black Caribs themselves, the power of older women is "masked" by the stated motive and goal of their collective action, and by the means they use to gain the compliance and cooperation of others. The stated motive is "duty" (not "rights"). Duty is culturally defined, primarily in terms of their own obligations and others' to lineal kin, living and dead. The stated goal is protection and care of others, or pursuit of common good (not personal gain). The usual means of gaining compliance are persuasion and the threat of supernatural harm from spirits, or, should that fail, shaming (not the threat or use of physical force). If their power is masked, it is nonetheless real. Any understanding of Black Carib kinship and ritual, and of women themselves, must take account of it. As Weiner (1976: 228f.) says,

> Whether women are publicly valued or privately secluded, whether they control politics, a range of economic commodities, or merely magic spells, they function within that society, not as objects but as individuals with some measure of control. We cannot begin to under-

stand either in evolutionary terms or in current and historical situations why and how women in so many cases have been relegated to secondary status until we *first* reckon with the power women do have, even if this power *appears* limited and seems outside the political field.

Ethnohistorical studies such as Jackson's (1971, 1979) of the Na-Khi and Wallace's (1971) of the Iroquois, among others, show how political incorporation by culturally alien states wrought fundamental change in indigenous kinship systems, eroding the traditional bases of female autonomy and power (also see Sanday 1981). As for the Black Carib, the historical record is riddled with gaps and missing links that make it difficult to assess changes in the social lives of women, past and present. Today, however, they do not categorically have a "secondary status" in their communities, where older women enforce the kin-based traditions that protect their interests and promote their well-being. When women enter the external labor market, in contrast, they do face categorical discrimination. It too has the sanction of tradition, but of a non-Carib one that lies beyond their control.

When I began my fieldwork with the Black Carib, I had some knowledge of their past, although it was largely confined to the events that led their ancestors from St. Vincent to Central America at the end of the eighteenth century. I saw little prospect of tracing continuity or change in any specific aspect of life, given their complex history of cultural (and biological) admixture. Two predecessors, Nancie Gonzalez and Douglas Taylor, had disagreed sharply about the feasibility of this task. Gonzalez limited inquiry to cultural elements that the Black Carib today visibly share with other peoples of the Afro-Caribbean. She described their culture as "a variant of Afroamerican" form, while Taylor stressed its Amerindian antecedents.[15] Despite their differing interpretations, I found no conflict in their data, but also very little overlap. Their substantive interests and analytical approaches were entirely different. Taylor (1951) had focused on language, ritual, and supernatural beliefs, attributing many traits to an ancient Amerindian source. Gonzalez (1969) had examined the effects of recurrent labor migration and economic insecurity on contemporary household structure. While Taylor explained much of the present in terms of a distant past, Gonzalez emphasized existing circumstance. In this respect, their works represent two major currents of ethnographic research in the Caribbean: one looking back in time for the cultural roots of contemporary life, the other concerned with the present social and economic conditions of that life.[16]

In this specific case, their ethnographies provide two accurate yet highly disparate accounts of the same people. In Belize I was to find several Black Caribs who were familiar with both books, and who described them as "true" in nearly all details. Yet there seemed to be no link between the two, no clear connection between the supernatural and the mundane—between belief and ritual on the one hand, social structure and economic conditions on the other. I hoped to bridge this gap by expanding the focus of my field research to the wider kinship system and ritual organization. Given his overriding interest in supernatural belief, in Taylor's account the major rites were dramas without personae. Gonzalez (1969: 49) had said little about ritual since households "were never autonomous in matters concerning the supernatural." I had no intention of venturing into the problematic areas of cultural antecedents at that point. As it happened, however, I later found some intriguing historical accounts of their ancestors in St. Vincent and Central America. I was struck by certain parallels between past and present, parallels between what I had seen in Belize and what I read in these old books and records. They raised as many questions as they answered. But they also suggested that women, to a greater degree than men, have held fast to many of the "ways" of their ancestors. This does not simply represent an inherent conservatism on their part. As I found during my time with them, these "ways" serve them well in the difficult circumstances that they face today—circumstances that differ from those of the past in degree rather than kind. For women, there is a close if not entirely seamless fit between pragmatism and cultural command (cf. MacCormack 1980: 4).

It is a truism that anthropological research is both personal odyssey and intellectual exercise. In retrospect, as in the course of fieldwork, I have found it difficult to separate these two elements. Certainly the questions that women and men asked me shaped those that I asked in return, and their answers offered insights with personal as well as academic meaning. The brief description of my fieldwork that follows clearly fails to capture anything of this subtle dialectic, but it does summarize the "facts" of what I did and did not see.

Fieldwork

Between 1973 and 1976, I spent eighteen months living in Belize. During my first visit I stayed for three months, traveling to all of the Black Carib settlements in the country and finally settling in one for about two months. I wanted to learn as much as I could in that brief time about women's work, especially wage labor. As circumstance had it, there was more to learn locally about kinship and ritual, which also fell into the category of women's work. During the course of my stay, I saw a number of rituals for the dead, and I grew increasingly curious about the prominence of older women in them.[17]

When I returned to Belize in 1974 for a year of fieldwork, I had decided to make one community the center of my research and to visit others periodically. To see social order in what initially seemed inchoate—a crowd of

people, most of them women, singing and dancing "for" their ancestors —
clearly required an understanding of kinship and community life. Excluding a town on the basis of its size and mixed populace, I chose a village in
Stann Creek District, where the Black Carib population is concentrated in
Belize. At that time it was the only village with a resident shaman. I also
made frequent trips to the other three Black Carib communities in the district, remaining for days or weeks at a time. Most of my visits were to attend death rites. Over a twelve-month period I took part in seven wakes,
twelve burials, eight novenas, ten ninth-night wakes, one end-of-mourning
ceremony, two Requiem Masses, and two *chugú*. I did not witness *dügü*, the
most elaborate of these rituals, during that year; and I saw only the final
portion of *amúidahani*, one of the minor rites. When I returned to Belize for
several months in 1976, I had the opportunity to take part in two *dügü*, one
in a village and the other in a town. I never encountered any resistance to
my presence at these rituals. In the three villages and the town where I witnessed them, people encouraged me not only to attend but to take part.
Women patiently taught me the dances but conceded that the songs were
"very hard." On more than one occasion, they insisted that I offer rum to
my ancestors: "You must do this for them. Speak to your grandmother."

During my year of fieldwork I also visited Black Caribs living and working in the other five districts of Belize and in Livingston and Puerto Bar-
rios, Guatemala. Except in one instance, I always traveled with women
who were going to visit their relatives in these communities. On these trips
I also interviewed non-Caribs: church officials and missionaries, employers
in various enterprises, and government officials. I spent about fourteen
weeks in these locales and the other Black Carib communities in the district
where my research was based.

The remainder of the time I spent in La Playa, a pseudonym for the
village that was my home. I lived in a small house and took my meals with
an adjacent household; a daughter of my host family lived with me. My
house was centrally located, near the school and church and with about a
dozen households in its immediate range. I observed daily life in this area,
but also spent time each day visiting other households in the community.

After I had lived in the village for several months, I took a household
census with the help of a paid assistant. Some people responded readily,
others with a certain reserve to my questions. ("Who lives in this house?"
"Do you keep a farm [*ichari*, cultivated plot]?" And so on.) Some time later,
one man confided to me that he had dreamed I was a Cuban *agent pro-
vocateur*, collecting information for dubious purpose. After all, I had written
it down. (According to rumors then current in Belize, Cuba planned to incite
revolution in the country, and an invasion by Guatemala was also imminent.
As for dreams, they are thought to reveal, often in oblique manner, hidden
truths about the world. In this case, the man assured me, he had "surely" mis-

understood the dream. But why had I recorded the information so carefully? I explained my purpose, as I had when I took the census, while his sister indignantly pulled him aside and told him not to bother this *"American* friend, *not* Cuban.") This was the only incident of the sort. But in order to allay any such suspicion in the other villages, I hired several former teachers, who had lived and taught in them, to collect census data for me there. I checked the accuracy of their figures with informants during my visits.

Several aspects of daily life remained beyond my direct view. My first effort to learn about fishing directly, by accompanying a fisherman, yielded a few interesting facts but so much suspicion that for months thereafter I confined myself to informants' accounts.[18] My understanding of male networks is partial and comes wholly from conversations with men. I have only secondhand knowledge of convivial drinking, which plays an important part in these networks.[19] On one occasion, when I was invited to share a drink, other women laughed scornfully at the offer and the implication that a lone female might accept it.

In this instance and others I listened to the women, and I spent most of my time in their company and their kinsmen's. Conversation often turned to the United States. Men inquired about wages and types of employment, and they spoke of their own work experiences in Belize and abroad. Women questioned me as closely about my birthplace and my family, whose small size elicited surprise and sympathy. ("Only *one* sister?") They gave lengthy accounts of their own relatives, including the names and whereabouts of a good number in the United States. ("When you go to California you will meet them.")[20]

One final point bears mention here. In this chapter and the following ones I use the name Black Carib rather than *Garífuna,* which has lately gained some currency in Belize. The women and men I knew referred to themselves both as Caribs and as *Garífuna,* depending on which language they were speaking. The term "Carib" may have a pejorative ring to non-Caribs in Belize, but it did not to the men and women of my acquaintance. "Black Carib" was almost never used locally, although it has been the standard designation in published ethnographic and historical works. In the course of later research at the British Library, I discovered that this name, if historical sources are correct, was of their ancestors' own choosing.

European explorers and colonists applied various terms, many of them unflattering, to the dark-skinned "renegades" who controlled much of St. Vincent in the eighteenth century. The British, during their initial encounters with them, betrayed confusion about this apparent anomaly: a population visibly of African descent but who spoke an Amerindian language and followed many of the customs of their "Red" neighbors. Unsure whether to believe their eyes or their ears, the British referred to them variously during the eighteenth century. They were the "free negroes of St. Vincent," "Black

Indians," "the Wild Negroes," and finally "Black Charibbs" (Anon. 1773). One colonial official claimed that the last name was self-chosen, "a title themselves arrogated" in their dealings with the British (Young 1795: 8). Whatever its source, it does capture the essence of their mixed biological and cultural heritage.

The historical record is silent about many aspects of their origins and history, but what it says about their past gives some perspective to the present. The following chapter traces the history of the Black Carib from their origins in St. Vincent through the century after their exile to Central America. It provides evidence of striking continuities in several areas of life: the selection of isolated, coastal areas for settlement; the differing orientation of women's and men's work, within and outside these communities; a religion that merged Roman Catholicism and various rituals for the dead. Regrettably, government correspondence and travelers' accounts offer only glimpses of the women. What they say reveals as much about the observers as the observed. Most confined comment to the marital status of women, their physical appearance, and their capacity for hard work. The first drew disapproval, particularly from clerics; the second, measured praise. The last inspired wonder.

Notes to Chapter 1

1. I use the term "older women" to refer to women between the ages of forty-five and seventy, who have passed the age of childbearing (see Bogue 1971: 5f.; Hafez 1978: 223). I knew of no Black Carib woman who had borne a child after the age of forty-four.

I have followed precedent in using the term "extended family" in this study. Previous works allude to "extended families" (Coelho 1955: 179; Gonzalez 1969: 85), and the term is used widely, although defined in different ways, in the literature on Afro-American family structure (e.g., see Laguerre 1978 and the other studies in Shimkin, Shimkin, and Frate 1978). Given their general composition, I initially thought of these groupings of kin as kindreds (cf. Davenport 1961). The term "kindred" has various meanings but usually refers to an ego-focused *category* or *network* of kin (e.g., Stack 1974: 30; Fox 1967: 167; Keesing 1966). In the case at hand, these groupings of kin have the structure of quasi-groups (see Mayer 1966, and Whitten and Wolfe 1973). Older women act as the focus and "activators" of nonresidential extended families.

2. See Bott (1957), Young and Willmott (1957), Willmott and Young (1960), Young (1954), Firth and Djamour (1956), Firth, Hubert, and Forge (1969), Mogey (1956), Geertz (1961), Potter (1977), Davis (1973), and Yanagisako (1977).

3. See Henriques (1968: 139) on the "maternal bias." Among many others, R. T. Smith (1956: 65, 142; 1973: 142), Greenfield (1966: 17),

Davenport (1961: 423), and Otterbein (1966: 119) mention the strength of the mother-child relationship, and the brittleness of marital bonds.

4. R. T. Smith (1971: 260; 1956: 152; 1960: 70), Mintz (1968: 315), and Wilson (1973: 134) refer to these groupings. M. G. Smith (1962b: 43) also mentions "strong materterine kinship bonds within a three generation range, especially between women." These groupings have not been the subject of study unless localized in so-called "grandmother households" (see Clarke 1966: 133f.; Henriques 1968: 113; Cohen 1956: 678; M. G. Smith 1962b: 243).

5. On fosterage by maternal grandmothers, see Clarke (1966: 151, 172f.), Otterbein (1966: 108), and M. G. Smith (1962b: 42, 62, 121, 158, 194). For mention of daughters' support, see Cohen (1971: 426), Davenport (1961: 444), Blake (1961: 66), Otterbein (1966: 119), M. G. Smith (1962a: 206), and R. T. Smith (1956: 167).

6. Herskovits and Herskovits (1947: 9), in an atypically explicit manner, do mention the position of older women in community life. Writing about a rural village in Trinidad, they remark that these women "figure importantly in the economic life in the community, they are paramount in matters having to do with family affairs, they are predominant in the religious life, and in any concern with magical control." Several other ethnographers also mention the prominence of older women in community groups, including burial societies, religious sodalities, social clubs, and other voluntary associations (e.g., R. Brana-Shute 1976: 166, 176; Horowitz 1967: 81f.)

7. For reviews of the literature on matrifocality, see Gonzalez (1970a), R. T. Smith (1973), and Slater (1977).

8. These terms are respectively used by Tanner (1974), Staples (1972), Firth and Djamour (1956), Young and Willmott (1957), Young (1954), Firth and Djamour (1956), Cumming and Schneider (1961), Poggie and Pelto (1969), and Yanagisako (1977), among others.

9. R. T. Smith (1956: 147, 223), for example, emphasizes the fact that lower-class Afro-Guyanese men *lack* significant occupational status or property of consequence; hence, they are "marginal to the complex of [domestic] relationships" (cf. Marks 1976: 64f.). Cohen (1956: 679f.), describing the "matripotestal" type of household (composed of a single woman, her unmarried children, and daughters' children) in Jamaica, writes that its "most striking characteristic . . . is the *absence* of a husband-father" (emphasis added). As Alexander (1977: 376) points out, "scholars analyze the matrifocal family as the result of what men, not women, feel and do." For specific studies, see the many references in Stuart (1979) and Comitas (1977 I: 417ff.).

10. For other gender-linked polarities, see MacCormack (1980). Social scientists often treat these as "objectively 'real' categories" rather than analytic constructs (Yanagisako 1977: 216). Some take them as psychobiological phenomena—as "natural" and presumably universal (e.g., Erikson 1964). Various feminist anthropologists view them as a matter of "cultural

interpretation, or cliché" (e.g., Rosaldo 1974: 30). As Yanagisako (1977: 217) notes about the instrumental/expressive construct, "Since we have no reliable criteria by which to uniformly distinguish instrumental from expressive tasks, the distinction appears more likely a reflection of fuzzy emic constructs that exist in the minds of the researchers." Rosaldo (1980) critiques the public/domestic dichotomy, and MacCormack (1980) the culture/nature construct. Implicitly, many of these gender-linked polarities amount to a distinction between "important" (male) and "less important" (female). They simplify the social roles and position of women, and relegate them to a secondary place in analysis.

11. As Yanagisako (1977: 221) suggests, "The tendency of previous researchers to ignore the normative basis of female centrality [in bilateral kin networks] may be a consequence of the manner in which normative expectations regarding female kin relationships are expressed and communicated." These expectations are rarely stated in clear, prescriptive terms. Instead, they are "embedded in people's notions . . . about what females do 'naturally' . . . . Yet however obscured these prescriptions may be, they carry powerful normative sanctions." I find it significant that Mogey (1956: 54f.) and Young and Willmott (1957: 33) mention that strong ties between mothers and daughters were expected and recognized, but not clearly "explained" by the subjects of their studies. As Mogey (1956: 54) puts it, "The people express themselves very vaguely [on this matter]."

12. The shifting and diverse composition of households has posed a primary analytical problem in Caribbean anthropology. Relations between residents have been described as "individualistic," as have ties with kith and kin outside households (see Mintz 1966: 932f.; Rodman 1971: 159ff.). Mintz (1966: 939) suggests that "the distinctive quality of Caribbean rural social structure may be its heavy emphasis on individual dyadic ties, as opposed to membership in groups having some corporate or institutional kin basis" (cf. Whitten and Szwed 1970: 45).

13. Men and women do occasionally mate with non-Caribs, however, and historical evidence indicates that this was not uncommon in the past (Kerns, in press).

14. Cf. Herskovits and Herskovits (1947: 8f.), who write that women in "Negro societies of the New World [are] . . . the principal exponents of the culture." They act as "the essential bearers of tradition, the primary agents in maintaining conventionally accepted modes of behavior."

15. See Solien (1959b: 307), Gonzalez (1965), and Taylor (1965a). Coelho (1955), a student of Herskovits, emphasized the African heritage of the Black Carib.

16. Studies of the former type have stressed the African heritage (Herskovits 1937, 1958), or the experience of plantation slavery (e.g., Matthews 1971) in explaining various features of contemporary life.

17. At the time, I was struck by their prominence because it seemed highly unusual. Several recent studies of women's roles in ritual have helped to dispel this notion and fill a gap in the anthropological literature (see Weiner 1976; Hoch-Smith and Spring 1978).

18. The suspicion was unanticipated because I had previously depended on men for transportation by boat to and from the village, without critical comment. Of course, in those instances my destination, purpose, and need were clear; in the case of fishing they were not. Later I discovered that a few women fished, and I accompanied one of them.

19. I do not think that my understanding of kinship suffered greatly on this account. Wilson (1973: 140, 145) summarizes the prevailing view in Caribbean ethnography when he describes men as "peripheral within the kinship sphere," and notes "the importance of kinship to females and the relative unimportance of it to males" (cf. Alexander 1977). On convivial drinking and male networks, see G. Brana-Shute (1976, 1979), Dirks (1972), and Wilson (1971).

20. I have used standard English rather than Belizean Creole for most quotations, and have followed Hadel's (1975) orthographic system for Carib words and phrases. Nearly all of the statements quoted were spontaneous ones, offered by men and women in the course of conversation and in the presence of others. I found that comments and observations made in this context were usually more reliable, and often more revealing, than responses to questions I asked privately, in informal interviews.

Chapter **2**

ANTECEDENTS

Black Carib history has two distinct parts and settings, but its origins are obscure. According to some accounts, it begins in the seventeenth century with the shipwreck of a European vessel on a voyage from West Africa to the West Indies. The ship carried the human cargo that filled so many holds during that era, but the slaves, who were intended for sale at Barbados, never reached that destination. At some point the vessel was blown off course or otherwise lost its way. It sank near St. Vincent, or perhaps Bequia, a small island several miles to the south; the records are contradictory on this point. At any rate, some of the Africans survived.[1]

The nature of the original meeting between these Africans and the Carib Indians, who controlled St. Vincent, is disputed. According to certain records from the following century, the Caribs welcomed the Africans; according to other sources, the Indians immediately enslaved them. Neither of these is strictly in keeping with their reputed practice of putting all captured men to death and keeping alien women as wives. Apparently the Caribs dispensed with custom in this instance. A European visitor to their island later in the century, in 1672, reported the presence of 600 black bowmen among 900 Carib warriors (Great Britain 1889: 392).

Whether the Indians acted as hosts or masters, the Africans quickly adopted the Caribs' language and many of their cultural practices. But the relationship between African and Indian was short-lived. By the end of the seventeenth century, the Reds and Blacks comprised separate groups. The story of their breach has several versions, all recorded by Europeans long after the fact. What is clear about this period is that the Africans survived and multiplied, and that having gained their liberty from their European captors first, and later perhaps from the Red Caribs as well, they were loath to surrender any fraction of it thereafter. A colonial official, writing at the end of the following century to his superiors in London, referred to the "ferocity" of the rapidly expanding Black Carib population. He reminded them that these unwilling subjects of the British Crown had long been "ac-

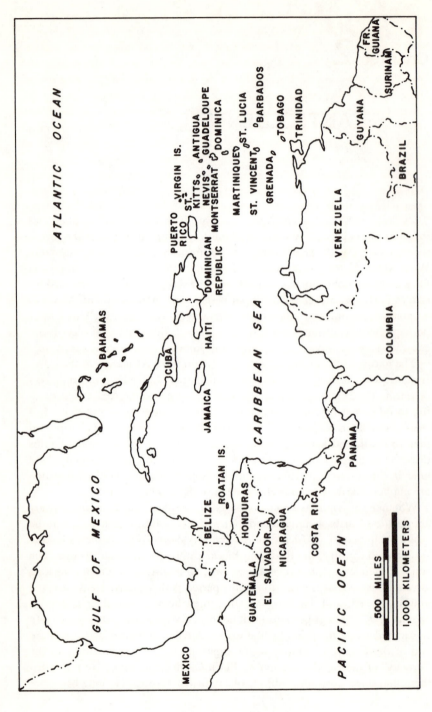

Map 1. Central America and the Caribbean

customed to consider themselves as perfectly independent" (Anon. 1773: 30; cf. Young 1795: 25).

The running battle between the British, who claimed hegemony, and the Black Carib, who claimed autonomy, was to end decisively with armed conflict in 1795 and the final defeat of the Black Carib in 1796. The second part of their story begins at this point, when the British transported the Black Carib en masse to the island of Roatán in the western Caribbean (see Map 1). From that island they rapidly spread to the Central American coast. By the early nineteenth century they had established settlements all along a narrow strip of shoreline, from Honduras to Belize.

Their descendants live there to this day. Asked where they came from, how they came to live there, the people tell a starkly simple story — of ancestors who left their homeland, *Yurúmai* (St. Vincent), "long ago," seeking a new home. A peculiar collective amnesia has erased most memory of their past, of the harsh events that led to their ancestors' exile from St. Vincent.

The Anglo–Black Carib conflict in St. Vincent is no more than a footnote in British colonial history, but an abundantly detailed one. Events that the Black Carib soon forgot were assiduously recorded for posterity by the British. The particular details of their conflict are unique, but the pattern is not. The early history of the West Indies is one of conquest and displacement, with Spanish against English, English against French, civil authorities against freebooters, Europeans against Indians, maroons against planters. In this veritable war of all against all, the Black Carib were sometimes victors, sometimes pawns. Ultimately they joined a long line of refugees left in the wake of the European drive for hegemony in the Caribbean and the rest of the New World. These refugees included their Arawak and Carib forebears, who were driven to the point of extinction before the Black Carib felt the full brunt of European expansionism.

Origins

When Columbus and his men sailed into the clear waters of the Caribbean Sea at the end of the fifteenth century, they found two groups of Indians, the Arawak and the Carib, living on most of the islands. The Arawak had settled on many of them before 1000 A.D., but they enjoyed brief sovereignty. Carib Indians, also from the South American mainland, followed close on their heels, dislodging the Arawak from smaller islands such as Dominica, Grenada, and St. Vincent. By their own tradition, recorded by the French missionary Father Breton in the seventeenth century, their Carib ancestors "exterminated all the [male Arawak] inhabitants, but kept the women, who have retained something of their [own] language."[2] In fact, the reverse was true when Father Breton wrote. It was the Carib men who "retained something," certain words from the language of their Cariban-speaking forefathers from South America. By the seventeenth century both men and women spoke a language with a "typically Arawak" structure, presumably acquired from the captive women. It was not mutually intelligible with the language of their Arawak neighbors.[3]

The earliest Europeans who entered the New World found the Arawak settled on the larger West Indian islands: in the south, Trinidad; in the north, Hispaniola, Cuba, Jamaica, Puerto Rico, and the Bahamas. According to the records of early Roman Catholic missionaries and archaeological evidence as well, the Arawak were an agricultural people who lived in permanent communities of some size. Arawak social organization was relatively complex and ranked, with chiefs who inherited office through matrilineal lines.[4] Their concentrated settlements, which Caribs raided at will for captives, made them equally vulnerable to the depredations of the Spanish. In the early sixteenth century, many Arawaks worked as forced labor in mines, where they perished from overwork, starvation, and disease. The friar Bartolomé de las Casas (1656, 1971) found their condition so pitiful that he was moved to advise the use of African labor instead (a proposal that he later regretted). When the Spanish system of forced labor finally ended in 1550, mere remnants remained of the Arawak population in the West Indies. Their demise and the need for plentiful labor had set in motion the importation of slave labor from Africa. This would culminate in the next century in the spectacular fluorescence of the sugar economy in Barbados and the quiet growth of a renegade population, the Black Carib, in nearby St. Vincent.

St. Vincent remained out of the mainstream of European conquest and settlement until the eighteenth century. As early as 1512 the king of Spain had authorized his subjects to enslave Caribs from that island and others of the Lesser Antilles. But they left St. Vincent largely unmolested in the sixteenth century and thereafter. The island lacked the precious metals they sought. Its dense forests and mountainous terrain made slaving difficult, as did the Carib settlement pattern of dispersed villages. Caribs were not to be so easily dispossessed of their territory or their liberty as the Arawak had been. Unlike the Arawak, whom Columbus commended in his journal as "gentle" and "unwarlike," the Carib had a reputation as a fierce and freedom-loving people. The few Caribs whom the Spanish took as slaves they considered "good for a lot of use, but hard to guard because likely to escape in canoes."[5]

In the seventeenth century, when the shipwrecked Africans reached St. Vincent, the Carib still held a firm grip on it, notwithstanding the formal claims of the French and English. In 1627, King Charles I had granted the various islands of "the Caribbees," including St. Vincent, to the Earl of Carlisle for the modest annual rent of £100 (Great Britain 1860: 85). But settlement of the islands, and particularly mountainous St. Vincent, was another matter. The French priest Père Labat, who visited St. Vincent in 1700, described it as "the headquarters of the Caribs" and noted that the island's only European residents were a fellow French priest and a companion of his (Labat 1970: 137). He found a few Caribs on Grenada and more on Dominica, but their numbers did not compare with those in St. Vincent. The Carib had vanished entirely from many other islands, which were then populated entirely by Europeans and Africans. Their aboriginal inhabitants had fled or had been exterminated by European settlers.

Unlike the Arawak, the Carib were an egalitarian people without hereditary chiefs. Père Labat (1970: 104) considered that there were "no people in the world so jealous of their liberty, or who resent more the smallest check on their freedom" as these Indians. By his account, they looked askance at the hierarchical relations of the Europeans: "They laugh at us for obeying and respecting our rulers, and say that we must be their slaves, and that since we allow them to give us orders we must also be cowards."

According to Père Labat and Father Breton, the Carib lived in villages ranging in size from thirty to a hundred people, each a matrilocal extended family. Every village consisted of several thatched structures: a men's house (called a *carbet* by the French), smaller houses for women and children, and storage platforms (see Illus. 1). Père Labat (1970: 87f.) described a *carbet* as "about sixty feet long by twenty-five feet wide and built something like a barn," with a floor "of beaten earth." Women's houses were about half this size and divided into two parts, one section serving as the kitchen and the other as a sleeping place for a woman and her children. Men and adolescent boys spent much of the day, and perhaps nights, in the *carbet*, and they took their meals there, apart from the women.[6]

Every Carib village was independent and largely self-sufficient. Women, related to each other by close blood ties, formed the stable core of each group. Their numbers were augmented by captive women, taken in raids on unallied villages. Père Labat (1970: 103) wrote that "when they capture women, no matter what race they may be, they always treat them kindly, and if they marry them regard them as belonging to their nation." Captive children were treated "as if they were their own." Male enemies were killed.[7]

Most men left their natal villages at marriage, replaced by others from allied groups who married in. A few men had several wives: in some cases sisters, in others women from other communities whom they visited in turn. Village headmen, "masters" or "captains" as the French referred to them, practiced virilocal residence, bringing some of their wives to live in their villages. Other wives of headmen remained in their own communities, sometimes on other islands.[8] By all accounts, headmen had very little authority. If the "master" were to issue any orders, Père Labat (1970: 104) remarked, he would receive "a very dry answer." Leadership appears to have been task-specific and achieved.[9]

Villages created and maintained alliances with each other through patrilateral cross-cousin marriage. Allied groups exchanged men, traded with each other, and joined in raids on unallied communities. Alliance apparently had a territorial dimension, since local groups tended to ally themselves with neighbors, on either the leeward or windward side of the island. Each side had its own "war chief," whose authority was limited to raiding expeditions. When men gathered to plan a raid, old women and the war chief addressed them, urging them to seek revenge for past wrongs committed by the enemy. Several women usually accompanied men on their expeditions, to prepare food and to paint them with *urucú* (a dye obtained from the annatto tree, *Bixa orellana*). In some cases, they traveled to distant islands to raid their enemies or to trade with allies. Caribs also traded with Europeans, exchanging food and baskets for tools, cloth, and rum.[10]

Land seems to have been owned in common by each community. Women in every village were responsible for cultivating, harvesting, and preparing food. They went to their gardens daily, and every evening a group of women fetched firewood. Many Europeans expressed dismay at the sight of women working together in the fields and carrying heavy loads, although their compatriots in other islands did not hesitate to set enslaved African women to the same tasks. The Carib women's lot in life was thus considered equivalent to a slave's. They "sustained every species of drudgery: they ground the maize, prepared the cassavi [manioc], gathered in the cotton and wove the hamack."[11] Their husbands and sons hunted, fished, conducted trading expeditions, and raided enemies, who eventually included the Black Carib.

Extant records make little mention of the Black Carib until the eighteenth century, when they began to command attention from occasional European visitors to St. Vincent. By 1700 the Black Carib were territorially and politically separate from the Red Carib. According to one account, the Reds had asked the governor of Martinique for protection against the Blacks, and he had complied by drawing a line to separate the island into two parts, the leeward side going to the Red Carib and the windward to the Black Carib (Young 1795: 9f.). In another account, a more plausible one, the Blacks simply forced the Reds out (Labat 1970: 137). However it happened, the island's traditional division into leeward and windward halves, separate and antagonistic, had gained an additional, racial distinction by the early eighteenth century.

The Red Carib quickly discovered that territorial separation from the Blacks provided little protection from them. When a certain M. de Bucq convinced the governor of Martinique in 1719 to send forces to St. Vin-

cent, with the idea of seizing the Black Caribs' land for a plantation and using them for slave labor, the Red Carib agreed to support the effort against
their aggressive neighbors. The governor sent several hundred men to St.
Vincent, but the expedition ended in defeat. The Red Carib reneged and
gave the French troops no support. The Black Carib defeated them, "and
thus ended this truly buccaneer enterprize, which was hushed up, and for
the time buried in oblivion."[12]

Hushed up it may have been in European quarters, but the Black Carib
certainly did not forget this effort to enslave them. When an English party
landed on the island four years later, in 1723, they reported parlaying with
separate leaders, "the Negro Chief" and "the Indian General," who respectively represented 500 armed Black Carib and 100 armed Red Carib
men. The English asked their permission to settle St. Vincent, which both
Britain and France claimed; but both chiefs refused to grant them entry.
Having been warned by the French that the British would try to enslave
them, they had "resolved never to put it in their Power, or any European,
to hurt 'em" (Uring 1727: 109). The Reds, unlike the Blacks, were not to
maintain this resolve.

Judging from records of the period, the Black Carib population grew
rapidly during the eighteenth century. Natural increase was augmented by
the steady influx of fugitive slaves from the nearby sugar islands of Guadeloupe, Barbados, and Martinique (Anon. 1773: 26f.; Labat 1970: 137).
Aside from these voluntary recruits, Black Caribs counted captive Red
Carib women among their number. During his visit to St. Vincent, Père
Labat (1970: 137) learned that "it is not possible for the [Red] Caribs to res-
cue them, as the negroes, who are a much braver race and in far superior
numbers, only laugh at them, ill-treat them, and possibly will one day
make them work as their slaves." Over the next fifty years, Red Caribs
gradually left St. Vincent and their troublesome neighbors. Some had relo-
cated on the sparsely populated island of Tobago before mid-century (Davidson 1787: 8; Young 1801: 292). By 1763 the Black Carib numbered
2,000 and the Red Carib only "one hundred families" (Edwards 1794
I: 400). The Reds no longer posed any threat to Europeans, who described
as "innocent and timid" the very Indians they had once considered a fierce
and formidable enemy (Anon. 1773: 6).

In the same year, 1763, the British and French formally resolved their
long-standing dispute over St. Vincent and several other West Indian islands. By the Treaty of Paris, St. Vincent assumed the status of a British
possession. But despite its formal political status, the French retained dominance, both in influence and numbers, in St. Vincent. Since the early years
of the century, the Red Caribs had allowed a few French at a time to settle
on the leeward side of the island, reportedly with the hope that these settlers
would act as a buffer against the Black Carib. Over the years, the French

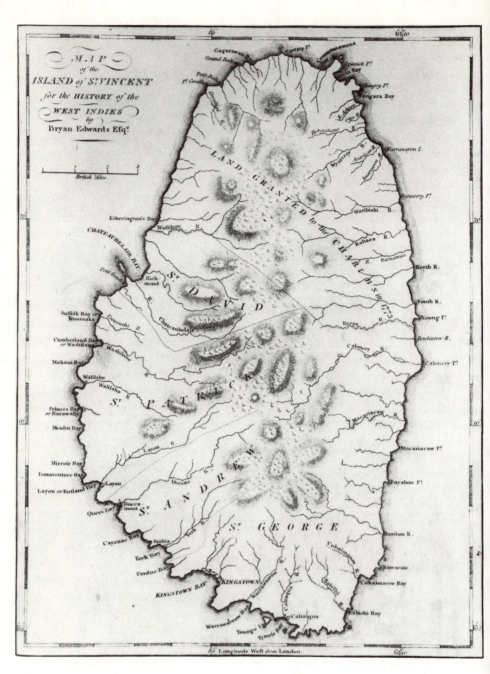

Map 2. St. Vincent, 1794

tried to extend their coffee and cocoa plantations unobtrusively while simultaneously cultivating the friendship of both the Black and Red Carib — by hosting them at "occasional hospitalities" on Martinique, by keeping them supplied with firearms, and by sending Roman Catholic missionaries among them "to dazzle them with ceremonies and entertain them with festivals" (Young 1795: 17f.). By 1763, the French settlers and their slaves outnumbered the combined population of Reds and Blacks but were wholly confined to the leeward side of the island. The Black Caribs were apparently not so easily wooed by French favors as the Reds. They accepted the French as allies and *compères* but remained vigilant against any encroachment of their territory. In 1752, when one M. Perain built a house on lands purchased from the Reds, on the border of their territory, the Blacks burned the house and plantation. This object lesson put a temporary halt to attempts to settle near them (Young 1795: 15).

The British assumed formal control of St. Vincent in November, 1763, and they made immediate plans to colonize the island, plans that centered on selling the land to British colonists and using the profits for "national purposes." Much to the dismay of the officials appointed to carry out this scheme, the Black Carib showed no intention of surrendering their land, even though the British repeatedly promised them "good, proper, and sufficient lands" and some money in recompense (Anon. 1773: 35). Indeed, the Black Carib refused to acknowledge the sovereignty of King George, and they actively opposed a British effort to build a road through their territory. In a memorial from the Council and Assembly of St. Vincent "on the Subject of the Charibbs in that Island," the settlers complained resentfully that the Black Carib "effect an independent neutrality, as well as an exemption from all civil jurisdiction or subordination whatsoever." They wrote that the Crown must decide either that it lacked any sovereignty over the Black Carib and their land — the Black Caribs' own view; or, alternatively, it must consider them "a nest of most dangerous and insolent rebels," and deal with them accordingly (Anon. 1773: 49f.).

Although accounts of the period stress that British honor was at stake, the fundamental issue was clearly that the Black Carib held a large portion of the island's cultivable land, and reputedly the best land at that (see Map 2). In reports sent to London this land was described as "the most extensive and finest part" of St. Vincent, and as "by far the more extensive, more level, and a finer country than the part already disposed of" (the land on the leeward side having been previously sold). For every correspondent who simply remarked that "the soil is perhaps the best in the world," another recommended it in more extravagant terms. One colonial official, who had met with the Black Carib in their territory, ruefully ended his report, "and for a time, I hope it will be short, I quitted that fine cream piece of this island, with a regret I cannot express to you" (Anon. 1773: 5, 7f., 24).

What especially rankled was that the Black Carib not only claimed this vast tract of fertile land but did not farm it intensively. Accustomed to intensive, fixed-plot agriculture, the British mistook swidden horticulture, with its extensive forest-fallow system, for near disuse. Observing that women did most of the field labor, they condemned the "indolent" men and commiserated with their wives. "No slavery can be conceived more wretched than that of the women," wrote one colonist (Davidson 1787: 11f.).

From the British perspective, Black Carib men showed no interest in the land and the women made scant use of it. No doubt their refusal to part with any portion of their territory seemed both unreasonable and perverse, blocking as it did the development of sugar plantations by eager British capitalists. Moreover, as the Council and Assembly complained bitterly to the king, the land provided neither taxes nor other revenue. Aside from such offenses as harboring runaway slaves and carrying on contraband trade with Martinique, the colonists wrote querulously, the Black Carib prevented "the cultivation of that valuable and extensive tract of land, which while in their hands lies almost entirely uncultivated" (Anon. 1773: 27).

This state of affairs, with British enterprise at loggerheads with Black Carib autonomy, persisted for more than three decades. They were years of treaties made and broken, of uneasy peace interrupted by British expeditions and Black Carib retaliation.[13] The fact that no chief could speak for all Black Caribs hampered negotiations with the British, who condemned them for being "subject to no law or discipline, and scarcely acknowledging subordination to any chief" (Anon. 1773: 6). The colonists, of course, equated society with hierarchy. Their social thought was summed up in Alexander Pope's *Essay on Man:* "Order is Heav'n's first law; and this confest / Some are and must be greater than the rest." The Black Carib vigorously rejected this tenet, both among themselves and in relation to the British colonists and king.

The colonists slowly realized that they would never be able to take peaceful possession of the coveted land. As for peaceably integrating these Black Carib "anarchists" into their rigid colonial hierarchy of rulers and ruled, that too seemed a vain hope. Indeed, one official concluded that only "a sufficient force to terrify them into obedience" would prove at all effective (Anon. 1773: 39).

But a sufficient force was a long time coming. The British government, occupied during these years with insurgents in their North American colonies, devoted little attention to St. Vincent. The settlers themselves lacked the weaponry and manpower necessary for any decisive victory; and on their side, the Black Carib had the advantage of rugged terrain and dense forest well suited to their guerrilla tactics. During the final decades of the eighteenth century, relations between the Black Carib and the colonists swung between peace by stalemate and open hostility. The Black Carib helped the French capture St. Vincent in 1786, but France returned the island to Britain in 1789. The Anglo-Black relationship of uneasy peace and mutual mistrust continued for a few more years, as the colonists gave increasingly serious thought to the idea of deporting the "insolent rebels."[14]

In the end, the Black Carib acted as unwitting accomplices in their own undoing. Some planters had questioned whether their land was not too isolated for profitable cultivation. They foresaw problems in shipping sugar from the island's windward side, given the strong surf and the difficulty that European vessels had in negotiating it. In the last decade or so of the century, Black Caribs solved the planters' problem. They agreed to carry cargo in their dugout canoes between shore and ship, for daily wages of "a Spanish dollar" each (Young 1795: 106). By hiring out, they probably added further fuel to the British desire to see the entire island under sugar cultivation.

The British encouraged all of the Black Caribs' entrepreneurial efforts, both in the labor market and in the marketplace, where they sold surplus produce and cash crops. Perhaps the colonists realized that the Black Carib might eventually, and unsuspectingly, integrate themselves into colonial society through such enterprise. "The Charaibbs thus begin to taste of money," wrote one official in the late eighteenth century. A man of obvious acumen, he observed: "Money civilizes in the first instance as it corrupts in the last; the savage labouring for himself, soon ceases to be a savage; the slave to money becomes a subject to government, and he becomes a useful subject" (Young 1801: 299f.).

But the Black Carib were not yet useful subjects when, with the aid of their old allies, the French, they finally staged a full-scale revolt in 1795. When the Black Carib chief Chatoyer fell during battle, the British allegedly found in his pocket a proclamation filled with the lofty rhetoric of the French Revolution. Dated "the 12th day of March and the 1st year of our Liberty," it entreated Chatoyer's fellow "citizens and brothers" to unite (Young 1795: 117).

In 1796, when the conflict finally ended, the British victors proceeded with the long-contemplated deportation of the Black Carib. Five thousand were transported to Roatán, an island off the coast of Honduras, and left there with a supply ship filled with provisions and agricultural implements. According to one account, the ship sank in the harbor, and the supplies with it (Roberts 1827: 273). When the Spanish visited from mainland Honduras soon after that, they persuaded most of the Black Carib to abandon the island for the coast. The few who remained at Roatán formed the first permanent settlement on the island (see Davidson 1974: 65ff.).

So ended one of the final chapters in the displacement of non-plantation economies, begun over a century earlier elsewhere in the Caribbean. As sugar became the leading crop in Jamaica and other islands, large plantations with African slaves had replaced small farms and white indentured labor. Hundreds of poor whites, pushed out during the latter half of the seventeenth century, took to the sea as buccaneers (see Floyd 1967; Exquemelin 1951). St. Vincent followed a similar pattern except that it was Black Caribs, rather than poor whites, who were dispossessed of their land.

A few Red Caribs remained in St. Vincent and in neighboring Dominica, as they do to this day; but a visitor in the 1830s described them as "a mere remnant of their race." More to the point, he characterized the land they inhabited in the mountains as "too remote and inaccessible to excite the envy or even the attention of the more civilized inhabitants" (Anon. 1834: 316). The same could have been said about the coastal settlements of the Black Carib in Central America.

The People: Before and After

A life begun on the island of St. Vincent in the eastern Caribbean ended abruptly with armed conflict and the forced transport of the Black Carib to an island in the western Caribbean. They had come full circle. Their African ancestors had been forcibly taken by Europeans from their homeland, across a sea to an alien island. So the descendants found themselves unceremoniously abandoned, like so many Robinson Crusoes, on an unknown island nearly 2,000 miles across open sea from St. Vincent.

With the loss of their long-coveted land, that "fine cream piece" of St. Vincent, Black Caribs disappear from the pages of West Indian history. For a brief time they were left in peace and obscurity. Little is known about the early years of their settlement in Central America. But within thirty years of their arrival, they had again engaged the attention of Europeans: in this case travelers, who mentioned the curious "Kharibees" or "Caribs" in published accounts of their journeys.

These nineteenth-century accounts, and the welter of government correspondence about the Black Carib in St. Vincent, offer a glimpse of their way of life before and after exile. They suggest a striking degree of continuity in men's and women's work: men's directed largely toward the outer, non-Carib world, women's oriented toward the inner world of community and kin. Regrettably, many other aspects of social life are ill defined or entirely missing from historical accounts, particularly those of the eighteenth century. In part, this is due to the fact that the Black Carib rarely permitted Europeans to enter their territory in St. Vincent. Like other maroons, they kept the enemy at bay. Even the portrait of Chatoyer, standing with five women identified as his wives, was probably drawn outside their own territory, perhaps as they returned home from market (see Illus. 2).

The territory of the Black Carib was bounded by the windward coast and the dense forest and mountains of the interior. These natural features helped to protect the Black Carib from European intrusion. The British themselves recognized that the isolated location of Black Carib settlements, far away from their own, was a matter of studied choice. It was, according to one colonial official, "a point they have always appeared to think of great importance" (Anon. 1773: 38).

If this isolation did not entirely discourage uninvited visitors, the Black Caribs' lack of hospitality did. An Englishman wrote of sailing near one of their coastal settlements, with the intention of visiting it. He sailed on when he saw his unwilling hosts on shore arming themselves. When he and his men tried to land at a point farther along the coast, they found a group of Black Carib men there "who all gave a squall when we came in view, and immediately began to fire at the boat, some from the bushes and others from behind the rocks" (Anon. 1773: 78). No doubt incidents like this one explain why descriptions of Black Carib settlements are both cursory and rare.

Whether the Black Carib ever adopted the localized, extended family system of their Red Carib neighbors is questionable (see Taylor 1951: 30). One resident of the island noted simply that "they live with their families in thatched huts, dispersed through the woods" (Anon. 1773: 6). Another described a coastal settlement with several houses, and with cultivated grounds at a distance of half a mile (Anon. 1773: 78). A third mentioned that some of the men had several wives, with a separate house for each (Davidson 1787: 11). One missionary wrote of passing "by their villages, [where] they stood at their doors in ranks, crying out *Bon jou, Bon jou* (a corruption of *Bon Jour,* a good day); others cried out *How dee, How dee*" (Coke 1789).

Although Black Caribs tried to keep most Europeans out of their territory, they sought contact with them elsewhere. During the eighteenth century they made frequent trips to the market in neighboring French Martinique. As early as the 1720s, an Englishman, who was conducting negotiations with the Black Carib in St. Vincent, had reported that "the Negro Chief spoke excellent French" (Uring 1727: 107f.). According to a British resident of the island later in the century, most of the Black Caribs were bilingual in French and Carib (Davidson 1787: 19f.). When William Young returned from a trip away from the island, several of the men appeared at his estate, asking "*quelles nouvelles de la France* and then *quelles nouvelles de l'Angleterre?*" (Young 1801: 274).

In the last decades of the eighteenth century, wage labor and marketing activities brought the Black Carib into frequent contact with the British and French, slaves and free negroes. No one could ever mistake the Black Caribs for the last two. One colonist wrote that "the black Charibbs are easily distinguished from any other negroes, by a custom they have of flattening the foreheads of their infants, in order that their race may be kept distinct" (Anon. 1773: 6; Davidson 1787: 10). They had adopted this practice from the Red Carib.

The economic pattern of the Black Carib, like that of other maroon societies, was quite diverse (see Price 1973: 10ff.). They were probably never entirely self-sufficient, and over time their dependence on marketing and wage labor increased. Men hunted and fished, earned some money shuttling cargo in their dugout canoes, and carried on contraband trade with Martinique.[15] A few marketed commercial crops, such as cotton and tobacco. Chief Chatoyer and his brother, Du Vallee, had large pieces of land cleared and planted in cotton, intending it for sale in the marketplace of St. Vincent. Loans from some of the island's European "gentlemen" permitted this enterprise, which eventually led one of them to describe the two men as "comparatively rich." Du Vallee himself owned nine slaves (Young 1795: 106f.).

There is no record of women working for wages in St. Vincent, nor were there many opportunities for free women with their skills. But their work was not confined to home. They provided the various root crops and cassava bread that were the backbone of the diet. Women also carried poultry, fruit, and cassava bread to sell in the marketplace of the capital, fifteen miles or more from their own settlements. Their marketing activities were so competitive with the slaves' own that the slaves hated them as rivals.[16] Black Caribs were not only producers and marketers, but also buyers. They depended on the market of neighboring Martinique for firearms and ammunition, weapons that kept them a free people in a hostile political environment. The men habitually carried cutlasses or "fowling pieces, which they usually keep bright and in good order" (Anon. 1773: 6).

The Black Carib maintained political ties with Europeans through their chiefs, who negotiated with Europeans and led expeditions against them. Early in the eighteenth century, the British showed some confusion about how to deal with these chiefs. In a report to his superiors in 1723, a Captain Braithwaite wrote: "I entertained them very handsomely and made the Chief some trifling Presents; but found he was a Person of no Consequence and that they called him Chief, to get some Present from me" (Uring 1727: 105). As the years passed, the British gradually realized that their political system was decentralized and egalitarian. One colonist wrote that they had no "established subordination" among themselves but organized together in the face of external threat. He spoke of "hereditary feuds and animosities which though ever laid aside in times of general war, and against a common enemy, were as constantly resumed in times of peace" (Young 1795: 22, 105). The various chiefs apparently had little power in local affairs: "Every district of two or three miles in length has its peculiar chief, who, however, has not the smallest shadow of authority except in time of war" (Davidson 1787: 18).

Little is known about the religious beliefs and practices of the Black Carib in St. Vincent, but they presumably incorporated some elements of

Roman Catholicism. French missionaries had tried to convert the Red Carib in the seventeenth century, and they later extended these efforts to the Blacks as well. When the British took formal possession of St. Vincent in 1763, they found that the Black Carib had asked a priest, one Abbé Valladares, to act as their "public agent" in negotiations with the British (Young 1795: 21). The Black Caribs' allegiance to the priests was so firm that they considered their new Protestant neighbors to be "Heretics" (Anon. 1773: 43).

Despite this allegiance, the Black Carib were not orthodox Roman Catholics. They probably shared some of the beliefs of the Red Carib: very likely, the belief that "their departed relations were secret spectators of their conduct; — that they still sympathized in their sufferings, and participated in their welfare" (Edwards 1794 I: 49). A British colonist, who described the Black Caribs' religious beliefs, wrote in very general terms: "They have some faint ideas of a Supreme Cause which created all things, but they conceive that God commits the government of the world to subordinate Spirits. They make use of several incantations against Evil Spirits, to prevent their malignant influence" (Davidson 1787: 9). He implied that the Black Caribs' commitment to Roman Catholicism was primarily political, and complained that the priests "took little pains to instruct them in Religion."

Of course national and sectarian bias colors this account. At the very moment that George Davidson wrote, a movement was afoot to establish a Methodist mission among the Black Carib. The legislature of St. Vincent had just granted 150 acres of land adjacent to the Black Caribs' territory for this purpose. Davidson hoped that his pamphlet would encourage charitable contributions to the mission from subscribers in England. Like many other British residents of St. Vincent, he wished to integrate the Black Carib into colonial society quickly and peacefully, and he considered education, as well as enterprise, to be the means to this end. "But we cannot expect to have much intercourse with these people," Davidson (1787: 19f.) wrote, "till publick schools are established to teach their children the English language, reading and writing, and they are afterwards brought up to husbandry, or some other trade or occupation." He recommended that the girls be instructed in domestic arts, rather than a trade: "The girls may likewise be brought up, and taught by school-mistresses in sewing and knitting stockings."

But before many boys had learned to read, or girls to knit, their fathers revolted. The British deported them all — men, women, and children — to the neglected margins of the Spanish empire, far away from Protestant missionaries and schools.

When the Black Carib established settlements along the coast of Central America in the nineteenth century, they again selected isolated settings (Young 1847: 125; Roberts 1827: 160). Uninhabited savannah stretched

for miles behind most of their villages. In front, the waters that they routinely traveled held hazards for outsiders, who lacked the Black Caribs' familiarity with the reefs and currents and their expertise with dugout canoes.

The isolation of their settlements in Central America, as in St. Vincent,
did not hinder the movement of Black Caribs themselves, although it made
visits by outsiders rather rare. But having lost political autonomy, the Black
Carib now welcomed the occasional European or North American visitor
with great shows of hospitality (Roberts 1827: 160, 272). Thomas Young
(1847: 133) wrote of them: "To any stranger they are attentive; but for a
white man, nothing is too good; and all are anxious, by kindness and hospitality, to make a favourable impression on him; in which they rarely fail."

This was a marked change from St. Vincent. During their last years on
that island, when they were well armed and numerous, intent on preserv-
ing both their land and liberty, they posed a physical threat to British security and an impediment to the settlers' financial interests. The colonists
described them in most unflattering terms, as "wild and lawless savages,"
"turbulent," "fierce," "uncivilized, lawless, disaffected, and of no use"
(Anon. 1773). But once dispersed along the Central American coast, in insular and unwanted areas, the European attitude toward them shifted. The
Black Carib were "peaceable, friendly, ingenious, industrious," "timid and
shy," "hardy and industrious," a "quiet, inoffensive people."[17] "Whatever
their ancestors of St. Vincent may have been, they are now honest and industrious," wrote an Englishman who traveled through their settlements in
about 1820, scarcely a generation after the exodus from St. Vincent
(Roberts 1827: 274f.). He also mentioned that they had abandoned the
practice of head deformation. Evidently they no longer found it useful or
necessary as a mark of ethnic distinction.

Whether the Black Carib were yet "slaves to money" when they were deported to Central America at the end of the eighteenth century is debatable.
But certainly a pattern of production for exchange and of wage labor in
non-Carib enterprise had been established in St. Vincent. In Central
America, they quickly acquired a reputation as a "good and useful laboring
population" (Squier 1870: 173). During the nineteenth century, men followed a variety of pursuits in Belize, Guatemala, and Honduras. Many
worked as woodcutters. Others enlisted in military service, hired out as
sailors, and worked on fruit and sugar plantations. Some earned money by
carrying contraband between Honduras and Belize; by hunting deer and
selling the skins; and by catching turtle and fish to market in Belize.[18]

Black Carib men had several advantages in the Central American labor
market. They were extremely mobile, the pre-eminent sailors of the coastal
waters. Many men, and women as well, were also proficient in several languages. Thomas Young (1847: 123) noted that "most of the men [are] able
to talk in Carib, Spanish, and English; some even add Creole-French and

Mosquito; and I have heard even the women converse in Carib, Spanish, French." Moreover, the men were versatile workers with a variety of skills. Young (1847: 124) wrote with evident admiration: "The men can hew and plant, hunt and fish, erect a comfortable home, build a good boat, make sails, &c.; some are capital tailors, and good carpenters; altogether, there cannot be a more useful body of men."

Few men worked at home in Black Carib communities. A traveler probably described most of their settlements when he wrote about one that it showed a "complete lack of [commercial] enterprise" (Brigham 1887: 29). Another visitor to a different town took note of the "scarcity of men," most of whom, he learned, "were away fishing or at work" (Stephens 1841: 30). In Belize, the Black Carib were known as a "coast tribe," but "ubiquitous over the colony," working at a variety of pursuits (Gibbs 1883: 166). Opportunities to earn money lay far afield, and men had to leave home to find them. Woodcutters might be absent for six months at a time, other workers for a period of weeks or months. They earned fairly uniform wages for wood-cutting and agricultural work. At mid-century, men in Honduras received $8 to $10 a month and rations. Wages in Belize were about the same.[19]

Women worked closer to home. Travelers describe them washing clothes beside springs and rivers; carrying heavy burdens of produce, balanced gracefully on their heads; cultivating and then processing cassava to make bread (see Illus. 3–5). Although men were obligated to clear land for their wives to plant, women otherwise took responsibility for the fields. Indeed, men did so little work at home that many visitors compared them unfavorably to their hard-working wives. One genteel traveler remarked with obvious consternation: "The women are often handsome and have a queenly gait; they frequently do the work while the men play the hero" (Sanborn 1886: 30). Another traveler, perhaps unaware that men worked for the most part away from home, used stronger language: "The lazy males are supported by their wives, who are much the more muscular and stalwart of the two" (Charles 1890: 114).

In truth, women did not support their husbands; but neither did they depend heavily on them for food and clothing. Every woman supplied her household with produce from her fields and then, "as the products are entirely her own, she . . . disposes of the rest to purchase clothes and other necessaries" (Young 1847: 123). Like their grandmothers in St. Vincent, the women carried surplus produce to market. They walked up to forty miles, with heavy burdens on their heads; on occasion they hired their husbands to take them there by boat.[20]

Toward the end of the century, women (and men as well) began to sell bananas for export, to the steamers that stopped at various ports en route to New Orleans. Women carried the fruit out to the steamers in dugout

canoes, which they managed "with wonderful skill" (Charles 1890: 118).
Eager to sell the fruit and receive payment, they evidently did not mince
words with the men on board: "Their tongues run like windmills; the purser
of the steamer must be a sharp one to battle with them." And again: "The
atmosphere surrounding the steamers while loading at Puerto Cortez, Sarstoon, Livingston, and so on up to Belize, is one of noisy profanity" (Charles
1890: 119).

Women also worked for wages during the nineteenth century, but in
comparison to men, they were restricted to a very few low-paying jobs. In
Guatemala, a number of women worked at sugar and banana plantations,
and others earned money as laundresses. Some women were probably employed as domestic servants.[21] Exactly when women began to work for
wages is not precisely documented, but it may have been by mid-century.
Young (1847: 107) alludes to this: "A [European] settler would find his advantage in employing Caribs to cultivate his ground," he wrote. "The
women would hire themselves to attend the plantations and to make
cassada bread."

When Young spoke of the advantages of hiring female labor, he no doubt
referred to their wage rates as well as to their skills. After recommending
the employment of Black Carib women to intended settlers, he described
the men's wages for agricultural work as "too high." They asked $8 to $10 a
month, and rations as well. Women of that era could be hired for much
lower rates, $3 to $4 a month (Young 1847: 115, 190).

Women apparently took little direct part in political activity. As in St. Vincent, men represented their people to the outer world. Along the Mosquito
Shore, every Black Carib town had a "captain" appointed by the Miskito
king; two "quarter-masters" served under him. Men also served as consta-
bles, with limited judicial authority. Similarly, every Black Carib settlement
in Belize had a government-appointed *alcalde* (mayor) and constable.[22]

Although Protestant missionaries attempted to convert Black Caribs in
Belize, and even translated biblical text into Carib, they enjoyed little success (Crowe 1850). When John Lloyd Stephens (1841: 28ff.) visited one of
their settlements with a priest in 1839, he saw figures of the Virgin and various saints in their houses, and characterized the Black Carib as "strict observers of the forms prescribed." But he also mentioned the priest's dismay
at finding so many mothers, babies in arms for baptism, whose marital
unions were unblessed by the Church. When the priest advised one woman
to take advantage of his visit and marry her child's father, she demurred,
saying that the man was away, cutting mahogany. Stephens himself noted
that "there was little to be done in the way of marrying, there being a scarcity of men for that purpose, as most of them were away fishing or at work."

However casual about formal marriage, the Black Carib went to great
lengths to see that their children were properly baptized (Young 1847:

128). They also devoted great effort to certain rituals for the dead, although the Church condemned these and civil authorities in Honduras attempted to suppress them (Conzemius 1928: 202). Non-Caribs pejoratively referred to these ceremonies as "devil feasts." Young's (1847: 131ff.) detailed account of one clearly identifies it as the ancestral rite *dügü*. Black Caribs came from as far away as Belize to take part in the *dügü* that Young witnessed in Honduras, probably in 1839.

In St. Vincent, men had joined together to make common cause against the British enemy; their unity was based on opposition. In Central America, ritual quickly replaced raiding as both the occasion and expression of cultural unity. Scattered along a narrow stretch of coastline crosscut by national boundaries, the Black Carib were a divided people. Dispossessed of land and political autonomy, they still shared a language, a distinctive culture, and their ancestry. Instead of joining together to spill blood, they gathered to celebrate blood ties. Women took active part in these rituals, as they still do today in Belize.

Portraits from the Past

Europeans, intrigued by the mixed heritage and the history of the Black Carib, not only wrote about them but tried to capture their likeness visually, first on canvas, later with camera (see Illus. 2-9). The first portrait, which like the earliest written accounts dates from the eighteenth century, is that of Chatoyer with his five "wives." It was reputedly "drawn from the life" by an artist and engraver named Agostino Brunyas (or, as he was more commonly known, Augustin Brunais).[23] Presumably this portrait was a commissioned work. Sir William Young, its owner, was a wealthy planter and colonial official in St. Vincent. Early in 1773, the same year that the portrait was made, Chatoyer and twenty-seven other "chiefs" had signed a treaty with the British, this after several months of armed conflict. Twenty years later, Chatoyer would be accused of treachery and ingratitude for "the most flattering attentions and hospitality" shown to him and his family by Young after the signing of the treaty (Young 1795: 107). Perhaps the portrait was the first of those "most flattering attentions."

Early in 1795, in what was the final but extended bout of Anglo–Black Carib conflict, Chatoyer was killed in battle. In March of 1796, six months before the Black Carib finally surrendered, a publisher in London issued a print of Brunais's portrait, no doubt with the intention of capitalizing on publicity about the ongoing conflict in St. Vincent. There is no reason to doubt the authenticity of the portrait or the publisher's claim that Chatoyer and the women posed for it. The women's attire conforms in most details to descriptions in contemporaneous accounts. Davidson (1787: 17), a resident of St. Vincent, wrote that Black Carib women clothed themselves with a piece of fabric about a yard long and a foot wide, worn around the lower torso and open on the left side. He also noted that women wore garters below both knees, unless they were unmarried or widowed, in which case they wore only the left garter. In the print made after Brunais's portrait, two of the "wives" carrying baskets are inexplicably without these garters. As for the baskets, Black Carib women regularly took produce, poultry, and cassava bread to market in the capital of St. Vincent, "laden like beasts of burden" and accompanied by an armed man (Young 1795: 99, 106). Chatoyer, as was the custom of Black Carib men, carries a cutlass at his side. Although his companions are unarmed, women often carried "cutlasses in their hands, and always knives by their naked sides" (Coke 1789).

In other aspects of physical appearance, Chatoyer and the five women also fit the descriptions in accounts from the period. Eighteenth-century writers consistently referred to the Black Carib as "negroes" and "black."[24] After alluding to their mixed Afro-Indian origins, Davidson (1787: 7) explicitly stated that "the negro-color and features chiefly prevail."

In Central America, the Black Carib were easily distinguished from neighboring groups, chiefly Miskitos and other Indians. Roberts (1827: 154, 275) described them as "darker in complexion," "of a dark red color approaching to, and not often easily distinguishable from black," and with "the short curly hair of the Negro." By 1820 the men wore "shirts and trowsers," but the women still dressed as they had in St. Vincent (Roberts 1827: 160). During the 1830s, when women went to market they wore calico bodices, patterned skirts, and headwraps, although they still appeared "almost in the costume of nature" at home (Young 1847: 122f.). In the second half of the nineteenth century, supposedly by order of civil authorities, women clothed themselves fully (Sanborn 1886: 30). They habitually dressed in skirts and blouses, "the head adorned with the inevitable handkerchief" (Charles 1890: 119; see Illus. 4). At present, as in the past, women can "always be distinguished from the Negroes" by this customary attire (Conzemius 1928: 191; cf. Gonzalez 1969: 27).

Nineteenth-century travelers consistently identified the Black Carib as "negroes" or "black" in their accounts.[25] One of them, who visited Trujillo, Honduras, in 1838, was perplexed to find that "a little apart from the town, there is a cluster of huts, twenty or thirty in number, inhabited by a little colony of negroes, called *Caribes,* a denomination for which I could find no reason, since they certainly have nothing in common with the Indians of the Caribee [Caribbean] Islands" (Montgomery 1839: 24). Likewise, a French visitor to Belize at mid-century was puzzled to learn that "all of the blacks who live along the coast of the Gulf of Honduras are called Caribs." He found it "difficult to justify this name" because these Caribs did not resemble Indians but were "purely African" in appearance (Valois 1861: 152).

Photographs from the 1880s and 1890s provide visual evidence that supports such assertions. Brigham (1887: 273), who photographed the Black Carib during his several trips to Guatemala, wrote that "all along this coast they are of distinct and uniform character, to the casual observer differing little from the negro type; of good stature, firm, muscular build and powerful limbs, — women as well as men." According to Brigham, this resemblance was less marked to the careful observer than to the casual. He enumerated some very subtle anatomical differences (ranging from the breadth of the mouth to the size of the finger joints), which he thought distinguished the Black Carib from "the African."

These features are not detectable, of course, in his photographs from Livingston, Guatemala, which include group portraits and scenes of everyday life — most of them taken at some distance from the subjects (Illus. 5–8). In "Weaving a Serpiente," a man looks up from his work, holding a half-finished *rugúma* (manioc squeezer, *serpiente* in Spanish). A finished *rugúma* is propped beside him in the foreground, while a cluster of curious children in the background gaze intently at the camera. "A Group of Black Carib Children" has an equally impromptu look, as if twenty children have been momentarily diverted from their errands and play. "Interior of a House" provides a glimpse of spare furnishings, the hammocks slung from high rafters and knotted during the day for convenience. In "A Street in Livingston, Guatemala," the sun casts deep shadows across a nearly deserted street, probably in the heat of late afternoon. Maudslay and Maudslay (1899) offer another scene from daily life in Livingston: a throng of men and women gathered around a returned fisherman (Illus. 9).

To anyone who has recently visited a Black Carib community, these photographs look strikingly familiar. They could be replicated in any village in Belize, save for some details. The everyday dress of many older women, like those in the photographs, consists of headwrap, blouse, and gathered skirt. Every community has at least one basketmaker, and fishermen still draw crowds of eager buyers. Curious children intrude in the margins of contemporary photographs, carrying younger charges on their out-thrust hips, or bowls and baskets on their heads. Even the faces, however indistinct in some of these old photographs, are not the faces of strangers but of friends, their grandchildren and great-grandchildren.

Notes to Chapter 2

1. According to Young (1795: 6), the Black Carib were descendants of Africans bound for sale in Barbados who were shipwrecked in 1675. A government correspondent writing in 1667, however, refers to the loss of two

Spanish ships in 1635 as the source of the "negroes" then living in St. Vincent with the Carib (Great Britain 1880: 534). "Black Indians" elsewhere in the circum-Caribbean have claimed ancestry from shipwrecked Africans (see Exquemelin 1951: 250; Henderson 1809: 181f.; Floyd 1967: 22; Whitten 1974: 40).

2. See Breton (1958: 1), and Breton and de la Paix (1958: 2f.).

3. Taylor (1951: 32, 41; 1961) discusses "sex-differentiated speech forms," which led many Europeans to conclude (erroneously) that the Carib in the West Indies, and later the Black Carib in Central America, had two languages, one spoken by men and the other spoken by women.

4. See Rouse (1948a) for a summary of achaeological and ethnographic data on the Arawak.

5. See Sauer (1966: 193f.) for Spanish correspondence about the Carib, and Columbus (1968: 58) on the Arawak.

6. According to Breton and de la Paix (1958: 61f.), men spent much of the day in the *carbet* but slept at night with women in the smaller houses. Presumably adolescent boys slept in the *carbet* (Taylor 1951: 28). Breton (1958: 15) described a *carbet* as about sixty feet by twenty feet in size and "oval" in shape. Rouse (1948b: 551) claims that the *carbet* was an "oval building, which later became rectangular." Also see Du Tertre (1958: 29).

7. According to many early accounts, the Caribs killed and ritually consumed male captives (see Breton 1958: 13; Breton and de la Paix 1958: 2f.). Labat (1970: 101f.), however, denies this. Arens (1979: 44–54) dismisses Carib cannibalism as myth.

8. See Labat (1970: 77), Breton (1958: 23ff.), Breton and de la Paix (1958: 13), Rouse (1948b: 558), and Du Tertre (1958: 16).

9. See Labat (1970: 101), Taylor (1946: 181), Rouse (1948b: 555), and Breton and de la Paix (1958: 17).

10. See Labat (1970: 77f., 112), Breton (1958: 13), Sheldon (1820: 405), Rouse (1948b: 554, 556, 559), Taylor (1951: 28f.), and Du Tertre (1958: 33).

11. Edwards (1794 I: 40), Breton (1958: 27), Labat (1970: 97, 105), and Bouton (1958: 2) comment on women's work.

12. See Young (1795: 12f.), Great Britain (1933: 244, 247), and Labat (1970: 138).

13. For detailed descriptions of the treaties and armed conflict between the British and Black Carib, see Shephard (1831), Young (1795), and Marshall (1973).

14. The idea of deporting the Black Carib had first been suggested in 1765 and periodically thereafter (Anon. 1773: 45, 69, 73f.; Edwards 1794 I: 402). Various sites were considered, including the coast of Africa. This was probably one of the earliest back-to-Africa plans, although it never materialized.

15. See Davidson (1787), Young (1795: 105f.), and Anon. (1773: 27).

16. Young (1795: 106), Davidson (1787: 11), and Edwards (1819 IV: 16) mention women taking produce to market.

17. See Young (1847: 122), Fowler (1879: 52), Bristowe and Wright (1890: 42), and Gibbs (1883: 166).

18. For description of men's work, see Roberts (1827: 271ff.), Young (1847: 124), Gibbs (1883: 166), Burdon (1935: 224), Sanborn (1886: 17), Fowler (1879: 52), Bristowe and Wright (1890: 212), Froebel (1859: 162, 177), Morlan (1892: 29), and Valois (1861: 153, 161). Floyd (1967: 185), Conzemius (1928: 199), and Gonzalez (1969: 23) mention contraband trade.

19. A number of sources provide information on wages, including Young (1847: 109, 124), Morris (1883: 120), Duval (1879: 58), and Great Britain (1870: 30).

20. For information on the marketing activities of women, see Roberts (1827: 123f., 274), Young (1847: 123ff.), Gibbs (1883: 166), Froebel (1859: 185), and Fowler (1879: 52).

21. See Morlan (1892: 33) and Gibbs (1883: 166).

22. See Young (1847: 127f.), Froebel (1859: 184), and Burdon (1935: 338).

23. To judge from the titles of his other works, Brunais was an itinerant artist who in the early 1770s visited a number of islands in the West Indies, where he painted both landscapes and portraits. By 1777 he was back in England, living in Soho and exhibiting such works as "A Sunday Negro's Market in the Island of Dominica" at the Royal Academy of Arts. He was variously known as Augustin Brunais, Agostino Brunyas, Abraham Brunais, and Abraham Brunias (See Benezit 1976 II: 357; Thieme 1953–62 V: 122; Graves 1970 I: 321).

24. For example, see Uring (1727: 107f.), Anon. (1773: 41, 53), Labat (1970: 139), and Young (1795: 6ff.).

25. Galindo (1833: 290), Pim (1863: 296), Squier (1855: 213), and Maudslay and Maudslay (1899: 155) described them in this manner. Young (1847: 123) did so as well, but noted variation in skin color, "some being coal black, others again nearly as yellow as saffron, although as a nation they are called the Black Carib," (cf. Brady 1895: 276).

Chapter 3

LIFE IN THE BACK OF BEYOND

Belize lies on the mainland of Central America, along the western margin of the Caribbean. Its narrow stretch of sandy coastline is backed by rolling savannah and dense forest in the interior. The Rio Hondo forms the northern boundary with Mexico, and in the south the Sarstoon River separates Belize from the Republic of Guatemala. Only maps mark the western border, where the forests of Belize merge imperceptibly with the forested lowlands of eastern Guatemala (see Map 3).

A wide expanse of open sea separates Belize from the distant West Indian archipelago. But the country has always kept its face toward the Caribbean and its back implacably turned against its mainland Hispanic neighbors. Ever since the British settled there several centuries ago, Belize has maintained stronger ties with geographically distant, English-speaking territories — Great Britain, the British West Indies, and North America. Historically, culturally, and linguistically, Belize has so little in common with the Central American republics surrounding it that the government has only recently sought to strengthen formal ties with some of them. It has expended even more effort in denying any links with neighboring Guatemala, which has long asserted sovereignty over the territory.

Belize has consistently rejected the Guatemalan claim, and innumerable attempts to settle it have all been for naught. In recent years scarcely a month passed without rumor of an impending invasion by Guatemala, and anyone who crossed the western border heard as litany, *Belice es nuestra,* "Belize is ours." Such rumor and refrain tended to heighten local loyalty to the United Kingdom. Although many people stated a wish for independence, they feared seizure by Guatemala as a consequence. A colonial status was preferable, they said, adding that the British had always ruled Belize with a light hand. This may have been as much a matter of appearance as a reality. The British military presence has long been welcomed for the protection it offers, and for the most part it has remained unobtrusive. The troops, posted in remote areas strategic for defense, have kept a re-

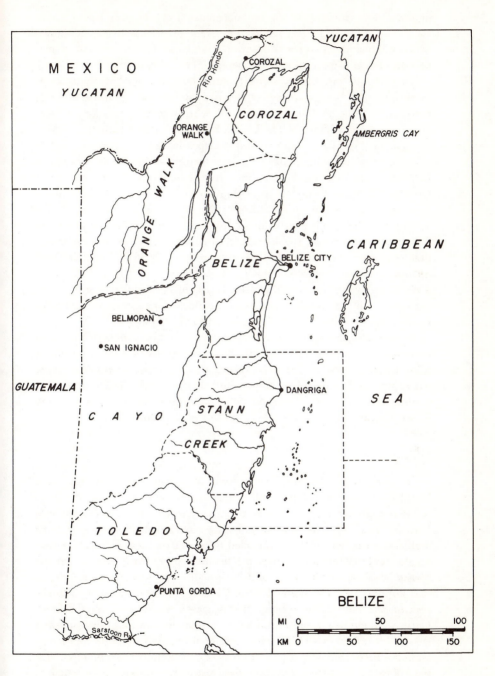

Map 3. Belize

markably low profile. British economic control has been even less visible to local eyes. Few people recognize the extent of private British holdings, which still include great tracts of forested land and some plantations. Colonialism always wore a deceptively benign mask in Belize.

Until recently the country seemed destined to retain indefinitely its status as an internally self-governing colony. A final attempt was made in 1981, however, to settle the Guatemalan claim; when it failed, plans for independence proceeded without it. The United Kingdom pledged temporary defensive support, and Belize celebrated its independence in September, 1981.

Aside from its political history, many features of life today distinguish Belize from the neighboring republics. Even casual visitors see striking differences. Crossing the border from Guatemala or Mexico, travelers enter a territory that some find reminiscent of the British West Indies before the advent of independence or tourism. English is the national language of Belize, and most people speak an English-based Creole as their first or second language. The country has a significant number of Maya Indians and Spanish-speaking mestizos, although the populace is largely of African descent. They live in zinc-roofed wooden houses of West Indian type, typically perched on stilts. Some settlements bear Spanish names, others such singular English names as More Tomorrow, Baking Pot, and Never Delay.

To outsiders, the most remarkable features of this small country are its isolation and cultural diversity. Its history suggests that the one follows from the other: over the centuries various peoples have sought refuge in the wilderness of the interior or along uninhabited portions of the coast. According to local lore, the first to do so were buccaneers whose common enemy, Spain, claimed all of this land but never colonized it.

Background

From the Spanish colonial perspective, the territory of Belize was quite literally "the back of beyond." It lay across a natural frontier line, the spine of high mountains that arch from Chiapas, Mexico, in the north to Costa Rica in the south. The Spanish quickly conquered the densely populated highland areas, which they controlled for centuries thereafter. Their hold on the lowland territory across the frontier, particularly Belize and the Mosquito Shore of Honduras and Nicaragua, was more tenuous.

Columbus formally claimed all of Central America for Spain. But the *conquistadores* who followed him left this coastal territory, which the Black Carib were later to occupy, uninhabited, unexploited, and unmissionized (Floyd 1967; Helms 1976a). The occasional Spaniards who traversed the territory discovered no resources worthy of exploitation and settlement. Explorers found the half-submerged coast distinctly inhospitable, a tangle of mangrove swamp intersected by estuaries and lagoons. Very few attempted to penetrate the densely forested interior.

The Roman Catholic clergy were more intrepid explorers. Drawn by the prospect of saving souls, they made some missionizing efforts among the sparse Maya population of the interior during the sixteenth and early seventeenth centuries. But eventually they too retreated, until missionization began again in earnest in the nineteenth century (see Buhler 1976). Throughout the early sanguinary period of New World history, while the Spanish were busy conquering and decimating aboriginal peoples elsewhere in the Caribbean and Central America, Belize languished. Only Maya Indians, seeking refuge from the Spaniards, and later the British, seeking profit, intruded into the uncharted territory.

The origins of the British settlement in Belize date from the seventeenth century. Logwood was to prove so profitable that the settlers soon claimed the territory for Great Britain. This British enclave at Belize was not unique. During the seventeenth and eighteenth centuries, small British settlements dotted the Caribbean shore of Central America—at Bluefields, Black River, the Bay Islands, and various other points, including Belize.

For years the Spanish ignored these settlements. They had retreated from the coast in the seventeenth century, falling back behind the frontier for defensive purposes. But by the latter half of the eighteenth century, the growing British presence so alarmed the Spanish that they sought to suppress it. After formal negotiation, Great Britain surrendered Black River to Spain in 1787, and most of the British settlers there re-established themselves in Belize (Floyd 1967: 166). Within a decade after the British settlers reluctantly vacated Black River, the Black Carib, whom the British had forced out of St. Vincent, began to spread out over the same coastline.

Belize remained British, despite sporadic Spanish attack. The last Spanish assault on the territory occurred during this period, in 1798, but the settlers and their slaves easily repelled it. According to a census taken a few years later, in 1806, the population of Belize included 150 whites, over 1,000 free colored and free negroes, and nearly 5,000 slaves (Burdon 1934: 90). The census counted neither Maya Indians in the interior nor the newly arrived Black Caribs, who had settled along the southern coast.

The Black Carib had first entered the territory in 1802. By the end of that year an estimated 150 were living there (Burdon 1934: 60, 146). The precise reason for their initial entry remains obscure. An account of the period alludes to the Black Caribs' antagonism toward the Spanish in Honduras, "whom they consider their most implacable foes" (Henderson 1809: 134). Employment opportunities for men in forestry, as well as trouble with civil authorities in Honduras, prompted later migration (see Young 1847: 139; Bristowe and Wright 1890: 42).

Because of the Anglo–Black Carib conflict in St. Vincent, the British in Belize mistrusted these early emigrés, but official efforts to prevent their entry were not very effective and soon ceased. Black Carib men soon proved useful as workers and soldiers in the labor-hungry colony, especially after the abolition of slavery in the 1830s. A French traveler who visited Belize around 1850 noted that the army was composed of 170 Black Caribs and only 25 Englishmen (Valois 1861: 153). In the 1860s census takers counted nearly a quarter of the Black Carib population in non-Carib locales (Colonial Office 1861). Presumably most of them were labor migrants. In order to assure their availability as wage laborers, the government decided to deny the Black Carib any title to the uninhabited land that they had settled in southern Belize (Bolland 1977: 133, 195).

Black Caribs continued to enter the colony until the end of the nineteenth century, when the flow declined.[1] Although they were probably the first immigrants to enter Belize in the 1800s, they were not the last. Many Spanish-speaking refugees entered from Yucatán during the mid-nineteenth century, fleeing the Maya uprising there, the War of the Castes, and settled in the northern area of Belize. During the latter years of the century, the population grew and diversified as more immigrants arrived: Chinese, Europeans, North Americans, East Indians, West Indians, and others (Dobson 1973: 177, 245ff.). The colonial government encouraged immigration, in the belief that economic development depended on population increase, and especially a ready supply of labor.

Since the middle of the last century, the government of Belize has considered underpopulation a problem, and one to be solved by immigration. It is a peculiar problem to have today, as many other countries in the Caribbean and Central America attempt to deal with overpopulation. With a land mass of less than 23,000 square kilometers, Belize roughly corresponds in size to Haiti and El Salvador. But in terms of population size and density, it presents a radically different profile. Haiti and El Salvador both have burgeoning populations, now numbering in the millions, with respective densities of 190 and 168 people per square kilometer. Belize has a population of about 130,000 and the lowest population density in Central America, about 6 per square kilometer (U.N. 1978: 69). Like its neighbors, it shows a high rate of natural increase, over 3 percent per annum. But emigration, especially labor migration, offsets this today as in the past. Formerly, most labor migrants traveled to other areas of Central America to find work, but since the 1950s their destination has shifted to the United States. A sizable number of Belizeans, especially Creoles and Black Caribs, now live in several North American cities.

The uneven distribution of population in Belize accentuates the impression of sparse settlement. A third of the country's populace resides in Belize City, the principal port and commercial center and the former capital of the country. Belize City is as remarkable for its congestion as the hinterlands are for their unbounded space. Some 40,000 people live in close quarters on a small peninsula that abuts upon the sea on one side and a mangrove swamp on the other. The city is a maze of narrow alleys, with wooden houses so densely concentrated along them that many seem perilously close to toppling into the open sewage canals that crosscut the city and empty into the sea. Rural people complain of the city's noisome odors and constant din, its congestion and oppressive heat. Many prefer to cope with provincial ennui than with these perils of urban life.

Still, Belize City attracts a constant flow of visitors and aspiring workers from the countryside. It offers jobs in the few non-agricultural industries that exist in the county; and as the commercial center of Belize, it has no rival in the services and supplies it provides. To walk along Albert Street, the city's main thoroughfare, is to mingle with a cross section of the country's population, a notably mixed one given its small size. The Creoles, who form the largest ethnic group in Belize, predominate in the city.[2] Many of the merchants are Chinese or Syrian. Other residents and visitors to the city include East Indians and Maya Indians, in from the countryside; Black Caribs, either visiting the city or working there; Spanish speakers from the west and north; and Mennonite farmers, whose somber dress as much as their fair coloring distinguishes them from the rest.[3]

Nearly half of the country's population is concentrated in Belize City, the new capital Belmopan, and five small towns that are administrative centers for their respective districts. The remainder live in villages widely dispersed throughout the country. Between settlements, and within a matter of miles from Belize City, stretch great tracts of land that are sparsely populated or virtually uninhabited, save for an occasional logging camp. From the air particularly, the interior has the lush and lonely look of wilderness. Only a russet line here and there interrupts the perpetual green of the forest. These are roads, many of them unpaved, crossing the flat or undulating land of the north and coast and hilly terrain in the southern and western interior. There are very few roads, most of them built since the 1950s. As late as the 1920s, roads were largely confined to the Belize City area, and even those were dismissed as "mere tracks" (Dillon 1923: 26f.). Half a century later, the weary traveler still finds these words apt. But the road system today, if not measurably improved, has at least expanded. It now links all six districts to Belize City, and nearly all internal travel is overland. The roadways also carry some international traffic. One narrow and sporadically paved road leads from Belize City to the Guatemalan border; another terminates at the border of Mexico. The country has limited internal and international air service as well.

Travel by air and by land are both relatively recent. In the past, people made most journeys within Belize or to points beyond by water. Rivers provided the traditional travel route in the northern and western districts until a few decades ago. Travel by river was never very common in the south, where all of the Black Carib settlements are located, because the southern rivers tend to be shallow, fast-flowing, and full of rapids. In the past, people in the south traveled mainly by sea. Since the recent advent of a road system into the southern districts, coastal traffic has declined, and it shows little sign of revival.

But the sea remains important to Belize, both as a major route for international trade and for the resources that it provides. The outstanding natural feature of the territory lies under water, a barrier reef some forty kilometers offshore. About 500 kilometers in length, the reef is the longest in the western hemisphere and the second longest in the world. Fishing in the adjacent coastal waters is superior; and marine products, especially lobster, are now a major export of Belize.

The barrier reef accounts for much of the publicity that the country attracts, and also draws many of its visitors: marine scientists or carefree travelers, bent on exploring or fishing in the crystalline waters around the reef. But tourism remains incipient, and the mainland still lies at a safe remove from the Caribbean and Central American tourist circuits. Mainland Belize has few of the extensive white beaches that lure North American tourists to so many West Indian islands, and it lacks the colonial architecture and accessible Mayan ruins that neighboring Guatemala offers. Although Belize can claim its share of Mayan sites, the internal transportation system is so unreliable and rudimentary that few visitors have an opportunity to tour them. For that matter, few see very much beyond Belize City and resort areas near the reef. Only an occasional intrepid traveler ventures down the Hummingbird Highway, a narrow strip of pavement that, after 160 kilometers, turns into the wider but unpaved Southern Highway. Near the head of the Southern Highway is the largest Black Carib settlement in the country, Dangriga. Well off the road lie several Black Carib villages, as well as a number of Creole and Maya settlements. The road runs on until it terminates abruptly at the southernmost town in Belize, Punta Gorda, also predominantly Black Carib. Beyond it lies another Black Carib village, accessible by water, and then the Guatemalan frontier. There is little industry in the south, and many Black Carib men and women travel this road when they leave their own communities to look for work.

Economy and the Labor Market

The insularity of Belize, which fostered Spanish neglect for centuries, has had a persisting influence on the country's economy and relations with the outside world. The novelist Aldous Huxley (1934: 35), after a visit to the colony, was prompted to describe it in a flourish of literary overstatement as "not on the way from anywhere to anywhere else." It is the sort of phrase that seizes the imagination of a distant reader, nettles local people, yet says little of substance about Belize.

A number of natural features, aside from its unfavorable location, account for the fact that Belize has limited industry, and none of it is large-scale. The country has no known deposits of commercially valuable minerals. Its position, off the major shipping routes, and the lack of a deep-water harbor make the importation of raw materials and their re-export in the form of manufactured goods impractical. The small domestic market cannot support any large-scale manufacture. Instead, industry centers on the production of consumer products such as rum and cigarettes for the local market, and the processing of primary products for export.

Like so many other West Indian colonies, Belize long had a one-industry economy (see Ashcraft 1973). But unlike the sugar colonies, forestry traditionally dominated Belize. The major employer of men until recently, it provided only seasonal employment, with a December-May working cycle at isolated lumber camps in the interior. Today forestry has declined in importance, in part because of the dwindling supply of commercially valuable wood. Citrus, sugar cane, and bananas have replaced lumber as the primary products for export, and agri-business (largely foreign-owned) is now the major employer of men (Dobson 1973: 259ff.).

From the workers' perspective, very little has changed. Most of them — about two-thirds according to official figures — remain in the manual labor and services sector, earning rather low wages. (Since most goods are imported, the cost of living is relatively high.) There is a chronic shortage of full-time, year-round employment, and many rural men and women still must migrate to find any work at all. These problems are particularly acute for women.

Women, like men, find work primarily in the manual labor and services sector. But in nearly every other respect, the work experience of men and women differs profoundly. The labor market is occupationally segregated, and men work in a wider range of industries and fill a greater number of occupations. Women find themselves confined to a handful of traditional pursuits, the principal ones same that they filled fifty years ago in Belize. For the most part, they work in urban areas as domestic servants, cooks, seamstresses, teachers, nurses, and shop clerks.[4] Recently, light industries have provided a few more jobs for women. In some cases these require learning new skills, but in many instances women simply continue to use old skills in commercial settings. Although a new garment factory near Belize City has created more jobs for seamstresses, it has not widened the occupational structure for women.

As a general rule, women earn lower wages than men, even when they do the same work. By union agreement, male citrus workers in 1975 earned a base rate of 38¢ per hour and females 28¢, or about $18.25 and $13.45 respectively for a forty-eight-hour work week.[5] The disparity used to be greater, with the female base rate about 60 percent of the male. In other occupations where men or women do comparable work, their pay also varies. Female shop clerks earn from $6 to $23 for a forty-five-hour week, about a quarter to a third less than the male weekly rate. A seamstress earns from $9.50 to $12 for a forty-hour week, again about a quarter less than a (male) tailor's wages. The government has never set a minimum wage, and the pay is dismally low in such strictly female occupations as domestic service. Domestics have probably always earned the lowest wages in the country, about $6 to $12 for a forty-eight-hour week. According to official figures, nearly 30 percent of all gainfully employed women work as domestics.[6]

Official figures on employment from the 1970 census indicate that the labor force is about 80 percent male and 20 percent female (see Table 1). But the way in which the unemployed are categorized tends to mask rather than to reveal the extent of unemployment among women (see Table 2). About 75 percent of all unemployed men are classified as actively seeking

TABLE 1
Employment Status of Men and Women in Belize, 1970[a]

Employment Status	Men		Women		Total	
	number	percent	number	percent	number	percent
Employed	25,192	81.6	5,684	18.4	30,876	100
Unemployed	3,991	14.4	23,776	85.6	27,767	100

[a]Employed men and women are those who worked "for most of the 12 months." They include employers, employees, own account workers, and unpaid workers in any business or farm operated for profit (Census Research Programme 1975 IV, pt. 16: ix).

TABLE 2
Categories of Unemployed Men and Women in Belize, 1970

Category	Men		Women	
	number	percent	number	percent
Seeking first job	873	21.9	182	0.8
Others seeking work	411	10.3	46	0.2
Wanted work & available	340	8.5	25	0.1
Home duties	341	8.5	22,352	94.0
Retired/Disabled	1,425	35.7	1,044	4.4
Other	601	15.1	127	0.5
Total	3,991	100.0	23,776	100.0

work (including those seeking first jobs), wanting work and available (but not actively seeking it), retired, or disabled. Only 5 percent of all unemployed women are so categorized, with 94 percent having "home duties." This category, which is "applicable to females mainly, indicates that the individual is essentially a housewife or some member of the household doing such things as cooking and cleaning but not receiving pay for it."[7] The implication is that domestic obligations keep most women from seeking work, that they neither want work nor actively seek it.

Anyone who talks to employers and women in Belize has reason to find this classification both biased and misleading. Nearly all women have home duties, including those who are gainfully employed. Indeed, women cite these obligations — the need to feed and clothe their children — as their reason for wanting work and as the main cause of female emigration to the United States. The classification of only twenty-five women in the entire country as "wanting work and available" grossly distorts the actual situation. More than twenty-five women who want work can be found in a single Black Carib village in the south.

The comments of both employers and women themselves suggest that a low demand for female labor, more than supply factors, explains why most women are unemployed at any given time. On their side, few women express any reluctance to work for wages, and it is the rare woman who has never done so.[8] But women point out that they have great difficulty finding any work that pays a living wage, and then keeping the jobs that they find. Effective contraception has never been readily available to lower-income women, who commonly complain that they are fired at the first visible sign of pregnancy, and without any assurance of being rehired. A number of employers, including the managers of several plantations, confirmed this, citing concern for the expectant mother's health and a ready supply of female labor as the reasons for this policy.

Unplanned pregnancies cannot, however, entirely explain the low employment rate of women, since the rate is about the same for those between the ages of thirty and sixty (see Table 3). Older women, who are past the age of childbearing, face a different type of discrimination in the labor market. The government has never set a compulsory retirement age, but many employers follow an unwritten policy of age discrimination in hiring. A few industries do have their own regulations. The citrus industry officially retires women at fifty-five, and men five years later, at sixty. But female employees claim that since the work is seasonal, with workers hired anew each season, management can and does discriminate against women before they reach this age. The banana industry follows a similar policy and rarely hires women over the age of forty to work as packers. Officials say that they have never considered hiring women to do anything other than pack bananas, and that they prefer to hire young women for this work. Since the

TABLE 3

Male and Female Employment in Belize, 1970: Proportion Employed by Age Categories[a]

Percent Employed	Age Categories									
	14–19	20–24	25–29	30–34	35–39	40–44	45–49	50–54	55–59	60–64	65 +

[a]The solid line indicates male workers; the broken line, female workers.

supply of female labor exceeds demand, they can enforce this preference. The hiring policy with regard to men is more liberal. Several ablebodied men in their late sixties and early seventies work on a regular basis at the plantation.

For the most part, women of any age occupy an extremely disadvantaged position in the labor market.[9] Jobs for them are scarce, and unplanned pregnancies pose problems for the few young women who are able to obtain paid work. Women past the age of childbearing have trouble finding work because of their age. Wages are very low in domestic service, which many women say is the only work readily available to them. They complain that they can scarcely support themselves, to say nothing of their dependents, with what they earn.

Because of these serious problems, many women are eager to emigrate to the United States. For them, the difference between wages in Belize and in the United States is vast. Domestic workers, for example, earn about six times as much abroad as they earn locally. Fifteen years ago, when there was a high demand for domestics in the United States, women found it easier than men to obtain visas and work permits; more women than men emigrated legally then (see Ashcraft 1973: 162). Now that the immigration policy has changed, the proportion of men and women who legally enter the United States from Belize is about equal. An unknown number of men and women also enter illegally, through the "back door." There are no reliable figures on the number of Belizeans working in the United States, since so many of them are illegal aliens. But the average local estimate is that about a quarter of all Belizean nationals live outside the country, most of them in the United States.

Many of the women who work in Belize or abroad have dependent children and require help with child care. Those who emigrate to the United States, like those who work locally, frequently leave their children in the care of female relatives.[10] This may partially explain why women are both the main donors and recipients of postal money orders sent from the United States to Belize. Receipts for money orders sent to Belize City during a four-week period in 1975 (the longest span for which they were available) showed that over 60 percent of the donors and 80 percent of the recipients were female. Over half (52 percent) of the remittances were sent to and received by women. Next in frequency (27 percent) were money orders sent by men to women. The remainder (21 percent) were sent by women to men, or by men to men. Unfortunately, there was no way to determine how regularly the donors sent money or the exact relationship between donor and recipient.[11] The average sum sent was $35, nearly equivalent to a fortnight's wages for a male manual worker in Belize.

Remittances sent from the United States are important to the national economy of Belize. One government official estimated that they amount to as much as 15 percent of the country's gross national product. The money and goods that migrants send home are also important at the local level, and especially in the underdeveloped southern region, where the Black Carib settlements are located.

Notes to Chapter 3

1. Thirty years ago, when the government last collected detailed information on the various ethnic groups in Belize, only 10 percent of the Black Carib population was foreign-born (see Central Bureau of Statistics 1948: xxix; also Metzgen and Cain 1925: 88).

2. In Belize, the term "Creole" generally refers to people of African descent whose first language is English or an English-based Creole. The term is also sometimes applied to whites born in Belize (cf. Dobson 1973: 256).

3. The Mennonites migrated to Belize from Mexico about twenty years ago (see Sawatsky 1969).

4. Of the women workers listed in the 1960 census, about two-thirds were employed as domestics, teachers, shop clerks, nurses, seamstresses, and cooks, in that order of frequency. An equal proportion (but far greater number) of male workers were concentrated in more than twice that number of occupations, and they filled ninety-two altogether (see Department of Statistics 1961: 206ff.; cf. CBS 1948: xxxvii).

Unfortunately, the 1970 census places all workers in eleven general occupational categories (e.g., "Transportation and Communication Workers") and alternatively in eight industrial groups (e.g., "Agriculture, Forestry, and Hunting, etc."). But even this broad classification does not obscure occupational segregation. The highest proportion (42 percent) of all male workers is in agriculture, forestry, and hunting, while 61 percent of all female workers are employed in services.

5. Belizean currency is tied to the British pound and has been unstable for the past few years. In 1975, when I collected most of the information on wages, the rate of exchange for one Belizean dollar was about sixty-six U.S. cents. All figures on wages, and in later chapters on ritual and other expenses, are in U.S. currency values as of 1975.

6. Information on wages and on domestic service comes from the following sources: Labor Department (1972), Ashcraft (1973), May and McLellan (1972: 132), and Carey Jones (1953: 85). According to Collver and Langlois (1962: 367), about a third to a half of the gainfully employed women in urban areas throughout the Caribbean work as domestic servants.

7. All data for 1970 are drawn from the census for that year (Census Research Programme 1975 IV, pt. 16.

8. I say this on the basis of comments made to me by the many Black Carib, Creole, and mestizo women with whom I spoke in Belize City and each of the districts. Most of them had worked for wages at some point in their lives. There may well be differences, however, in the employment rates for women of different ethnic groups. No current data are available, but thirty years ago between 20 and 25 percent of all Black Carib, Mayan, "European," and "African" (Creole) females over the age of ten were classified as gainfully employed. For the categories "Mixed/Colored" (presumably including mestizos) and "Asiatic," 15 and 12 percent respectively were employed (CBS 1948: xxxi).

9. Only the few women with education past the primary level can hope to find full-time, year-round work with a measure of job security. Those who finish secondary school have the prospect of finding a white-collar job, usually as a stenographer or typist, with the high salary (for women) of $35 a week. Educated women can also earn higher than average incomes as teachers and nurses, the only two professions traditionally open to them.

But employer policies about pregnancy also pose problems for these women. A married teacher who has twice had maternity leaves may be granted further leaves or, "in the interest of maintaining the efficiency of a school," may be terminated (Ministry of Education 1972).

10. Sanford (1971) discusses child care and fosterage at length, particularly among Creoles and Black Caribs.

11. When Ashcraft (1973: 165) collected data on remittances, the relationship between donor and recipient was specified, and receipts were available for annual periods. His figures parallel mine, but are more detailed. Over a three-year period, and for the country as a whole, the recipients were female in 80 percent of the cases. About 95 percent of the money orders were exchanges between parent and child. The average amount sent was $30. Ashcraft does not specify the gender of donors.

Chapter 4

SHIFTING SANDS

The men and women who live in any of the Black Carib villages of southern Belize can speak eloquently and at length about the unique qualities of their own community. Civic pride notwithstanding, the variation that they describe is a matter of degree rather than of kind. Certainly there are geographic differences among these settlements — especially in their distance from markets, plantations, cultivable land, and transportation routes. But the villages share a number of defining features. They are all residential communities. To do almost any income-earning work — fishing, cultivation, or wage labor — requires leaving the confines of the village. Although some food is produced locally, most households also purchase food on a daily basis, using money earned elsewhere. The need for money is unremitting, but most income sources are remarkably unstable. Many jobs are seasonal, and others end when enterprises fail, a common event in Belize.

These villages stand on shifting sands in a double sense. But the quixotic nature of the labor market troubles men and women far more than the slow erosion of the beaches where they have always built their houses.

Locale

The Black Carib settlements in Belize are located in the south, in Stann Creek District and Toledo District (see Map 3). Black Caribs and Maya Indians, both minority groups, predominate in the southern region, which was the last, and remains the least, commercially developed area of Belize. Creoles and Spanish speakers — who respectively make up about a half and a third of the country's population — are concentrated in the more prosperous districts of the north and west and in Belize City, where employment is more plentiful and wages higher.

Five of the six Black Carib communities in Belize are scattered along a 200-kilometer stretch of the southern coast. The single interior settlement

Map 4. Distribution of Fifty-three Black Carib Settlements in Central
America. Stars indicate settlements. (Source: William V. Davidson)

was established by the government as part of a resettlement plan after the severe hurricane of 1961. These communities are the northernmost of some fifty-three Black Carib towns and villages, unevenly dispersed along a narrow strip of coastline. Aside from the six communities in Belize, there are two in Guatemala, forty-three in Honduras, and another two in Nicaragua (see Map 4). An estimated 80,000 Black Caribs live in these communities (Davidson 1976a: 89).

Few of those in Belize realize the total number and full extent of these settlements. They consistently underestimate their number, and very few know of the settlements in Nicaragua. They do, however, perceive of themselves as a minority group, demographically as well as socially. Black Caribs represent less than 3 percent of the national population of Honduras, where their settlements are concentrated, and less than 1 percent in Guatemala and Nicaragua. In Belize they number only about 10,000 but form 8 percent of the small national population.[1]

Over half of the fifty-three Black Carib settlements are villages, with fewer than 1,000 inhabitants each. Most of the remainder have populations under 3,000. In Belize, the four villages range in size from roughly 200 to 700 inhabitants. The two towns are much larger and, unlike the villages, have mixed populations, with sizable minorities of Creoles and other non-Caribs. Dangriga, the oldest and largest Black Carib settlement in Belize, probably dates from the 1820s (cf. Davidson 1976b: 471). With some 7,000 inhabitants, the town serves as the administrative and commercial center of Stann Creek District, the only district in which Black Caribs outnumber non-Caribs. The town of Punta Gorda, with a population of about 2,000, is the administrative center for Toledo District.

The distance that separates Black Carib communities varies from only a few kilometers between some villages in Honduras to as many as 80 kilometers between settlements in Belize. The social boundaries between these communities are nearly as sharp as the physical. Localism is so entrenched that Black Caribs consider birthplace to be a fundamental aspect of social identity (cf. Coelho 1955: 52). No matter if a man left his home community several decades ago, he still claims to "belong" to it, and often regards his residence elsewhere as merely temporary. More than blind loyalty underlies this claim. Regardless of how long he may live in another Black Carib settlement, he will always be regarded to some degree as a *teréncha,* stranger, by its native residents. Many young men and women, who will spend years of their adult lives living and working elsewhere, declare their intention to "go home" eventually, just as their own parents and grandparents have done.

Localism manifests itself in other ways as well: in assesssments of character, of linguistic competence, even of musical skills. The people of one particular village regard those of another as quarrelsome and quick-tempered. Town residents pride themselves on their "progressiveness" and consider village life hopelessly rustic. But they also commend villagers for their supposed expertise in the Carib language, complaining that the town-born prefer speaking Creole to their native tongue. It seems that every settlement also claims to have the best drummers, dancers, and singers. Residents of any given community consistently disparage the musical abilities of others.

The government of Belize, like the Black Carib themselves, considers each community entirely separate from the others. Every village and town has a statutory council or board, made up of locally elected officials, which deals directly with the national government. The single occasion when they cooperate with each other is a ceremonial one, Settlement Day. Celebrated on November 19 every year, Settlement Day commemorates the arrival of the first Black Carib settlers into Belize. During this annual event, which is now a national holiday, Black Caribs gather to celebrate their common ancestry and culture.[2] Settlement Day is celebrated in all of their communities in Belize, although Dangriga is the center of the festivities. Many Black Caribs who work in other districts return home or go to Dangriga to take part in the celebration.

On Settlement Day, and on other calendrical holidays and ritual occasions, visitors pour into Black Carib villages.[3] But even on an average day many people come and go. Given the insular location and economic pattern of these settlements, their populations are ordinarily in a state of flux. People come to visit kin. People leave to look for work.

Work and Residence

A century ago many Black Carib men left their villages seasonally, to work as woodcutters in the interior of Belize. Today, forestry has suffered such a decline that it provides little employment. Most men now work at banana, citrus, and sugar plantations, mainly as unskilled manual laborers; very few fill supervisory positions. Other men pursue various trades in urban areas, or find work as stevedores and sailors.

The few professionals are nearly all teachers. Black Caribs teach in primary and secondary schools all over the country, particularly in Roman Catholic schools, although a few teach in schools run by other religious denominations or by the government. They have long served as the mainstay of the rural teaching force, because of their willingness both to live in remote areas and to learn other languages. Teachers in rural Belize often find that they must help their students learn to speak English before they can instruct them in anything else.

Perhaps the most important change in male employment patterns in recent years is that a number of men now have permanent jobs. Some, particularly the better-educated, have found jobs with the government. They work at all ranks and in various departments, including public works, social development, customs, and the health department. Many young men have joined the police force and are stationed all over the country. One elected representative in the national government is Black Carib.

Women also leave their home communities to look for work, but they usually meet with less success since the demand and wages for female labor are so low. Still, most women do work for wages at some point in their lives. The greatest number of them find seasonal work on plantations or in domestic service. Others are employed as shop clerks, seamstresses, teachers, and nurses.

Over thirty years ago, when census figures on ethnicity and employment were last collected, a quarter of all Black Carib women had earned a wage during the previous year.[4] Writing about one particular village, Taylor (1951: 55) estimated that "most of the men and nearly half of the women between the ages of eighteen and fifty" were away for several months annually, doing seasonal work. A census taken twenty years ago showed that only 11 percent of all adult Carib speakers claimed to live in non-Carib districts.[5] The proportion today may well be higher, to judge from the number of men and women who go home for holidays. At Christmas, one village of 450 people grows to half again its normal size when many of its native sons and daughters visit, some from other places in the district, others from a greater distance. Their number does not include some seventy migrants working abroad, most of them in the United States, and over half of them women.

While it is difficult to estimate the exact number of migrants from any particular community, it is virtually impossible to determine the precise value of money and goods that they send to their village kin. Cash remittances vary in frequency and value, and contributions often take the form of foodstuffs and goods as well as cash. Very few households are entirely supported by migrant kin, but many households receive some "help." This is to be expected, since local wage-earning opportunities are so limited.

Only a handful of villagers are self-employed or find full-time employment within the community; and except for the occasional female teacher, they are all men. Local teachers and policemen, who work for external institutions — church or government — have the only stable, year-round incomes. Every village has one or more self-employed shopkeepers, but they tend to be retired teachers who depend as much on their pensions as on their shops for income.

Most of the men in these villages, including part-time residents who work nearby, earn roughly the same wages. A beginning teacher and manual laborer have monthly incomes of about $80. A few older men who have devoted twenty or thirty years to teaching have incomes triple that figure. But only these senior teachers have an income level much higher than that of most working men. Marked income differences exist only between very small minorities at opposite ends of the financial spectrum: at one extreme a head teacher who earns several hundred dollars a month; at the other a destitute old man, without children, who subsists on the food and occasional coins that his late sister's daughters give to him. Although most men occupy the middle ground, households do vary in the level of security that they enjoy. The most secure people live in households that have a number of contributors (not necessarily residents) working at a variety of pursuits, locally, in other areas of the country, and abroad (see Chapter 8).

The few women who find employment in the vicinity work irregularly and for lower wages than those earned by any man. A nearby banana plantation hires young women only on a weekly basis, to pack fruit for shipment. The women must work twice as long to earn as much as their husbands and brothers do for a day's work in the fields. Several women from one village also work as domestics in a nearby Creole settlement, but for wages that they consider a mere pittance, about $30 a month. Domestic work and fruit-packing are the only jobs open to women in the immediate area.

Men find steadier employment at the banana plantation, and many return home on weekends. Banana cultivation, unlike citrus, sugar, or forestry, requires a year-round labor force rather than a seasonal one. But bananas are vulnerable to drought, and when production falls off, shipments cease. Women lose the opportunity for temporary work, and many men are laid off until conditions improve. Some men leave the area to look for employment elsewhere. Others return home, where they can fish in the interim, supplying their households with fish and selling the surplus.

Fishing provides a regular income for some men, but its importance in the village economies varies, depending largely on the distance of the community from a larger market. In one village, far from any marketplace, only a few men fish regularly, and none of them are young. Probably most of these men could find wage work elsewhere, but they prefer to live at home. It is a preference that they can afford since they no longer have a large number of dependents to support; their children are grown and their parents deceased. In this particular community, young men consider fishing a temporary pursuit, suitable only for periods of unemployment. They claim that the profits from fishing are too small for them to make it a full-time occupation. In another village located near Dangriga, where fish fetches a higher price and demand seems always to exceed supply, more men fish on a regular basis. Fishing provides a major income source, although many men supplement their income with occasional wage work. (The third village, located inland, obviously has no full-time fishermen.)

Food purchases easily qualify as the major expense of most households in these three villages. Many women buy fish on a daily basis, and they regularly purchase a variety of other dietary staples: flour, sugar, rice, beans, condensed milk, salt, baking powder, and yeast. Households vary in their dependence on purchased food, but none is self-sufficient. Even households that farm small plots of land, which they lease from the government for a nominal fee, produce a limited amount and variety of food, much of it for their own consumption, the surplus for sale. Common cultigens include corn, plantains, rice, cassava, and other root crops.

Twenty years ago, a British survey team, studying land use in Belize, characterized the inhabitants of one Black Carib village in Stann Creek District as "agriculturally-minded" and those of another as "not very diligent" (Romney et al. 1959: 136, 150). Productive land lies closer to the former village, and today nearly three-quarters of its households do some farming. To reach cultivable land from the latter village requires a trip of several hours each way, first by dugout canoe and then by foot. Only one in every ten households in that community now cultivates any land.[6] The villagers routinely complain about the high cost of living and the scarcity of such traditional staple foods as plantains and cassava.

Despite these differences in local economies, all of the villages share a fundamental dependence on the labor market, on money earned by male and female workers in non-Carib enterprise. They also show the effects of labor migration in their skewed age-sex profiles. About 70 percent of the population of any village is under twenty or over sixty years old, most of them economic dependents. The sex ratios are also quite low (cf. Gonzalez 1969: 55).

As Table 4 shows, there are fewer males than females in each community, even including part-time residents (who work elsewhere but return home regularly, on a weekly or monthly basis). The sex ratios are based on all residents, full- and part-time. (They do not include migrants, men and women who rarely or irregularly return to their home communities.) On weekdays, when many young and middle-aged men are away at work, the proportion of males is even lower. On a daily basis, there is an average of only forty-seven adult males (over the age of twenty) to every hundred adult females in the three communities. Nearly all of the women are full-time residents, since very few can find paid work in the immediate vicinity. In contrast, almost as many men are part-time residents as full-time ones.

If village-born Black Caribs are divided into these three categories—full- and part-time residents, and migrants—then the composition of any village appears to be in a constant state of flux. From one month to the next, some men and women leave to look for work, and others return home for indefinite periods. The pattern of movement seems highly idiosyncratic, a matter of individual choice, made on the basis of personal circumstance and in the context of chronically unstable employment. If the work (and migration) histories of men are complex and variable, it can at least be said that employment prospects and a relentless need for income govern their decisions

TABLE 4

Sex Ratios by Decade of Life in Three Black Carib Villages

Age	Males Full-time Residents	Part-time Residents	Total	Females Full-time Residents	Part-time Residents	Total	Sex Ratio
Village I							
0–10	82	0	82	80	0	80	1.025
11–20	43	2	45	47	0	47	.957
21–30	9	12	21	25	0	25	.840
31–40	3	16	19	18	0	18	1.055
41–50	7	11	18	17	0	17	1.059
51–60	10	4	14	25	0	25	.560
61–70	9	5	14	20	0	20	.700
71 +	9	3	12	10	0	10	1.200
Total	172	53	225	242	0	242	.930
Village II							
0–10	50	0	50	50	0	50	1.000
11–20	27	2	29	40	0	40	.725
21–30	2	0	2	6	0	6	.333
31–40	2	6	8	17	0	17	.470
41–50	2	12	14	4	0	4	3.500
51–60	2	3	5	7	0	7	.714
61–70	2	0	2	7	0	7	.286
71 +	3	1	4	1	0	1	4.000
Total	90	24	114	132	0	132	.863
Village III							
0–10	155	0	155	174	0	174	.891
11–20	79	9	88	83	1	84	1.048
21–30	4	14	18	31	1	32	.562
31–40	17	11	28	25	0	25	1.120
41–50	20	5	25	31	0	31	.806
51–60	10	3	13	9	0	9	1.444
61–70	8	1	9	12	0	12	.750
71 +	8	1	9	6	0	6	1.500
Total	301	44	345	371	2	373	.925

to migrate. Women's decisions are more complicated. They depend on many other factors, among them their age, marital status, level of education, the number and ages of their dependent children, and the willingness of kinswomen to foster those children.

A more parsimonious and ultimately more meaningful way to categorize village-born Black Caribs is as temporary or permanent residents of their home communities. The vast majority, for most of their lives, are temporary residents. They maintain a strong sense of identification with their home village, visit it frequently, even live there for many years at a time, but inevitably leave to find work elsewhere. Their number includes virtually all children and most men and women under the age of fifty. The children will grow up and eventually leave the village, some to attend secondary school, most to look for work. Like their own parents, they will spend many of their adult years living and working elsewhere. The only permanent residents of these villages are older men and women, who have little prospect of finding employment. Growing older means, for most of them, finally settling in their home community — this after many years divided between home and workplace.

Black Carib villages are best described as residential communities populated by a small but stable core of older women and men, and by a larger, more or less transient population of young men and women, and children. Many young people say that they prefer to live at home. But they add, with a wry smile, that sand buys nothing — this in allusion to the landscape and its most plentiful resource. Having nothing to sell but their labor, migration is a fact of life for the men and women who live in the village of La Playa and the others of Stann Creek District.

Village Landscape and Life

La Playa stands on a narrow strip of beach facing the Caribbean Sea, with the closest houses only a stone's throw from the water. Behind the village lies an elongated salt-water lagoon that, like the sea, functions both as fishing grounds and travel route. Nowadays most traffic into and out of the village is across the lagoon and then by road through the interior.

Geographically La Playa is an isolated settlement. Only a Creole fishing village, some seven or eight kilometers away, is accessible by land. Forty kilometers to the north lies another Black Carib village, and after that the town of Dangriga. But these cannot be reached by foot along the coast. The beach deteriorates to mangrove thickets, and estuaries intersect it here and there. In the past, people traveled by sea from La Playa and the other Black Carib settlements, either sailing in their dugout canoes or in one of the commercial vessels that plied the coast. The road system, however, has changed the pattern of travel today. Overland travel is far more common and reliable than sea transport, and four of the six communities are now directly accessible by road.

To reach the nearest road from La Playa requires crossing the lagoon, about a two-hour journey by dugout canoe, through a maze of shallow, narrow mangrove corridors. Alternatively, and for a fee, one can make the trip more quickly in a large dugout canoe, equipped with an outboard motor, that carries passengers and cargo between the village and the largely Creole town on the other side of the lagoon. People from La Playa frequent the town because of the services and supplies it offers. It has two large general stores and a new bank that opens one day a week for those who want to cash their paychecks or remittances. A bus also stops there twice a week on its way to Belize City. The only other means of public transportation is a freight truck that makes weekly trips to Belize City and carries some passengers. Whatever the mode of transportation, the trip requires eight to twelve hours of bone-shaking travel over partially paved road. Since the advent of internal air service several years ago, the local airline has scheduled regular stops at an unpaved airstrip a few miles from the town. But only the most prosperous travelers can afford the fare.

Very few people, aside from returning fishermen, approach La Playa from the front, by sea, these days. Those who do see the village spread out before them in the linear pattern that most Black Carib settlements share. The village has a small population that hovers around 450 most of the year, with houses strung out at irregular intervals down a kilometer-long stretch of sandy beach. La Playa has a spacious look because of this linear pattern, and also because the villagers keep it cleared of the natural growth that otherwise abounds along the coast. This is partly a matter of aesthetics, a "bushy" yard or village being equated with an ugly one. It also has a pragmatic side. The coastal villages of the Black Carib are entirely open to the near-constant trade winds, and they have few of the noxious insects, the blood-sucking black flies and mosquitoes, that plague the interior. There is a striking difference in the level of comfort between the southern coast and the interior during the rainy season, from about June to October. Nature is so extravagant inland that keeping the land clear is impossible. During the wet months the luxuriant vegetation provides a haven for biting and stinging insects, and the land itself turns into a morass. Throughout the season of inland misery, Black Caribs congratulate themselves for having the good sense to live on the sandy and well-drained coast. Anyone who has experienced the discomforts of the southern interior will agree that this is not mere conceit.

Visually, also, there is much to commend the southern coast. To visitors from the temperate zone the area has a sometimes startling beauty, especially on those brilliant days when sea and sky share the same clear shade of azure and only the pelicans and an occasional white sail interrupt the horizon. On a rare day the trade winds subside entirely. The sea then assumes the appearance of a vast lake, gray-green and glassy-smooth, the breakers reduced to mere ripples. An oppressive heat stifles the coast on those days, and people speak longingly of the accustomed "sea breeze."

Having been so long bleached by sun and rain, the village of La Playa cannot compete with the natural beauty of its setting. But it has a pleasant aspect, with its houses, pastel or weathered silver, scattered along the beach. Most of the houses are lumber, roofed with zinc. They stand poised on wooden stilts, from three to seven feet high. Before the severe hurricane in 1961, which devastated Belize City and other coastal settlements, nearly all of the houses were the rectangular palmetto-and-thatch type.[7] Since this type of house sits directly on the ground, many of them washed away during the storm. After the hurricane, the government offered loans and grants for the construction of sturdier wooden houses, and today these predominate in La Playa and the other Black Carib settlements (see Illus. 10, 11).

Houses vary somewhat in size, the smallest having two rooms, others three or four. House size bears little relation to household size, though, which may fluctuate from one month to the next. Since houses function primarily as sleeping and storage places, not as living spaces, even the smallest can easily accommodate a half-dozen children and adults.

House furnishings are similar but not uniform. Most houses are furnished quite simply, with a small wooden table, a few chairs and benches, and perhaps a cabinet or some shelves in the front room; and in the bedrooms, a wooden bedstead, and usually a trunk or large basket for storing clothing and linens. Since the government's plans for providing electricity in La Playa remain a goal rather than a reality, every house has a kerosene lamp, and most have a battery-powered radio.

In some houses, one room or a corner of one serves as a kitchen and is equipped with a kerosene stove. But most women still cook in hearths over open fires, in separate structures. Their kitchens, usually of the traditional palmetto-and-thatch construction, are well ventilated and relatively cool, even in the intense heat of the midday sun and dinner preparations.

The new lumber houses hardly differ in basic construction or furnishings from those in Creole and mestizo communities. But the thatched kitchens contain all manner of traditional tools and utensils: sturdy radial baskets, used for storing and carrying food; heavy stone-chip graters, some for coconut, others for cassava; round woven strainers and sieves; rough-hewn mahogany mortars and the pestles used for pounding plantains; and all of the paraphernalia to process cassava and bake cassava bread.[8] Many of these items are virtual antiques and nearly irreplaceable, due to a shortage of materials or of craftsmen who know how to make them. Women who own the large and shallow mahogany bowls that were once *de rigueur* for breadmaking prize them now. But for many other culinary tasks, they often express more enthusiasm for imported plastic or aluminum ware than for traditional tools.

Thirty years ago, Taylor (1951: 139) wrote that "technology remains what it was three hundred years ago." The same cannot be said today.

Many of the utensils and tools that people now use were made and purchased elsewhere. The flow of imported goods is most pronounced at Christmas, which brings a veritable deluge of clothing and other gifts from migrants, especially those in the United States. The gifts range from common items, such as aluminum pots, to more expensive and coveted goods: cameras, phonographs and records, watches, and the like. Except for these latter, and the few outboard motors, most imported tools and furnishings are simply manufactured substitutes for what was once made locally. Every kitchen and house contains some of these.

Most houses stand on small, separate lots that villagers lease from the government for an annual fee of a few dollars. Every yard has a wooden washstand, built under a fruit tree to shade women while they launder, and most have a small lumber bathhouse adjacent to the kitchen. A number of communal wells scattered throughout the village provide water for washing. Pure drinking water comes from the large, government-built cistern and several smaller, private ones that fill to capacity during the rainy season. Most yards also have a fruit tree or two, usually coconut palms, sometimes a mango, citrus, or breadfruit tree. About half have tiny gardens, planted with some cassava and other starchy tubers. Aside from these kitchen gardens and the occasional hibiscus bush, yards are clear of vegetation. Women meticulously sweep the sand around their houses to keep it free of extraneous materials, deposited there daily by the wind and by children.

Waste disposal is simple but effective. Villagers burn dried vegetation — leaves fallen from trees or weeds they have uprooted from the sand. They throw other incombustible and inedible waste into the sea. Scavenging animals, especially dogs and chickens, devour all edible trash, such as the grated coconut that women routinely throw out onto the sand after expressing the liquid to use in cooking or baking.

Many women keep a few chickens, both for their eggs and their flesh, but they have little else in the way of livestock. A few people have a hog or two penned, intended for the menu of some future ritual event. Villagers do not "own" dogs so much as they tolerate them as hangers-on. Cats fare somewhat better, there being enough rodents in the village to keep them well fed and sleek. The only feral animals that live in the village or its immediate environs are birds, various small reptiles, and legions of insects.

The few nonresidential structures in the village function as public meeting places, either by happenstance or design. Several petty shops do a small but steady business throughout the day. Mothers often send their children to the shops to buy a few cents' worth of baking powder, a box of matches, or perhaps a piece of salted pigtail or snout on days when fish is in short supply. Sometimes women make the purchases themselves, lingering for a few minutes to talk to the shopkeeper or his wife or to some of the other customers. One of the shopkeepers sells rum, and near his shop a small number of men often gather on Saturdays and Sundays, sitting in the shade and sharing a bit of rum or just conversing.

The village church and school are also community meeting places. Everyone is at least a nominal member of the small Roman Catholic church, and many women and children attend the weekly "Mass" (without sacraments) conducted by one of the teachers. Even more attend when, several times a year, the district priest visits the village. The adjacent school is denominational, like most in the country, partially funded by the government, but primarily administered by the Roman Catholic Church. Lay teachers, all of them Black Carib, staff it. By law, every child in Belize between the ages of six and fourteen spends weekdays in school, save for a short break at Christmas and a longer one in July and August.[9]

The delegated local head of church and school affairs is the principal, often a native of the Black Carib village to which he is assigned. He has diverse duties. Aside from teaching and managing the school, he conducts "Mass" and burials when the priest is unavailable. He sees to the maintenance of the school and church buildings, and he acts as an advisor to the women's religious sodality.

Like the sodalities in other Black Carib settlements, this one devotes some effort to fund-raising and uses the proceeds for various worthy causes, including church maintenance and contributions to burial expenses of members. The members also organize celebrations of Roman Catholic calendrical holidays. Voluntary associations, with female memberships, are common in the Black Carib communities of Belize, and in Guatemala and Honduras as well.[10] About forty women belong to the sodality in La Playa. Although membership is open to all women in the community, very few young women have chosen to join. The average age of the members is fifty-two. Most of these women are permanent residents of the village.

Another building that functions occasionally as a community meeting place is the *dabúyeiba*, temple (Illus. 43). A *dabúyeiba* has the same construction as a traditional palmetto-and-thatch house except for two details: it lacks any partition inside the main structure, and it has in addition a small *gúle*, sanctuary, which adjoins the back. It is there that the shaman "works" during *dügü*, the paramount ancestral ceremony. In the past, people built a new *dabúyeiba* for every *dügü* and then destroyed it at the bidding of their ancestors. This particular temple was built a number of years ago and has been the site of several *dügü*. The ancestors have never requested its destruction.

The oldest residents of the village recall watching the construction of temples as children, and they also remember a palmetto-and-thatch church and school, built around the turn of the century. Some of the other public buildings have no precedents. The health station and police station are fairly new, government-financed buildings. The former often stands vacant these days due to a national shortage of nurses. (Many have emigrated to the United States.) The community center and concrete hurricane shelter were also built with government funds, both during the past twenty years. Social events and meetings of the village council are held in the buildings.

About half a dozen men and women, elected biennially by other adults in the community, serve on the village council. Council members select one among themselves to serve as village council chairman. Frequently they choose a teacher or retired teacher, a man who has a higher level of education and a wider range of personal contacts with government and church officials than other villagers. Any adult in the community is eligible for election to the council. Although most council members are men, an older woman or two also typically serve. The posts carry no salary and are largely advisory.

Under the previous system of local government, an appointed *alcalde* represented his village, settled cases involving minor infractions of the law, and organized the *fajina,* the communal labor program for cleaning the village (see Dobson 1973: 293f.). The duties of a village council chairman are roughly similar, but he has more limited powers than *alcaldes* had. A chairman is the village's representative to the national government, and the government's agent in presenting and administering matters of public policy. He registers voters, petitions government aid for community self-help projects (which have now superseded unpaid, communal efforts), administers these projects and distributes government aid, plans the local ceremonies held on national holidays, and hosts government officials on their occasional visits to the community.

These various corporate groups — school, church, village council, and sodality — share one distinctive feature. All of them articulate with non-Carib, external organizations, Church and government; and each depends on one man to represent it to these external agencies. With the exception of the sodality, they are not self-sustaining groups. The village council and school have as their primary task the distribution of resources that come from *outside* the village. These range from disaster relief, which the village council chairman distributes (after hurricanes), to education, which teachers dispense daily in the schoolhouse. The religious sodality differs in at least one respect. The funds contributed to it, and distributed by it, come from *within* the community, from the women themselves and from fundraising events, although the money was earned outside the village. The community has no strictly local corporate group.[11]

These extralocal institutions help to counteract the geographic insularity of La Playa and other Black Carib villages in Belize. The few non-Caribs who visit these villages with any frequency are government and church officials. No other non-Caribs have any reason to do so, except for occasional visitors from other settlements in the vicinity who decide to "take a li' walk," as they say, and see the village for themselves. The mobility of village residents, past and present, is a more powerful force that works against isolation. However insular the villages, the people who live in them are not isolated because they are inveterate travelers, mobile by necessity but also, to judge from their relish of travel, by choice.

To different degrees, all of the men and women in La Playa and the other villages are familiar with urban centers and city life. Since many have traveled widely within the country and some quite extensively outside it, they have firsthand knowledge of a number of other places and peoples. The scarcity of wage labor in the south accounts for much, but certainly not all, of this travel. Women over the age of forty-five or fifty are unemployable, but not sedentary. They make frequent trips to other Black Carib communities to visit kin and to take part in ritual events there. The need for goods and services not available in villages also prompts travel to and from urban centers. Medical care beyond the level that rural nurses can provide is only available in the district towns, the capital, and Belize City. Postal service to rural villages is so limited that anyone expecting a package from kin in the United States must travel to the district town or to Belize City to claim it. Since local shopkeepers stock only staples, the need for so small an item as a particular kitchen tool or specific type of battery may require a trip to town or city to purchase it. Some women, whose children attend secondary school in the district towns or Belize City, accompany them and leave the village for months at a time.

Given this mobility, the "rustic" Black Carib villager is in one sense more cosmopolitan than the city dweller in Belize. Every villager has visited Belize City countless times, but few city residents have ever seen a Black Carib village. Only a handful of non-Caribs in Belize have any degree of knowledge about the Black Carib, and of those who profess such, many gained it entirely from hearsay. Some tell strange tales about their rituals, grossly distorting both aim and format.[12] Few can claim to base any of their information on direct observation of village life, which bears little resemblance to the common run of these accounts.

Daily Life

Daily life in a Black Carib village, like any residential community, centers on domestic routine. Its rhythm is punctuated by the comings and goings of villagers and migrants, and by the round of rituals and calendrical holidays. But the average day passes at measured pace, with familiar cadence.

The day begins earliest for a few men who leave in the cool, pre-dawn darkness, paddling their dugout canoes alone or with a companion out to sea or into the lagoon. A few of the fishermen will return early, around the time of the morning meal (*bacháti,* tea). Most will not return until midday, particularly if they left just before sunrise.

The next to stir are the women, sometime between 5:00 and 6:00 A.M. Children wake soon after. As soon as they arise, most women slip on bright cotton dresses or gathered skirts and blouses, their everyday garb; and many, especially older women, tie a *músue,* headwrap, over their hair. They spend the next hour at a number of daily tasks: chopping firewood with a machete into small pieces suitable for fuel, and using a coconut broom or a manufactured one to sweep the yard. They take a few minutes to sweep yesterday's accumulation of sand from the floors and steps of their houses. Once a week women spend considerably more time and energy scrubbing the same surfaces thoroughly with soap and water.

During these early-morning tasks, their thoughts turn to the morning meal. They consider which variety of quick bread to make and, more problematic, where to find fresh fish to serve with it. One of the first questions a woman puts to her neighbors is whether any fishermen have returned yet and whether they have any fish for sale. If the answer is affirmative, she quickly dispatches one of her children or grandchildren, or walks herself, to the fisherman's house, hoping to purchase at least a few fish for tea. If he has a good catch, she may be fortunate enough to buy an amount sufficient for the day's needs, relieving her of this time-consuming chore for the rest of the day.

Even before a woman asks the whereabouts of fishermen, she greets her neighbors, who greet her in return. There is a stock sequence of questions and replies with which, as a matter of politeness, one adult greets another during their initial encounter each day. It begins with an inquiry about the other's well-being and typically ends with an affirmation of the speaker's own. But if the woman's neighbor is not in good health, the morning inquiry may prompt her to describe her symptoms at length. Her listeners commiserate with her, and perhaps suggest a particular remedy or advise her to talk to one or another of the oldest women in the village, some of whom have special expertise in "bush medicine" made with local plants.

Morning is also the time when anyone who has had a vivid dream during the night relates it to others. If the dream seems to have numerical significance, it will figure in conversation throughout the day, as people speculate whether it might be a winning number in the daily or weekly national lottery.

From 7:00 to 9:00 A.M., yards are the scene of noisy activity. Women work energetically, taking advantage of the morning coolness. They send children in various directions: one to a nearby well to fetch water, to wash dishes left from the previous night's meal; another to a shop to buy a few matches or a bit of baking powder. Mothers pacify their hungry youngest children with a piece of bread left from the day before, and then perhaps send them to a well or the sea for a bath, usually in the custody of an older brother or sister. On any morning there are apt to be a dozen small bodies at a time bobbing in the gentle surf; later, they up-end buckets of well water over each other to wash away the salt.

Chickens and dogs contribute to the general hubbub, browsing about busily in anticipation of the grated coconut that women throw out on the sand, and the fish bones that human diners discard there. Inevitably an expectant chicken or two intrudes into the kitchen and immediately departs in a flurry of feathers and curses. But women devote most of their attention to the task at hand: making a quick bread, either flour tortillas or "fry jack," a bread fried in coconut oil; frying fish, preferably in coconut oil or, lacking that, in lard; and boiling water for "tea," made with commercial tea or coffee or a local herb, and drunk well sweetened with sugar and condensed milk. The cook does not sit down to eat until she has handed plates of food to others in her household as they appear in the kitchen, usually starting with the youngest children, who remain constantly underfoot until their stomachs are filled.

Sometime during these early hours, a few women walk down the beach to cut firewood. They leave the village in pairs, or perhaps three or four together, each laden with a machete, a piece of rope, and a cloth to cushion her head from the bundle of wood she will carry back to her yard. They stride off purposefully; but their return, in the late-morning heat and with upwards of fifty pounds of wood balanced gracefully on their heads, is at a more leisurely pace. This is a weekly chore for them, although those few women who own small kerosene stoves require less wood, using it only when they bake bread over open fires.

By 9:00 A.M. most of the children are playing in the schoolyard. Here and there a dilatory girl submits to her mother's or older sister's hasty efforts to finish plaiting her hair before the bell rings; and a young boy, reluctantly following his mother's orders, takes off his old khaki shorts and puts on a more presentable pair for school. When the bell rings at 9:00 or shortly after, one-third of the village population crowds into the confines of the school building, and the level of noise immediately subsides. The village is suddenly and startlingly quiet, and has an almost vacant look. Women continue to work at various tasks in their kitchens and yards, and the occasional man who walks by greets them and perhaps lingers for a few minutes to talk. There is little work for men to do locally, and men who choose not to fish on a particular day spend it relaxing or working casually, seeing to various house repairs, mending a tool, and the like.

Women, both young and old, never face the prospect of empty hours to fill. If they are not busy finding food and preparing it, the interminable task of laundering always awaits them. The equipment is minimal: a laundry tub made of mahogany or, in the new tradition, aluminum; a wooden washboard; and plenty of soap and muscle. Women launder on a daily basis; holidays offer the only respite. And every day they routinely express both astonishment and dismay at the ability of men and children to soil so much clothing. Laundering is solitary work, but not an isolating task. Women have a clear view of their neighbors in adjacent yards; and when they make a trip to the well for another bucket of water, they may linger for a half-hour visit there with a kinswoman or friend on the same mission.

While various tasks occupy their hands during the morning, women's thoughts turn to dinner, which they will serve at noon or after, depending upon when they acquire the needed ingredients. Throughout the morning women interrupt their work repeatedly to walk down to the beach and scan the horizon for signs of returning fishermen. They stop anyone who walks by with a string of fish, to inquire where it was bought and if some remains for sale. Even before a woman has found fish, she optimistically begins to prepare the foods that will accompany it: usually either rice and beans; boiled or fried plantains or green bananas; or "ground food," starchy tubers such as yams or sweet cassava.

When a fisherman does come in, usually before noon, the news of his arrival spreads to the other end of the village before he reaches his house. A crowd of several dozen buyers may gather there within minutes. Sizing up his catch—perhaps a large jewfish and several strings of small snappers if he has had a good day—they can see that demand exceeds supply and that not everyone will be able to buy some fish. Despite the banter and jokes that pass between the fisherman and expectant buyers, people appear anxious and impatient. The women are trying to calculate how much fish they can hope to buy. Some express regret that they decided not to buy salted meat, because of its expense, earlier in the day. A few reassure themselves and the others with the thought that more fishermen will surely return soon, perhaps with even larger catches. Buyers call out their preferences to the fisherman as he cuts up the jewfish: "I want the head, *yau* [uncle]," or "Save two pounds for me, *nidúhen* [cousin]." When he hands the pieces to his wife for her to weigh on a small scale that hangs from the kitchen rafters, the buyers turn toward her: "I want three pounds, *naúfuri* [aunt]." Some walk away with obvious satisfaction, fish in hand. Others leave disgruntled, empty-handed or with a portion of fish that they consider insufficient, complaining that the fisherman or his wife has been stingy with them.

Back home, the women gut and scrape the fish hastily, scattering the glittering scales around them in the sand as they work. Then they boil the fish in *lesúsu*, coconut milk seasoned with pepper and onion, or some other sauce, depending on the ingredients at hand. Between noon and 1:00 P.M., while school is recessed, schoolchildren eat whatever the women have prepared.

In early afternoon the heat intensifies, and the sand grows white-hot underfoot. People seem to move in slow motion, until torpor overtakes even the women, who cease work for an hour or two, some resting in hammocks that hang under their houses. Small children give up their frenetic play and fall asleep in a shady spot. Here and there small clusters of men and women gather, trading banter or earnest talk about topics of universal and perennial interest: the high cost of living, and the scarcity of jobs with good wages; the whereabouts of various migrants; the number likely to play in the national lottery; the latest local scandal.

These are quiet hours, save for the murmur of conversation and the sound of a few radios tuned to Radio Belize. Recorded music, a mix of Jamaican reggae and plaintive Spanish ballads, alternates with announcements: usually death notices or personal messages for people in remote rural areas who otherwise would require days or weeks to contact. Villagers may first hear of the death or illness of an absent relative by radio; and many women listen with keen interest to these announcements, shaking their heads over the personal tragedies of unknown people in distant and obscure places. During the afternoon lull, some of them also take a few minutes to draw water from the well, then retire to bathe. Later, as they talk together, they occupy their hands by plaiting their hair or a companion's. On a Friday, conversation may turn to husbands and sons, due home for the weekend from the banana plantation.

By 4:00 the afternoon heat has begun to subside. Women start to prepare the evening meal of fried fish, bread, and tea. About once a week they make yeast breads, waiting for these cool hours to begin the hot and smoky business of baking wheat bread in covered pots over an open fire. Less often, a few of the women who plant manioc will bake cassava bread, a much more elaborate and lengthy process (see Illus. 14–23).

Between 5:00 and 6:00, women serve food in their kitchens, usually on a first-come, first-served basis. As darkness falls they are finishing the last bit of cooking. After the women eat, they stack the dishes and pans by the dim light of the embers in the hearth, store any leftover food in sturdy, rodent-proof baskets suspended from the rafters, and close up the kitchens. A kerosene lamp illuminates each house, its windows closed against the cool night breeze and, some say, against the malevolent spirits that frequent the village in the darkness.

During the early hours of the night, *gúñon*, between 6:00 and 9:00 P.M., small clusters of people congregate outside if the moon is bright, or if someone has made a bonfire of trash, illuminating the yard. There is a steady flow of traffic toward the shops that sell lottery chances for a few cents apiece.

Most women and children have retired to their houses by 8:00 P.M. or so, and men join them soon after. By 9:00 the village is quiet, save for the low and constant undertone of the surf. Many people say that spirits always wander about the village during the night, especially between 9:00 and midnight, *áriabu,* and the even more dangerous period between midnight and 2:00 or 2:30 in the morning, *iráwina áriabu.* If so, they encounter few humans outside on an ordinary night. When a rooster first crows at about 2:30 A.M., the dangerous time has passed. A few fishermen awake and dress, pulling on khaki pants, cotton shirts, and hats, ordinary working attire for men. They walk to their dugout canoes, untie them from the moorings, and paddle away, leaving fleeting trails of phosphorescent bubbles in the opaque water. Above them they see the moon and a scattering of stars, still visible but waning. Before the sun has risen, another day begins.

Notes to Chapter 4

1. These percentages are figured on the basis of Davidson's (1976a) estimates of settlement size and total population of the Black Carib. Since Davidson does not include migrant Black Caribs living in non-Carib locales in these estimates, their total population size (and proportion of national populations) may well be somewhat higher. The 1970 census for Belize offers no help in this matter, as it groups Black Caribs in the category "other races" (CRP 1975 VII: 31–33).

2. Until recently, Settlement Day was a public holiday only in the two southern districts where all of the Black Carib settlements are located. The 1975 celebration was considered the 152nd anniversary of the settlement, although documentary evidence indicates that the first Black Caribs arrived in the colony in 1802, not 1823 (see Burdon 1934: 60f.). It may be that 1823 is the date when Dangriga (formerly known as Stann Creek Town and reputedly the oldest Black Carib settlement in Belize) was established.

3. Hadel (1972: 54ff.) describes various calendrical holidays, including National Day, Settlement Day, Christmas, Easter, and a number of holy days.

4. This figure comes from the Central Bureau of Statistics (1948: xxxi) and is based on all Black Carib females over the age of ten.

5. The Department of Statistics (1961 I: 184ff.) provides figures on the distribution of adult (fifteen years and older) Carib speakers in Belize. The 1970 census does not furnish comparable information.

6. Taylor (1951: 58), who did his research in the former village, estimated that "rather less than half" of the households actively maintained a "farm," as these cultivated plots are called in Belize. Many of the people in the latter village who told me that they leased land were not cultivating it. A number of women complained that they had no ablebodied men in their households to clear the land, or that the men were employed during the season when the land is cleared (generally between March and May). See Beaucage (1970) and Chibnik (1975) for detailed accounts of horticulture.

7. Taylor (1951: 70ff.) provides a thorough description of these houses and other aspects of traditional material culture.

8. Taylor (1951: 62ff.) describes in detail how cassava bread is made (also see Roberts 1827: 272; Swett 1867: 26; Conzemius 1928: 195-97; 1930: 873-75).

9. Ashcraft and Grant (1968) provide a brief but comprehensive account of the educational system in Belize.

10. Religious sodalities, or other voluntary associations whose memberships are largely or exclusively composed of older women, are mentioned by Gonzalez (1970b: 167f.), Coelho (1955: 158f.), Adams (1957: 375), Taylor (1951: 88), and Chamberlain (1979: 82).

11. This is true, as Mintz (1966: 939) remarks, of many rural communities in the Caribbean. Dirks (1972) points out that some of those communities lack a stable local resource base, a prerequisite for such groups.

12. Taylor (1951: 113n, 132) mentions one particularly long-lived and lurid piece of hearsay that still has currency among some non-Caribs in Belize: namely, that *dügü*, the paramount ceremony for the dead, has elements of "devil worship," including human sacrifice (cf. Coelho 1955: 49; Conzemius 1928: 204). Young (1847: 131), over a century ago, referred to *dügü* as a "Devil feast," no doubt having learned that term from non-Caribs. To the best of my knowledge, there is not a shred of documentary evidence that the Black Carib in St. Vincent ever ceremonially consumed human flesh, as the Red Carib reputedly did. But even John Lloyd Stephens (1841: 29), who was otherwise so judicious and perceptive in his comments, described an old woman in one Black Carib settlement who "looked as though, in her youth, she had gloried in dancing at a feast of human flesh."

1. A Carib family (late eighteenth century).

2. Chatoyer and five women (late eighteenth century).

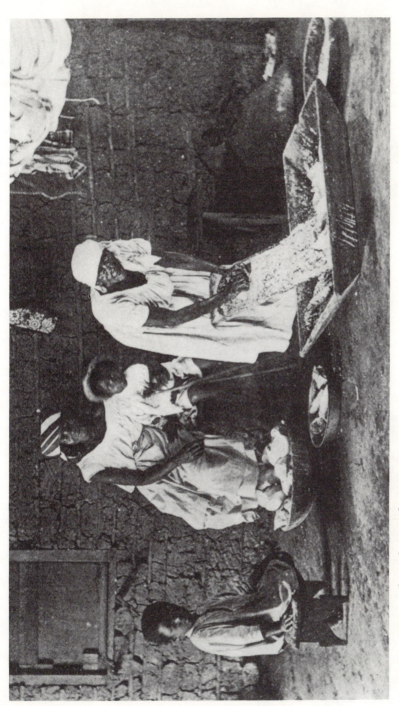

3. Grating cassava (late nineteenth century).

4. Two young women.

5. Weaving a serpiente.

6. A group of children.

7. Interior of a house.

8. A street in Livingston, Gautemala.

9. Buying fish.

10. A village house.

11. Houses in Dangriga.

12. A traditional thatched house.

13. The usual mode of inland travel.

14–23. Baking cassava bread.

Chapter 5

PERSONAL AUTONOMY

Women often admonish their children with the homily, "You must fight for yourself." The expression has multiple meanings, both figurative and literal. It refers at once to the necessity of self-reliance, the nature of work, the structure of conflict, and the value of personal autonomy.[1]

This well-founded piece of folk wisdom springs from the fact that social organization is fundamentally dyadic: rooted in relations of reciprocity between individuals, who control their own labor and its products.[2] While men and women universally recognize their financial obligations to primary kin, meeting them is another matter. Obligations to others are very diffuse. In either case, no one can compel anyone else to "share." The only resort is all manner of friendly persuasion or, should that fail, a threat or show of personal force. For the most part, individuals decide what and with whom they will share. Reputation is almost wholly based on personal (not collective) evaluations of an individual's "generosity," and of other personal qualities such as honesty, wit, and mettle. People are held responsible for their own conduct from early childhood, and judged accordingly. Most conflict is interpersonal and generally centers on exchange: how individuals choose to share money and other forms of personal property.

Labor and Property Ownership

Wherever they work, for the most part men and women work individually. They have done so (in the wage economy at least) ever since their ancestors consented to carry cargo from ship to shore for daily wages of a "Spanish dollar" per man. Even at home no *daily* work requires cooperative effort. A small group of women may go off to cut firewood together, but only, they say, for the purpose of sociability or for protection against wandering spirits in the bush who attack lone individuals. Women do not pool the firewood unless they live in the same household. Any mutual aid is limited to helping each other lift the bundles of wood onto the head for carrying. Although a small number of kinswomen usually cooperate in processing manioc to make cassava bread, a woman can accomplish this without assistance and occasionally does so. Other domestic tasks, from laundering clothes to preparing food, can be done single-handedly. Likewise, men often fish alone, and most of their other work is solitary.

For the most part, property is personal and portable: clothing, tools, furniture, and the like. Black Caribs do not commonly own property of value exceeding the means of an individual and requiring joint purchase and joint ownership. Even spouses generally keep their finances separate and claim little property in common.

Inheritance of houses and of land pose the only exceptions to the general rule of individual ownership. In theory, the spouse and descendants inherit property equally and in common when the owner dies. In fact, however, the surviving kin and other villagers refer to the deceased person as owner. Usually the spouse and children simply continue to live in the home. In the occasional case in which the owner was childless and widowed, one of the next of kin claims it but still names the deceased as owner. In one such case, the woman who had borne most of the expense for her paternal aunt's burial, and other rituals after the woman's death, claimed the house; but she still refers to it as her aunt's house. No one has contested her claim, probably because houses are not in short supply.[3] Due to labor migration, as many as a quarter of the houses in these communities stand vacant for much of the year.

As for land, ownership of productive acreage is exceptional. Less than 1 percent of all adults (in the three villages surveyed) own a piece of land that they purchased. In most cases the holding is small, a few acres at most. The property is not on productive land, and equivalent house-lots are available from the government for an annual rent of a few dollars. There are only two pieces of land that were purchased several generations ago, in the 1890s, and people still refer to the original purchasers as the owners. All lineal descendants of these two men have the right to build houses on their land, but few have done so. By all accounts, occupation of one piece of land has proceeded peacefully. The other has a complex history of displacement that is difficult to reconstruct, with several contradictory versions. At present, two houses stand on the land; a woman, her spouse, and several of her children and daughters' children live in the houses. The woman's maternal grandfather purchased the land.

Inheritance is not an important means of acquiring most property. Men and women obtain money and goods through their own efforts: either directly, through wage work or other productive activity, or indirectly, by persuading others to honor their obligations and to share with them. Direct acquisition of cash and goods occasions little dispute. Individuals own whatever they earn or produce. What *is* often problematic is sharing. There are no specific "rules" that govern it, aside from the general obligation to help support lineal kin and spouse, and to be as generous as possible with others. The ethos of generosity is so expansive and diffuse that a broad range of kith and kin request occasional "help" with money or food. In many cases they demand it, and publicly if necessary. Whoever fails to press a claim for help courts neglect — whether that be an aged parent, a woman who is financially dependent on her husband, a man who wants the bottle of rum passed his way, or even an ancestor who asks attention from living descendants.

Thus, a woman who had complained several times to her husband about the pittance he gave her each payday finally lost her patience. Her husband had once again handed her a few dollars for food, not enough for the week. Turning a deaf ear to her protests, he departed with the balance of his money, to enjoy the day with friends. The woman was washing clothes and brooding over the matter when her sister stopped to visit. With this sympathetic audience of one, the woman was moved to complain about her husband's neglect. She began in a conversational tone, enumerating his faults. But as her anger increased so did the volume of her voice, until finally she was announcing to everyone in the vicinity that unless her husband changed his "ways," he would soon find himself without a wife. She described his probable discomfort in lavish and colorful detail, and to the great amusement of her listeners in adjacent yards. The "news" soon reached her husband's ears, and a few weeks after the fact, the woman said that her husband was taking his financial obligations to the household more seriously. Commenting that some people must be reminded of their obligations, and shamed when they neglect them, she summed up her own actions by saying, "You must fight for yourself."

Conflict

From early childhood, people learn to "fight for themselves." Women train their sons and daughters to be self-reliant, to confront adversaries. They do not reward submission or retreat, even by very small children. When a young woman saw her cousin's boy throwing sand in the face of her four-year-old son, she did not move to his defense. The child quickly fled to her because his cousin was clearly superior in size and strength, but the woman did not comfort him or scold the other boy. Instead, she stooped down and picked up the nearest missile at hand, an old can, and sent her son so armed out to battle. "If he beats you, you must beat him back," she instructed. At the sight of the can and the little boy's determined face, the older boy flung a final handful of sand, then took to his heels.

Like these children, adults may threaten attack but they rarely come to blows. To outward appearances, villagers enjoy cordial relations with each other. People pause to exchange pleasantries and banter throughout the day. Inquiries about health are pro forma, as are expressions of friendship and esteem. But many complain privately that others are jealous and hypocritical, that they pretend good will but harbor old grudges and ill feelings. Past quarrels provide the usual evidence marshaled to support this view. It seems that axes are never buried, and even minor disputes linger on in memory. Years after the fact, men and women can relate the occasions and circumstances of old quarrels in minute detail.

Most conflict centers on exchange, the manner in which people share, or refuse to share, with each other. Observation supports the common claim that jealousy, *emeídini*, and envy, *gimúgaü*, lie at the root of most interpersonal conflict. Exchange is dyadic, and so are most of the quarrels that spring from it. Occasionally conflict spreads to include others — particularly a parent, sibling, or child of one of the disputants. But most quarrels directly involve only two people. The use of collective sanctions, such as ostracism or concerted physical force, is exceptional.[4]

This is cause for regret in some instances. A young woman, near the end of her first pregnancy, complained one day that the father of her unborn child refused to support her, and that it would be at least six months before she could leave her baby with her mother and look for work herself. If she were Spanish [mestizo], she said, her father and brothers would force the man to marry her. "That is why the Spanish all marry while so many of us must fight for ourselves," she concluded.

If men and women find it difficult to enlist others in their cause, neither can they resort to the use of economic sanctions. As a general rule, no one controls a material resource, such as land or employment, which is indispensable to the security and well-being of many others. The only obvious exception to this general rule is shopkeepers, who, since they extend credit for goods, can easily withdraw it. This tactic of withdrawal is an effective one, and villagers usually follow a circumspect course in their dealings with shopkeepers. They need credit and take care not to offend the men who dispense it.

As for legal action, villagers very commonly threaten to seek restitution in court for such minor crimes as petty theft, but few actually do so. The expense of transportation, if nothing else, discourages legal redress. There are other more economical and effective means of retaliation.

The common sanctions, available to virtually all men and women, are slander, assault, and sorcery (cf. Coelho 1955: 68ff). Slander is rampant in villages, where indignant reports of misbehavior, barbed jokes, and critical commentary fill daily talk. Whether accusations have any foundation in fact is largely irrelevant. They are usually impossible to verify, in any case, because they center on private or covert acts. Women are most often charged with sexual misconduct, men with neglect of financial duty, men and women alike with "stinginess" or dishonesty. The fact that slander is nearly impossible to disprove and that the burden of disproof rests on the accused (who is guilty until proven innocent) gives it special strength. The slandered person's only recourse is to deny the charge, often in public and to the accuser's face.

Nearly all men and women complain that they are victims of slander. They regularly suspect others of talking against them, secretly calling their characters into question. This happens publicly on occasion, when one person confronts another and "rails up" about some offense, impugning the other's honesty, generosity, or sexual conduct. Some of these confrontations end in assault. Threats of attack are quite common, but actual instances are not, and very few result in serious injury. Although disputants may arm themselves — with a machete, harpoon, or bottle — most weapons are props, more often brandished for effect than used. Cases of assault between women, typically sexual rivals, are often sent to the district court by the local police. No matter the particular circumstances, the judge is said to rule in favor of the legal wife, or the woman whose relation with the man is of longer standing. Cross-sex assault also occurs, usually between current or former sexual partners (and sometimes initiated by the woman).

More cases of assault and threats of attack involve two men, and in many instances rum is both the catalyst and the object of dispute. The usual circumstances are as follows: A man has bought a small amount of rum to share with a few friends, and another man intrudes. The self-invited guest expects a drink, the buyer fails to offer it, and the disappointed guest accuses him of stinginess. Very often the two men are already intoxicated and in no mood to be "interfered with," as they put it. As they argue and begin to threaten physical harm, someone inevitably runs to inform kinswomen of the disputants, usually an elder sister, mother, or aunt, who appear quickly at the site. Each seizes her kinsman's arm and urges him to leave, saying *Kaímau águyu,* "Let's go home." If that fails, she tries to scold him into compliance, saying *Nubúsi-garítibu,* "You are shameful." Mothers reprove errant children with the same words.

Women act as mediators in such disputes, but their intervention does not usually resolve them. They simply try to separate the hostile parties, to prevent them from harming each other. Tempers cool, and in a matter of days the disputants no longer openly show antagonism. After some weeks or months they may pretend friendship. But by most accounts, old quarrels languish rather than die. Very serious ones may rekindle years later, when one of the parties is stricken by some misfortune, especially a wasting illness. People recall old quarrels and grudges, and they speculate that sorcery, *abíñagaü,* is the cause of this affliction.

In some respects sorcery is a matter of everyday concern. People often speak of it, and some take daily "precautions" to protect themselves. Many women claim to count their laundry when they lay it out to dry and again when they collect it, to make sure that none is missing. They explain that an enemy could take a piece of clothing to a sorcerer or sorceress and pay to have it "worked on."

Sorcery does not necessarily require the skills of a specialist. The use of ordinary poison is also categorized as sorcery, and people commonly claim to exercise caution in accepting food and drink from any but those whom they fully trust. Observation does not entirely support this claim, since men rarely refuse any drinks offered to them. But of course men who die suddenly and unexpectedly are often said to have been poisoned in precisely this way.

Few men or women ever admit openly to the use of poison or another form of sorcery, that being tantamount to an admission of attempted murder. But they readily threaten its use. A woman whose prized rooster disappeared one night confronted the man she believed had taken it and demanded payment. When he denied her charge and refused to compensate her loss, she swore to see a "wise man" (a diviner, assumed to be a sorcerer as well) in the district town. A few days later the man sent her partial payment, which the woman said was not entirely satisfactory but certainly better than nothing.

Since most sorcery is covert, it may seem a piece of fiction to an outsider. While most people deny ever using sorcery to harm others, many admit that they have paid sorcerers goodly sums for protective "medicine": as much as $30, well over a week's wages for the average male laborer. (The cost of simply asking a question of a diviner-sorcerer is far less, about a dollar). Furthermore, even men and women who profess not to believe in many other supernatural phenomena consider sorcery a real and dangerous threat.

Sorcery and slander are both weapons that are equally available to, and effective against, nearly everyone. Slander, the lesser of the two, is rife, and works to level reputations, just as the system of exchange levels economic differences.

Reputation and Exchange

Reputation, the assessment of personal worth, is based on an individual's conduct with others (cf. Dwyer 1978: 233). Villagers agree that a "decent" person is generous and honest; a "worthless" person is dishonest, stingy, *hángi-,* or poor, *magábari-* (literally, having no life). But people's evaluations of specific others differ, since their personal relations with them vary.

Generosity, *araíni,* is without doubt the most admired trait in a man, woman, or child (cf. Coelho 1955: 86). This positive quality is often phrased negatively, in terms of being not stingy, *mángi-.* The definition of generosity also has a negative cast: a generous person is one who responds to a request for help without protest, without expecting an equivalent return — ideally, without ever asking a return. Obviously, no one can be generous with everyone without being reduced to destitution; and to be poor, incapable of generosity, is little better than to be stingy, unwilling to share. Hence, the circle of men and women whom any person describes as generous and decent is small and personally defined. At the center, forming a stable core, are some (but not necessarily all) of the person's lineal kin. Exchanges with them are distinctive in two respects: they may be asymmetrical, and the returns long delayed. On the periphery are others, kin and friends, whose numbers are usually in flux. Exchanges with them tend to be balanced. A man who shares rum with his friends assumes that they will soon reciprocate in kind; if they fail to do so, his openhandedness with them ceases, and his opinion of them plummets.

One of the most common causes of severed friendships and personal animosity is default on petty loans of cash. Although most men and women try to present themselves as generous people, they complain openly about outstanding debts. They may warn their debtors with the maxim *Máma rügünei ábán wáiasu labúserun mégu lúmari,* "It's not only once monkey wants his woman." In other words, no matter how great their future need, they will have to look elsewhere for help.

Some etiquette also surrounds exchange, and much of it has the apparent purpose of emphasizing the donor's generosity (or, to take a cynical view, trying to force it). One woman explained the proper presentation of food this way. If she has just finished cooking when she has unexpected visitors, it is rude to ask them, "Would you like some fish?" or "Are you hungry?" or "Have you eaten yet?" All of these questions indicate reluctance to share with them: that is to say, stinginess. Instead, she should serve whatever food she can "spare," setting this before her guests and letting them decide whether to decline or to eat the food. Either is a suitable response.

Acceptance also has its various points of etiquette. The expectation of reciprocity is generally tacit, and one rarely hears expressions of gratitude or thanks between adults. The recipient may comment favorably on the size or quantity of the item, or indicate pleasure at receiving it, but not thankfulness. An expression of gratitude is inappropriate because it suggests that the exchange is complete, that there will be no return. Gratitude also connotes subordination, and men and women usually present themselves as equals in their dealings with each other, whether they ask for help or give it. No one subscribes to the notion that people are entitled only to what they directly earn, and receiving does not inevitably imply inferiority. On the contrary, people tend to interpret what they receive from others as material evidence of their esteem. (Perceptions of an exchange may differ, depending on whether one is on the giving or receiving end. While recipients consider themselves well liked, the donors very often complain after the fact about their "begging habits.")

Only in the few cases of acknowledged inequality do subordinates routinely express gratitude. After each meal, children thank adults in the household for the food they have eaten. This is a point of etiquette and a sign of good training. Mourning and other ritual obligations to deceased kin, especially elder lineals and spouses, also count as tangible expressions of gratitude. And in church, the prayers offered to God are full of thanks.

Because most exchange is dyadic, evaluations of generosity often vary enormously from one person to the next. Ritual sponsorship provides nearly the only instance in which there is community consensus about personal reputation. People who cannot, or choose not, to sponsor a required rite for one of their ancestors deny food and drink not only to the dead but also to other villagers, the incumbent guests. Showing "gratitude" to the dead necessarily entails the display of generosity to the living.

Men and women who do sponsor rituals, particularly very lavish ones, often enjoy a fleeting taste of community esteem. Reputation is intrinsically unstable, and slander plays a major role in its decline. Villagers use "collective" slander on an everyday basis, to level reputation. Rumor and gossip work against the development of any fixed system of ranking and prestige. Many people speak of it as "wickedness out of nothing" (that is, unfounded malice). Gossip is not necessarily a response to any specific offense, but simply "idle talk," as they call it, part of the daily and informal exchange of information about others. To be the subject of gossip and rumor is, everyone agrees, emotionally painful. Some say it can even cause a type of physical illness, *idáhadu*. As one man defined it, *idáhadu* is "a sickness caused by criticism and ill intentions," especially when that criticism is whispered privately by hypocritical people who pretend publicly to be one's friends.[5]

Villagers complain bitterly about this sort of slander and backbiting, and they even sing about it. One song begins with the ponderous question, "What am I going to do to please my fellow Caribs?" and continues pessimistically: "Even when you are on good terms with them / They will always have something to say against you" (translation by Hadel 1972: 199).

As this song suggests, virtually no one can maintain an unblemished name. Everyone occasionally suffers as the victim of gossip, and some habitually. These latter, also the targets of the most spiteful gossip, are the few men who enjoy some financial advantage: shopkeepers, head teachers, and, to a lesser extent, other teachers. Scarcely a week passes without a rumor that one or another has committed some sexual impropriety or act of ungenerosity. What distinguishes this gossip from the common run is its virulence, not simply its hostile humor, which figures in all manner of social criticism. It is these men whom others so frequently accuse of serious misconduct. Whatever the original charge of such a rumor, it worsens with each telling. Thus, according to the "news" circulating one day, a teacher was to be disciplined for having gone to school drunk. By the end of the week, the rumor had several embellishments, including alleged acts of sexual perversion.

When they are not the subject of current "scandal," these men must contend with constant and belittling humor. One village council chairman, whom others resent for his attitude of superiority, has the nickname *gáyu*, chicken; and except when he is within earshot, everyone refers to him by this name. It derives from his (alleged) theft of a chicken one night when he was (allegedly) drunk. "He acts high," other villagers say, laughing scornfully, "but he is really just a common chicken thief." This man and the others try to dismiss such ridicule, putting it off to jealousy. Their fellows do not like to see anyone "above" them, they say.

Generosity, like other aspects of the sensitive matter of giving and taking, also has a prominent place in humor. Anyone returning home after an extended trip hears one question from nearly everyone: *Ka buíti banúgabai nun?* "What good thing did you bring for me?"[6] The traveler's stock reply, *Níkata*, "Nothing," always provokes uproarious laughter. This standing joke never tires with the retelling.

Generosity and stinginess occupy a central place in morality as well as humor. Most men and women pride themselves on their generosity, and many consider it a distinctive cultural trait (but by the same accounts not equally manifest in all). Stinginess they regard as reprehensible. To be stingy is to stockpile food and money beyond immediate needs, and to refuse all requests for "help." Evaluations of stinginess, like judgments of generosity, vary. Only the few notoriously stingy people, who fail even to share with spouse and lineals and who entirely neglect ritual obligations, fall prey to community ridicule and contempt.

Because people find it virtually impossible to meet every request for a small loan or gift of cash or food, they use various techniques to circumvent them. The primary means is to conceal money and food, the theory apparently being that others will ask for what they can see. A woman who purchases a ten-pound tin of lard elsewhere, for example, usually carries it back to the village concealed in a box or bag. Once home, she does not leave it sitting openly on a shelf or table in her kitchen; to do so is to invite requests from needy neighbors. Instead, she puts it in a back room of the house, which only others in her household or close kin enter without explicit invitation; and she measures out the amount she needs each time she cooks. Consequently, only she knows precisely how much she has and whether she can "spare" some to any petitioner.

Other strategies to ward off requests without appearing stingy also entail creating the appearance of absolute equality, of having no more food or money than one's fellows. One means is literally to dispose of food or money immediately. Children, given pieces of candy, often consume them on the spot, regardless of appetite. Likewise, women commonly buy staples in small quantities and use them immediately. Most purchase only a few cents' worth of baking powder or salt or matches at a time. In theory, they would save money by buying in bulk. In fact, purchasing small amounts proves more economical in the long run — especially for those who are loath to appear stingy, and who prefer to say honestly that they have none to spare.

Still another defensive technique, a less common resort, is simply to deny proprietary rights. Refusing a request for food or money with the words *máma náni,* not mine, is equivalent to saying "I don't have the right to give it to you." Like any other refusal, this one does not always convince petitioners. Two young girls, sent to their neighbor's house on an errand one morning, arrived just as she was removing *tableta,* a type of coconut candy, from the hearth. They both asked for a bit, *murúsun,* the word often used in requests for anything divisible. The woman demurred, saying that it was her husband's; he had purchased all the ingredients and asked her to make it. The girls left, disgruntled and unconvinced. *Hángitu,* "She's stingy," they said. For her part, the woman explained that if she gave the girls some candy, she would find all of the children in the vicinity at her doorstep, asking for *murúsun.*

Despite this elaborate system of defense, generosity is not simply a figment of the cultural imagination. There are certainly many instances when people share widely, but these tend to be either ritual occasions or to involve highly perishable foods — for example, the wild grapes that women and children gather seasonally. And in many cases people conceal their possessions, they say, not because they are ungenerous but for fear of incurring the jealousy and malice of other people. This seems to be true enough where nondivisible goods are concerned, and concealment is not entirely a defense against sharing. In one such case, a woman handed her ten-year-old son a few dollars one morning and sent him to her sister's house for a cooking pot. She had asked her sister to buy an aluminum pot for her in the district town, and the woman had just returned from her trip. A few minutes later the boy returned, dangling the pot by its handle. When he carried it to his mother in the kitchen, she boxed his ear and rebuked him angrily: "Why didn't you put it in a bag? Do you want everyone to see what we have?"

The fact that not all property can be concealed is a matter of regret. A woman whose hog died suddenly and without apparent cause believed that one or another of her envious neighbors had poisoned the animal. She pointed out that she was the only person in the community with valuable livestock; the others had only a few chickens. "If people here see you try to improve yourself," she said, "they will step on your luck."

Like this woman, other villagers often complain that no one can "get ahead" locally. They point out that few jobs are available within the community, and they add that any income a person ekes out is prey to so many requests from kin and other villagers that it soon vanishes. Anyone who accumulates property of value, they say, puts life in danger by inciting the jealousy of others. Migrants who have achieved financial success often claim that they cannot live in their natal communities, where they would have to contend with sorcery, slander, and incessant requests for aid. Many men and women observe darkly that it is impossible to "improve" themselves in *any* settlement where they are surrounded by other Black Caribs.

They must choose, in short, between an outer world, which is governed by hierarchy and permits the accumulation of a surplus, or life in a community that opposes both. Few Black Caribs have cast their lot entirely with the outer world, in part because the means to the desired end—a higher standard of living—eludes most women and men.

Personal Autonomy

Outside their own communities, villagers accommodate themselves to an entrenched socioeconomic ladder, on which they usually occupy the lower rungs. They have little choice but to tolerate hierarchy in inter-ethnic relations and their workplace. But what they reluctantly accept in the outer world they firmly reject at home.[7] Those who pretend social superiority, or who attempt to exercise leadership, find their pretensions mocked and their efforts at leadership thwarted. The assertion "Nobody rules me" is the common response to anything remotely resembling an order from a peer.

For the most part, villagers act with easy familiarity toward each other. Except for teachers, whom they address with the Spanish term *maestro* (or the Carib derivative, *maísturu*), men and women address their peers familiarly: by given name, nickname, or, particularly in the case of women, by teknonym. They address their elders as *yau*, uncle, and *naúfuri*, aunt. These courtesy terms imply respect but not social distance.

Even children, who are somewhat circumspect with their elders, do not treat them with marked deference. Indeed, in some circumstances adults tolerate and even encourage defiant or insolent behavior. One such instance occurred as two women were talking together during their afternoon respite from work. Conversation waned, and one of the women began idly teasing the four-year-old daughter of her friend, telling the child that she was so ugly that no man would ever want her. The little girl, playing quietly nearby with a piece of string, simply ignored the woman. After a few moments, her mother threw a small stick to get her attention. "Tell her she is ugly too," she said to her daughter as the woman began teasing the girl again. "How did your mama get such an ugly little girl?" the woman asked. Finally provoked into action, the child filled her hands with sand and began to throw it at both of her tormentors. They laughed, jumped to their feet, and ran away in mock fear. "She's *rude*, you know," her mother said, grimacing, but with amusement and a trace of pride.

Men and women react just as strongly to "interference," whether it takes the form of an implied slight or an overtly hostile act. They regard the exercise of authority, especially by peers, as particularly disagreeable. When candidates for national political office campaign in these villages, they invariably seek out the chairman and council members as supporters, assuming that they carry influence in the community. But other villagers, and even council members themselves, clearly take a more skeptical view of their authority and influence. One council member observed with some rancor in a public speech, "No matter what we do, people talk and criticize it. They try to spoil anything that is good for them." More to the point, later in the same address he remarked that an effective chairman is a "worker and not an order-giver. He must work together with the people on any project in the village and not put himself above them."

Authoritarian leadership, as this council member implied, guarantees the failure of any project. Issuing orders only antagonizes others, by casting them in the distasteful role of subordinates. A chairman who wishes to gain compliance in any pursuit is well advised to use personal persuasion and to share equally in the work. He lacks any means to compel obedience. His leadership, like others', is task-specific and achieved.

Even astute chairmen find that more than effective leadership is needed in such purely voluntary projects as the *fajina,* which is notoriously difficult to organize. They enjoy greater success with "aided self-help" projects, for which the government provides funds to pay workers. Although the monetary return for labor is quite small, the difference in the level of cooperation and enthusiasm for an aided project, as opposed to a purely voluntary one, is vast. Some see a contradiction in the fact that people who value generosity can be so "greedy," as one chairman put it, unwilling to work for community benefit without personal reward. Yet this is entirely consistent with the system of balanced exchange and work for individual gain.

The practical advantages and drawbacks of this system are well within the ken of most villagers. One elderly man explained what he called his "philosophy of sharing" in these words: "If I have something and I share it, it is soon finished. But if I keep it for myself, it will finish anyway. So it is better to give. Then if I am in need some day, I have hope of getting help from people I have helped."

Nearly everyone needs help occasionally because most income sources are unreliable. Men, who resent the fact that their earnings are prey to incessant demands and requests, most often say, with a trace of bitterness, that no villager can hope to "get ahead." Women and elderly men, who cannot realistically aspire to that themselves, are more apt to point out that no one needs fear going hungry.

Notes to Chapter 5

1. Following Leacock (1978: 247), I use the term "personal autonomy" to mean that individuals display significant decision-making powers over many aspects of their personal lives and daily activities. This term seems preferable to "equality." As Leacock points out, the latter "connotes rights and opportunity specific to class society and confuses similarity with equity. Strictly speaking, who can be, or wants to be 'equal' to anyone else?" In this sense of the word, Black Caribs certainly do not. Indeed, individuals actively cultivate a "personal style," a distinctive persona expressed in speech, dance style, and sometimes in self-selected nicknames.

2. Cf. Whitten's (1974: 146ff.) discussion of dyadic ties and exchange in an Afro-Hispanic setting.

3. The inheritance of houses is also not an issue in these villages because most houses are occupied by their original owners, who have had them built within the last twenty years. This is true of the district as a whole: 75 percent of the houses have been built since 1960, and about the same proportion are occupied by their owners or are lived in rent-free by others — presumably kin in most cases (CRP 1975 IX, pt. 2.: 114f.). As for the past, it seems unlikely that the inheritance of houses ever occasioned many disputes. According to my informants, traditional houses cost rather little and rarely stood for more than thirty years. Natural elements, including hurricanes, usually took their toll within that period of time.

4. The primary exception to this is the collective criticism aimed against adults who neglect ritual obligations (see Chapter 10) or *openly* flaunt moral standards. The only case of ostracism I learned of had allegedly occurred many years before when a man and woman, first cousins, formed an incestuous union and then moved away from the community. (This is a common response of principals in a very serious "scandal.") They have since returned and still live together. Most villagers, who told me *sotto voce* of their "unnatural" relationship, now treat them with the same degree of civility that they extend to others.

5. Taylor (1951: 170) refers to this as *idáhadu* and defines it somewhat differently as "a kind of spell brought about by others' envy." Most of my informants who cited cases of *idáhadu* referred to men and women long dead as the principals. None could recall a recent case, but many still believe that it can potentially cause sickness.

6. Cohen (1955: 287) mentions that a common greeting in the rural Jamaican community he studied was, "And what are you carrying for me today?"

7. Many years ago, Conzemius (1928: 200) noted about the men: "They make very gay soldiers, but are considered unreliable, *will not submit to rigid discipline,* and their fighting qualities compare very unfavorably with those of the Ladinos" (emphasis added). Some employers today make similar complaints about the men as workers.

Chapter 6

AGE AND GENDER

A fifty-three-year-old woman who was wont to describe herself as old, past the age of childbearing, bristled when a male acquaintance
teased her one day about being too old to have any interest in a man. "I'm
still hot!" she retorted, then slyly suggested that the man himself was
fulúaru, impotent.[1] Later she commented that she was still sexually active
and intended to remain so until she grew "old, old," very elderly.

Sexual activity changes over the life cycle and serves to define the different
life stages. At any age, men's and women's expected conduct and attitudes
about sexuality also differ. For a man or woman to seek sexual pleasure is
regarded as "natural," yet women face certain constraints in this pursuit.
Females learn to exercise more control over their sexuality from an early
age. They show greater modesty about their bodies; ideally they confine
themselves to one sexual partner, preferably for an extended period of
time; they are expected to take certain "precautions" to protect others from
the harmful effects of their menstrual blood. Men and women hold responsibility for their own sexual conduct, but a woman's reputation depends on
sexual restraint, while a man gains esteem for sexual initiative and prowess.
A man known as a "breeder" (the father of many children, especially by
different women) enjoys prestige among other men.

People usually speak of sexual misconduct by women as irresponsible
and therefore shameful. They express disapproval and speculate about the
supernatural harm that it may cause. That this supernatural harm usually
affects people other than the negligent woman is significant. Throughout
life, women hold major responsibility for the well-being of others. Their
care can protect and sustain others; their carelessness can endanger lives. A
responsible woman creates and sustains life; a negligent woman may inadvertently jeopardize or destroy it. From their earliest years, girls learn hard
lessons about their responsibilities for others. When they neglect these, they
suffer the consequences at their mothers' hands. Women place fewer fetters
on their sons.

Male and Female

Boys and girls are dressed differently from a very early age. Some women dispense with diapering their infant sons, and they do not consider shorts obligatory as everyday garb until the age of four or so. Younger boys may simply wear shirts when they play. To the age of ten or twelve, boys usually bathe nude in the sea. Little girls go directly from diapers to under-clothing and shorts, and usually blouses, for everyday wear. Some sort of covering between waist and thigh is always required, even when they bathe in the sea. Older children and adults ridicule any little girl who appears in public unclothed, but their teasing is gentle and their shock feigned if she is only two or three. Women reprimand their older daughters for any show of immodesty.

When they are five or six, children begin to help their mothers at home, usually running errands at first and gradually assuming more difficult duties. By the age of eight or nine, girls regularly help with many chores: washing clothes, doing dishes, scraping and cleaning fish, caring for younger siblings when their mothers cook. While household work occupies many of their hours outside of school, boys have fewer responsibilities and spend less time at home. Many women complain that their sons devote most of their free time to "drifting about" with male friends, usually on ven-tures that carry them down the beach, away from the village. As a rule, only firstborn sons, especially those without sisters, help their mothers very much. Girls with several older sisters also have fewer duties at home. Still, most boys find more opportunity to play with friends, while their sisters spend time at home in the company of kinswomen.

In nearly every respect, women are more permissive with their sons than with their daughters. No mother encourages her son to "drift about," but she often tolerates in a son what she will not brook in a daughter. When a boy neglects home duties, his mother may complain with mild exaspera-tion—"That boy is *upstart!*"—or merely shrug and reassign the task to another child. But if he chronically evades work, his mother's patience will finally wear thin and she will retaliate with a long-threatened lashing, using a length of rope or a belt and applying it with vigor.

A girl who neglects her duties, however, can always expect a severe scold-ing at the least, and perhaps a lashing to underscore the point. She soon learns that, unlike her brothers, she cannot evade duty without suffering immediate punishment. Women act as the primary socializers and discipli-narians of their children and grandchildren. Men show greater indulgence, sometimes reprimanding or swatting a child for misbehavior, more often ignoring it altogether.

During early childhood, boys and girls play freely with each other, but from the age of five or six, boys begin to spend more time with male peers, and girls with kinswomen of all ages. This pattern persists throughout life. Even at public gatherings, men tend to congregate with men and women with each other and small children. When a crowd of about forty buyers waited early one morning on the beach while a fisherman slaughtered a sea turtle, the men clustered together to one side, and the boys to another. Nearby, women and girls of various ages stood together, talking among themselves. Within minutes, however, several of the men and women began to exchange sexual banter. Repartee of this sort flavors nearly any social occasion and arises as often among men or women as between them.

Sexuality figures in jokes, gossip, and general conversation. Men and women alike consider sexual relations natural, desirable, and even healthful. No one appears to place any particular value on virginity, and the concept of frigidity is quite alien. People regard abstinence as unmitigated hardship. When a woman who had recently separated from her husband complained of headaches to other women one day, they advised her to find another man or go back to her husband. Then talk shifted to other complaints caused by sexual abstinence, among them backaches and weight loss. Several women recounted stories about acquaintances who had tried to be faithful to migrant spouses, but with ill effects. In their view, corpulence indicates health and vigor, especially in women; but these unfortunates had grown listless and increasingly slender. The women agreed that no medicine could cure this malady. Practically speaking, the only recourse was to find a man.

Both men and women are thought to possess a strong sexual urge, but young women (of childbearing age) are expected to exercise greater control over it. Many of them claim not to drink rum (which supposedly heightens the desire for sexual relations). Rum is the staple drink of nearly all ritual occasions, and many men insist that major ritual events provide a convenient cover for trysts that they ordinarily find difficult to arrange and keep secret. Women, who protest that men exaggerate the frequency of illicit relations, do not personally admit to having more than one sexual partner (although many suspect other women of infidelity). They complain that men often slander women unjustly, claiming them as illicit partners just to boost their own reputations among other men.

By all accounts, men also suffer sexual victimization, but of a different sort. People say that women can use supernatural means to "tie" men to themselves. Some techniques supposedly insure that a man will be impotent with any other women. If a woman wears a black pin on her underclothing, she has this intent. Or she may put secretions from her body or other substances into food that her man eats.[2] Men claim not to possess such effective techniques themselves.

All of this is in the nature of hearsay, since no woman admits to these covert practices. But nearly everyone understands why a woman might take such measures. If her spouse should leave her for another woman, she has no assurance of soon finding another man. Certainly the sex ratio of the community is not in her favor, nor can she find employment locally. The prospect of being left literally holding the baby troubles many young women. Female competition for men is nothing less than fierce, but whether women actually employ such ruthless means to hold their men remains open to question.

Men suspect women of using sorcery not only to "tie" them but to control them unnaturally in other ways as well. Ideally, they say, "Men rule women," a global statement with the highly specific meaning that a woman should defer to her spouse. Women dismiss any such notion with the standard retort, "Nobody rules me." They view the marital relationship as a partnership between equals.[3] But they agree that while a submissive woman is merely uncommon, a submissive man is abnormal. If a man openly defers to his spouse, other people suspect that she has used sorcery to make him compliant.

Male fidelity also provokes suspicion. A man whose eye never wanders is considered a likely victim of sorcery. Most men hold a matter-of-fact attitude toward their own infidelity. They explain that men "naturally" prefer to have more than one woman. Women take a different view. They criticize the sexual rivalry and conflict that men create among women, and point out that multiple liaisons also make a man "greedy" (for money to support the women). But they regard these problems, however deplorable, as inevitable. Most express greater disapproval of an unfaithful woman than man.

Since restraint is woman's duty, and pursuit man's privilege, for a woman to "court," to make overtures to a potential sexual partner, is unseemly. (Taking sexual initiative with a spouse is another matter.) Initially, a woman should refuse a man's advances. Or she may always refuse, telling him that she does not love him but regards him as a "social friend," and if she has a spouse, reminding him of that fact. Women dismiss persistent overtures lightly and derisively, saying that the man is "begging for sex." "Begging" for anything connotes shame.

In sexual matters men and women seem to share only a general premise: that everyone enjoys sexual relations. Otherwise, their expectations and attitudes diverge and often conflict. Women claim to choose a sexual partner on the basis of love, but many men portray them as indiscriminate and calculating, interested only in financial gain. Men criticize contraception as "unnatural," while some women express regret that they have no effective means of birth control. Men complain that women show no discretion about sexual affairs, but women blame them for kindling the gossip that does damage to their reputations.

Relations between men and women show clear elements of opposition and contest, but women give no evidence that they see themselves as lesser opponents, or men as having (outside the labor market) any final advantage over them. They express pride in their strength, their capacity for strenuous work and childbearing. Women often speak of their ability to endure the "terrible" pain of childbirth; men, they say, could not tolerate such pain. (Many men share this view.) They also claim (and men concede) that women can carry heavier burdens, which they place on their heads, than the average man can. Custom dictates that men use their shoulders.

Most women are undaunted by physically demanding work, and many explain the division of labor as a matter of learned skills and tradition, not as conditioned by the greater strength of men. In any case, the division of labor is very flexible.[4] If need be, a woman will readily undertake a task that "properly" belongs to a man. Thus, a man who had long promised to dig a well near his house, for his wife's convenience, returned from fishing one afternoon to find her drawing water from a well that she had dug herself. She had grown impatient with her husband's delays. Another man, whose wife spent several weeks visiting her sister in another community, cooked for himself during her absence. Such temporary "role reversals," based on expedience, occur quite often and cause little comment. Even the few older women who fish are admired for their unusual skill rather than criticized for violating tradition.[5]

The social experience of men and women varies visibly in its orientation, with men's directed toward the outer world and women's toward kin and community. Employment takes men away from home and brings them into daily contact with non-Caribs. Many men also belong to lodges, with ethnically mixed memberships and headquarters in Belize City or the district towns. Although many lodges accept female members, few women join them. Some cannot afford the cost of membership; others show no interest in them. Men clearly benefit more from membership in these groups. Lodge brothers help each other find employment, and may make small loans to a member who finds himself out of work temporarily. Some lodges also function as burial societies. When a member dies, lodge brothers who live nearby are expected to attend the funeral and contribute to burial expenses.

If a man seeks security by cultivating a wide network of male friends, a woman finds it within a rather narrow circle of kin.[6] Women bitterly resent their spouses' spending money on friends, dissipating scarce funds for such a "worthless" purpose. From their perspective, men stint women and their children when they "spree" (drink convivially with male friends). One young woman, as she reproved her husband for drinking, reminded him that he would soon be old. (He was forty-three.) If he neglected his dependent children, she said, they would neglect him in his old age. He shrugged and made ready to leave, planning to spend the afternoon with his friends. Unwilling to surrender the point, his wife demanded, "Who will bury you?"

The man retorted that he would work until he died (as many men do), and that his lodge brothers would help to bury him.

Other women, like this one, also use persuasion to obtain support from men, prodding them with reminders of obligation. Should that fail, they reputedly resort to other means. Unlike men, who earn money directly and approach a potential sexual partner directly, women follow a more oblique course in matters of money and of heart. If this indirection prompts men to speak of women as "softer" and "more tender-hearted," it also leads them to perceive some women (their sexual partners, not consanguines) as calculating and manipulative, using covert means to achieve their ends. People suspect women of using sorcery more often than men — particularly female affines or sexual rivals.[7]

In keeping with their expected restraint, women pride themselves on attracting many visitors but claim not to "drift about" the community as men do, aimlessly visiting others (and perhaps arranging a tryst). For a young woman to do so, they say, invites criticism and raises suspicion about her virtue. She should leave her yard only with a specific destination in mind: a shop, a kinswoman's house, a social event. (If she leaves the village to cut firewood or collect wild fruits, she should do so in the company of other women.) While they spend most of the day working near their houses, women are not at all isolated. Older women can visit freely, and the young find reasons to leave their own yards when they wish. Child care does not restrict them greatly because children are welcome nearly everywhere, including most social events. Most women also have mothers, sisters, or other kinswomen at hand who can relieve them of child care and other household duties if need be.

Throughout life, women's work centers on caring for others. But as they grow older, the means by which they provide that care changes.

Life Stages

Chronological age bears loosely on social age, and birthdays usually pass with rather little notice. Seniority, or relative age, has more importance in interpersonal relations. The terms *ñũgi-*, young, and *wáia-*, old, have relative rather than absolute meaning as used by most people. A forty-year-old woman is young in relation to her mother's generation and old in relation to her children's.

The transition from one life stage to another occurs gradually and hinges on physical changes and social criteria rather than absolute age. Table 5 shows the life stages, their markers, and approximate age spans. From adolescence, most women enter each of these at an earlier chronological age than men.[8]

TABLE 5
The Life Stages

Life Stage	Approximate Life Span	Physical Markers	Events
Prenatal	9 months before birth	conception, pregnancy	— — —
Infancy	birth to 1 year	birth	christening
Childhood	1–12 years	growth	school
Adolescence	12–16 years	puberty	onset of sexual activity
Early adulthood	17–44 years	reproduction	parenthood, employment, marital relationships
Late adulthood	45–70 years (or age at death)	end of reproductive capacity	grandparenthood
Old age	over 70 years	physical disability	retirement from work, great-grandparenthood
Afterlife	— — —	death	death rituals

Changes in sexual activity define the life stages from adolescence through old age. The onset of sexual activity occurs during adolescence, and most men and women reproduce during early adulthood. With age, sexual and reproductive capacity decline, as does physical vigor. People often use the term "impotence" figuratively, to mean old, worn out, finished. The very elderly, others near death, and the dead are thought to have lost all capacity for work and for the sexual act, the source of life.

Life is thought to begin before birth, with coitus, conception, and the growth of a fetus, *dága*, in the woman's womb. If the mother miscarries or has a stillbirth, the fetus is buried without ceremony, unlike an infant, *kriatúra*, who survives even a matter of hours. An infant who dies receives a formal burial and, depending on the hour of death, perhaps a very small and simple wake.

Infants, and especially the newborn, are considered constitutionally weak, susceptible to sickness and death. People explain this by saying that the baby's "heart is soft," *ñülüti lanígi*. Some older women tell of having borne a dozen children, of whom less than half survived to adulthood.[9] Even today many women lose at least one child, despite the many "precautions" they take to protect their health.

Most infants are christened some weeks or months after birth. The parents (or the mother only if she has no spouse) ask another couple to act as godparents to their child. The godparents must pay for the christening ceremony, the infant's christening dress, and a private fête held in the home after the ceremony. With the christening ceremony infants receive a set of parent figures as well as fictive siblings, whom they will refer to as god-brothers and godsisters. Sexual relations will be prohibited with them, as also between the parents and godparents. Following the ceremony, the latter always address each other as *comadre* and *compadre* (unless they are close relatives, a common circumstance).

The transition to childhood occurs gradually, with increasing independence from the mother. Children are weaned during their second year if not before. They make their first attempts to master the difficult arts of walking and talking, encouraged by older children and adults, who show amusement and pleasure at their efforts. Most young children learn to use toilets by the age of three, but more painfully and largely to avoid the taunts of other children and scoldings of the women, who slowly lose patience about cleaning up after them. Children enter school at the age of six and continue their formal education until fourteen. Those few who pass the required examinations and have the financial means go on to secondary school in the district town. Before they leave school, children undergo confirmation, usually between the ages of seven and ten. Each gains a new godparent, a woman for a girl, a man for a boy.

Childhood has its somber side. At an early age boys and girls learn the fundamental facts of life and death, which adults discuss openly in their presence. When a relative or neighbor dies, children hear about it directly and immediately. A woman who had just learned about the death of her infant nephew told her three-year-old daughter that the baby, the child's first cousin and classificatory brother, was dead. *Hiláti bamúlen,* "Your little brother is dead," she said. Uncomprehending, the girl asked where he was, and her mother repeated, "He's dead, he's gone." "I want him back," the child said, pouting. The woman replied simply, "You *can't* have him back. He's dead." Later she took her daughter to see the body of the infant, laid out for burial in his christening gown.

Like infants, children who die are buried with simple ceremony. School-children attend brief prayers in the church and then form the procession to the burial ground. If the deceased child was very young and the coffin is light, several boys act as pallbearers. Another child carries the *palma,* a wreath made of brightly colored paper which symbolizes the deceased child's chastity. (This is never used in the burial of an adult.) Aside from the schoolchildren, only a teacher, who reads the prayers, and several close kinswomen of the deceased child attend the burial.

Adolescence begins between the ages of twelve and fifteen for girls, when they menstruate for the first time. Some women who claim not to have known about menstruation as girls were alarmed by their first menstrual flow. Only then, they say, did their mothers explain menstruation and instruct them about its danger.

Menstruating women are said to pose a threat to others because the scent of menstrual blood attracts malevolent spirits, variously referred to as *winâni* and *máfia*. These spirits do not harm the woman who attracts them, but they can injure and even kill those around her — not only infants, who are particularly vulnerable to harm by spirits, but also children and adults.[10] The polite term for the verb "menstruate" is *anúra múnada,* literally "sit at home." This is precisely what mothers should instruct their daughters to do during their menstrual periods. They also warn against carelessly dampening the abdomen when laundering, since they believe that this makes the womb cold and causes painful menstrual cramps. Aside from this measure, little can be done to prevent cramps. Women who suffer from them usually drink various "bush teas" to alleviate the pain. Finally, mothers instruct their daughters about proper disposal of the water used to cleanse the cloths they wear while menstruating. Since the water is full of blood, only a careless and irresponsible woman discards it in her yard, thereby attracting spirits to it. Instead, she should pour it in a hole dug in the sand, then cover it, or throw it on the beach near the water's edge.

Many women say that they "sat at home" only during adolescence, at their mothers' insistence. Later, they moved about as freely when they were menstruating as not. But nearly all women agree that they refrain from participating in *dügü,* the paramount ritual for the dead, when they menstruate. This is supposed to be offensive to the ancestors (cf. Taylor 1951: 131). Attendance by menstruating women is also said to provoke attacks by the spirit of the drum, *wayáganbui* — again, attacks against others around the woman, not against her. (Few young women choose to take part in rituals for ancestors other than their own; see Chapters 9 and 10.)

Some adolescents become sexually active soon after puberty, but in most cases their relations are covert (although the subject of speculative gossip and jokes). In a very rare case, a girl of fourteen or fifteen openly has a young man, who may even sleep occasionally in her home. But most women look askance at a mother who permits or encourages this, accusing her of being "greedy," expecting financial contributions from the young man for the girl's support. They also criticize the mother for putting her daughter's health at risk. They know that girls can reproduce at this young age, and often cite the example of Maya women who marry at fourteen. But they point out that Maya women are not noted for their longevity. As for boys, they rarely father a child before the age of eighteen or twenty, and many are older when their first child is born. A fifteen-year-old boy who had an infant son was considered exceptionally precocious and virile. Men and women often pointed him out, remarking with a smile how strange it was that "such a small boy is really a man."

Early adulthood begins with employment and parenthood. By the age of twenty most men have begun to work regularly, and many women have borne their first child. In the months before birth both parents customarily observe certain restrictions to protect their unborn child (cf. Taylor 1951: 89). Pregnant women avoid eating shellfish and game animals, as well as the black pepper that they usually add liberally to the cooking pot. Some do not eat sugar cane, saying that it causes a newborn baby to cry excessively. During their first pregnancy, many women are uncertain about which foods to avoid. They depend on the guidance of their mothers and other older women with experience in these matters. Some pregnant women openly dismiss dietary restrictions as "superstition," and others express doubt about them. Still, they usually observe them, if only to avoid up-braidings from their mothers and other older women who criticize such negligence.

During the prenatal period, both parents should observe certain activity restrictions. These too have the purpose of protecting the health of the unborn child. (Neither parent, for example, should wring a chicken's neck, lest the child be born with a neck limp like the chicken's.) More restrictions apply to the mother-to-be than to the man. If a pregnant woman quarrels or sees strange sights, her child may be "marked" by these experiences, born with a congenital defect. Women agree that staying at home as much as possible prevents such injury, but they do not show equal caution in this regard. Pregnant women are certainly not housebound, and most work as usual. Some experience occasional nausea, while others say that they feel particularly vigorous during this time. Many men report symptoms that parallel their partners'. These include morning sickness, "fever," and food cravings.[11]

During pregnancy a woman should also have regular sexual relations with the father of the unborn child. This benefits the fetus. The father's semen (but only his) "nourishes" the unborn child. Infidelity by the woman can harm the fetus and make her infertile, people say.

Birth occurs either in the woman's house, with the assistance of a local midwife or nurse, or in a hospital in the district town. Today many women go to the hospital for their first delivery or if they anticipate difficulty. Others express reluctance to do so, citing the indignity of exposure in the presence of strangers (the doctor and other hospital personnel). A delivery in the home is very much a female affair, usually with the woman's mother and perhaps some of her sisters in attendance. If her mother-in-law and any of her sisters-in-law are fond of her, they may be present as well, "to help her bear the pain," they say. A woman takes pride in having a number of concerned kinswomen and friends around her during labor and childbirth. "If you are a courteous and generous person," said one pregnant woman, "you are never sick alone." The only man who may be present is the woman's spouse. Intercourse during labor is thought to hasten delivery, and a midwife sometimes instructs the couple to have sexual relations (privately) for this purpose.

When women give birth at home, they have nothing medicinal to ease the pain of labor or childbirth. If they have difficulty expelling the after-birth, the midwife tries several remedies: she may have the woman hold salt in both hands, blow into a bottle, or drink the urine of another woman. The midwife buries the afterbirth secretly, in the belief that if an enemy found it and turned it upside down or put salt in it, the woman would never bear children again.

A woman who delivers her child at home customarily remains in the house for nine days. Several observances, restrictions on activity and dress, protect the health of the parturient woman. She does no laundry for several weeks. (Another woman washes for her during this time.) The coldness of the water is harmful, given the "heat" of the woman's body after childbirth. The woman should also keep her body well covered to protect it from any cold. She wears a headwrap and clothing to cover her arms, torso, and as much of her legs as possible. Many parturient women object to this, saying that they do not want to look like an "old lady." (Women over the age of forty or so often wear loose-fitting dresses, or "gowns," and headwraps; their daughters usually choose form-fitting clothing and prefer plaiting their hair elaborately to covering it.) But most young women accede to these "rules," however reluctantly. They sacrifice personal appearance to avoid the browbeatings of their elders.

From the time the woman resumes sexual relations (several months after birth) until the child is finally weaned, she should confine herself sexually to the child's father. If she has relations with another man, she may suffer a wasting disease called *amímidiha*. The symptoms of this sickness reportedly include weight loss, the loss of hair, an insatiable appetite for fish, and a vaginal discharge. *Amímidiha* is thought to be caused not only by infidelity but also by neglecting certain dietary restrictions during the postpartum period — particularly the taboo on eating tarpon and barracuda. Some people say that if a woman is careless about these restrictions, her child will be afflicted as well.

For several weeks after birth, the father of a newborn infant should also limit his activities. Specifically, he must refrain from strenuous labor that requires any jerking movements. (The classic example is wood-cutting; more recent ones include shifting gears on a machine and starting an outboard motor.) The man is prohibited as well from having sexual relations with other women. This also could cause his child to sicken and even die. These restrictions, and many of the new mother's observances, are said to protect the infant's health. The parent-child bond is so close that the activities and diet of the parents directly affect their offspring, both before and after birth.[12] To ignore these amounts to child neglect.

When an infant or any very young child dies, speculation about the cause of death almost invariably centers on the parents' behavior. Perhaps the infant's mother, who was sad about the death of a close relative, inadvertently "poisoned" the baby with her breast milk. Or perhaps the infant's father did not sufficiently restrict his work. If the child is older, others may conclude that the mother simply waited too long to seek medical help, and that this particular act of negligence caused the death. Even in the rare case in which people blame sorcery for a child's death, they explain it as the act of a malicious person who wanted to hurt one of the parents.

Although most men and women reproduce, some do not.[13] Others regard them with pity and even some suspicion as they consider infertility both unfortunate and unnatural. People offer physical and supernatural explanations for barrenness. One childless man was said to have a crooked penis: his semen never entered the womb of his partner. A woman who had never borne children was thought to have a dormant fetus lodged in her womb, which prevented the growth of another. People suspected a sexual rival of having caused this with sorcery. Other repugnant acts that explain female infertility include attempted abortion, and physical abuse of or infidelity (by the woman) during pregnancy.

To a degree, men and women can compensate for childlessness — men by forming unions with women who have children, women by fostering children. But in some respects they can never entirely overcome this deficiency. Others will never address them by teknonym and, lacking direct descendants, they will probably receive only the sparest ritual attention.

By the age of forty-five women have borne their last children, and by their early fifties they reach menopause. They speak of menopause as "a change in the blood" with physical effects beyond the inability to reproduce. Physical strength, they say, declines, and they report feeling tired more often and with less exertion. (Questioned about their stamina at ritual events, where they sometimes sing and dance from dusk until dawn and then work the following day as usual, they merely laugh.)

As a physiological process, senescence is usually defined as a decline in strength, fertility, and activity.[14] Socially, however, the activities of these women change but do not necessarily decline. As older women feel their own physical strength diminish, they show increasing interest in health and sickness. For many years they cared for their own children. Now they offer advice to their daughters and other young women, and some acquire a local reputation for their ability to cure certain minor ailments.

Most older women also involve themselves in ritual activity, which has the specific stated purpose of curing physical affliction and caring for the dead. They do not take more active part because, as elders, they remember traditional lore that younger people do not. Many of them claim to have been skeptics or to have had no interest in ritual affairs earlier in life — statements that their own daughters, speaking of themselves, often make independently. Older women commonly say that their personal experiences over the years finally conquered their doubts. As one explained her gradual conversion, she could not discount the fact that over and over again she had seen shamans and rituals cure what medical doctors could not. Eventually she began to take part in rituals herself, learning more and more through participation in the full range of rites.

Men and women generally define aging in terms of a decreasing capacity for sexual relations, reproduction, and work. By these criteria, men and women age differently. Few women at the age of fifty can find employment, but men rarely retire from the labor market until physical disability compels them to do so. Some men work until shortly before they die, unless they have a prolonged terminal illness. Those who do retire in reasonably good health occupy themselves with fishing, selling the surplus for profit.

While women do not bear children after their mid-forties, men in their fifties occasionally father children by younger women. The decline in sexual activity, rather than reproductive capacity per se, defines aging in men. Those past the age of fifty-five or sixty commonly boast that they "played havoc" with women during their younger years. Their voices contain an unmistakable note of pride mixed with regret for those lost times. Since they equate virility with sexual prowess, the loss of sexual potency troubles them. People commonly joke with each other about being *fulúaru,* impotent, but for older men this joke has a special sting. Others often speculate privately about their sexual capacity. Indeed, people express nearly the same intense, even anguished, curiosity about the sexual activity of older men as about that of young women. (But the underlying question differs. For young women the question is *"Are* they?" and for older men, *"Can* they?")

The loss of sexual potency signals the end of a favored period in the lives of men, a time when they met the very specialized definition of manhood, when they were sexually active and independent. As they sense a decline in physical vigor, they turn their attention to the past, reminiscing about sexual adventures and their experiences as workers.[15] A man who in one breath gives account of all his children by various women in the next recalls his work abroad, as a sailor or woodcutter.

Older women rarely dwell on past experiences unless prompted by direct questions. They display less concern about their sexuality, few express regret about menopause, and some say that they welcomed the end of childbearing. People often speak of childbearing as a mixed blessing for women. Although they want children, they think that childbearing itself is quite wearing, and causes women to show the physical marks of age before men. In any case, the end of childbearing does not bring an end to childrearing. Many older women have young children, their last-born, and foster some grandchildren as well.

With age, women also express greater satisfaction with their marital relationships. They feel secure in the knowledge that their men will not leave them for a rival. If a couple has lived together for many years, the man has grown accustomed to his partner's "ways." He would not be satisfied with another woman's cooking and other domestic habits. Women also point out that a man's sexual capacity declines with age, especially if he is careless about his health.[16] His interest in other women inevitably wanes, and with it a major source of marital conflict. Later in life, women say, spouses become like siblings or mother and child. They trust each other, and over the course of time their affection has deepened.

Overall, the later years of adulthood pose more difficult shifts for men than for women. Men lose some measure of their former independence, but women have had their whole lives to learn the lesson of interdependence. Some of their burden eases with age, in fact, as their sons and daughters grow up. They expect support from their grown children, and many assure it by fostering grandchildren. Some achieve greater financial security than they have known before, since they receive "help" from several children and perhaps support from a spouse as well. Such women may even accumulate small savings, holding the money in reserve for the hard times that they have learned to regard as an inescapable fact of life.

Few men and women reach an advanced age, over seventy or so. Some especially vigorous old men continue to work for wages; others fish. Despite their age, many younger people describe these men as "not so old" because they remain economically active. Women of this age, and disabled men, are by consensus old, *wáia-*. Most of them depend on kinswomen, their daughters or granddaughters, for care.

Many of the very elderly suffer some physical disability, especially "palpitations of the heart" and "pressure" (hypertension). But whatever the state of their physical health, they have a special strength that others lack. Because they are so near death, they enjoy immunity to certain supernatural forces that can harm or even kill younger people. On ritual occasions they can eat food offered to the ancestors, food that would cause younger men and women to sicken and perhaps die.

Afterlife, the final stage of existence, begins with death. The dead reluctantly surrender their place in this world and undertake a long and arduous journey to the next, the "other side."[17] They never entirely sever ties with the living, however, particularly with their descendants. As ancestors, *gubída,* they will continue to take interest in the affairs of their descendants, and to demand ritual attention on occasion. Their descendants must care for them or suffer misfortune for their neglect. Ritual and kinship share a central meaning: the interdependence of the generations and the lifelong responsibility of women for lineal kin.

Notes to Chapter 6

1. The word *fulúaru* literally means flour, and figuratively impotence. (The penis of an impotent man is said to be limp like bread dough.) Creoles use the word flour in the same sense.

2. A woman can lace a man's food with menstrual blood or with water she has used to wash her genitals, and thus "tie" him (cf. Gonzalez 1969: 64; Taylor 1951: 134f.; Coelho 1955: 169f.; Bullard 1974). People also say that the longer a couple has sexual relations, the more "tied" the man is to the woman.

3. Men apparently do not say "Men rule women" to women. When I mentioned this phrase, women invariably snorted and said, "Nobody rules me." Coelho (1955: 86) notes: "The position of the woman in the family is in no way to be conceived as subordinate, the principle involved being one of partnership under equal terms, not of one person commanding and the other obeying."

4. According to the formal division of labor, men fish and hunt, clear land for planting, repair houses and tools, and navigate boats; women cultivate and harvest (or otherwise procure) food, prepare it, and take responsibility for child care and most household work. Cf. Taylor (1951: 55f.) and Gonzalez (1969: 46ff.).

5. In one village, two women fished regularly and were known as "good fisherwomen." They had fewer home duties than most women. Each had only one son (a school-age boy and a young man in his early twenties) and a spouse who worked at a plantation during the week. Neither of the women fished for profit. Both had been avid fisherwomen since childhood, when they had accompanied elder brothers who taught them the basic skills.

6. Wilson (1971), Dirks (1972), and G. Brana-Shute (1976, 1979) discuss male networks in other areas of the Afro-Caribbean.

7. I collected information about seventeen cases of alleged sorcery. The aggressor was female in 65 percent of these, and 65 percent of the victims were also female. Nearly half (47 percent) of the cases involved two women, many of them sexual rivals. Of the remainder, 29 percent involved a man and a woman, and 24 percent two men.

8. Since I have no figures on life spans, I do not know whether women also die at an earlier average than men. It is commonly said that women generally live longer, and that the elderly are disproportionately female (Cowgill and Holmes 1972: 332), but Amoss and Harrell (1981: 7) question this "popular stereotype." Men over the age of seventy outnumbered

women in the three villages where I collected census data (see Table 4 in Chapter 4).

9. Infant mortality has declined sharply over the past fifty years in Belize, from about 190 to 50 per 1,000 (Dobson 1973: 244).

10. Taylor (1951: 103) states that *máfia* harm the menstruating woman herself, but my informants claimed that this is not so.

11. These symptoms and the father's activity restrictions have been categorized as couvade and interpreted in various ways: as a psychological "buffer which absorbs the shock and emotional agitation inherent in a delicate transitional situation" like birth (Coelho 1949: 53); as "a means of guarding against spiritual powers harmful to men" (Taylor 1951: 92); as an indication that "in former days a strong bond existed between father and child" (Gonzalez 1969: 48); as a manifestation of "low male salience" in early childhood and consequent cross-sex identification by males (Munroe, Munroe, and Whiting 1973); as a symbol of the "social unity and . . . egalitarian status of the sexes" (Cosminsky n.d.); and as a means of acknowledging and clarifying paternity (Kerns 1976).

12. The observances that relate to sexual relations may also serve to strengthen a weak link between the parents of the child, who do not necessarily live together.

13. Official figures on maternity by different ethnic groups in Belize were last collected over thirty years ago. At that time, 92 percent of all Black Carib women forty-five years and older had borne children (CBS 1948: xxiii). According to the figures I collected from women in two villages, about 89 percent of those forty-five years and older had borne one or more children. Most of the remainder had fostered children.

14. For example, see Comfort (1956: 1).

15. Cf. Coelho (1955: 76) on the reminiscence of old men. MacMahan and Rhudick (1964, 1967) interpret reminiscing as a coping device used to deal with personal loss.

16. Among the habits said to hasten aging in men are heavy drinking and "walking about in the dew" at night (usually while "spreeing" with male friends or philandering). These pursuits run contrary to the interests of a man's spouse, who commonly invokes the threat of premature aging to persuade him to stay at home.

17. See Coelho (1955: 135ff.) and Taylor (1951: 102ff.) for detailed accounts of beliefs about death.

Chapter 7

KINSHIP

Black Carib villages are communities of kin, and villagers commonly assert that they are "one family," *ában rása.* In its broadest sense, the term *rása* encompasses all Black Caribs. *Harása garífuna* is the Black Carib family, people, or, as it is sometimes translated, race.[1] In a narrower sense, *nirása,* my family, includes all known blood relatives, who may also be referred to as *nidúheñu,* my relatives. Those from the maternal side are *tidúheñu núguchun,* my mother's relatives. Paternal relatives are *lidúheñu núguchin,* my father's relatives. Anyone without a known blood tie is *mútu baúgudin giñe,* a person from outside. In the course of daily life, village women associate most closely with their children and female consanguines, while men who work outside their home communities routinely find themselves in the company of "people from outside" and other "strangers," including non-Caribs.

Consanguinity

In the bilateral kinship system of the Black Carib, genealogical knowledge tends to be shallow but broad. Most people can name their grandparents and some of their grandparents' siblings. Many can name several of their great-grandparents. Remembrance of great-great-grandparents is selective and rather rare, however, and knowledge of their descendants, including an individual's third cousins, is partial. A cousin of any degree can be referred to as *nidúhen,* which is translated either as "my cousin" or "my relative." Black Caribs commonly specify degree of cousinship although their terminology does not. Introducing a woman as his cousin, a man might explain, "Our grandmothers were two sisters: one mother, one father," or "My grandfather and her grandmother were brother and sister: one mother." Full blood ties are considered stronger than half-blood ties, although the same kin terms are used.

Genealogical knowledge varies from one person to the next, but few are so well informed that they can fully document the assertion that their natal village is "one family." Since mating tends toward local endogamy in these villages, people commonly count many other villagers as their first, second, or third cousins on their mothers' or fathers' sides. They may also refer to others as cousins, but without being able to specify the linking ancestor or the degree of cousinship. Asked to explain the connection, they can only say that the person is a maternal or paternal relative. If need be, one or another of the very elderly women who have an extensive knowledge of local genealogy can usually clarify the relationship.

How many relatives any person can name depends on a number of factors others than reproductive success. The most apparent of these are the individual's age, gender, and degree of interest in genealogical matters. As a general rule, women display more interest than men, and genealogical knowledge increases with age. Older women and men can usually identify more distant relatives than their juniors.

Although the outer boundaries of kin networks vary, they share a uniform internal structure. There is a clear-cut division between the core of close blood relatives and the periphery of distant kin. All lineals and classificatory lineals — lineals' siblings and ego's first cousins — are close relatives. Descendants of grandparents' siblings — second cousins and their issue — are described as "not so close," and exempt from the few specific "rules" that pertain to close relatives.

Close kin are prohibited from mating with each other. Sexual relations between lineals, real and classificatory (including first cousins, who are classificatory siblings), are uniformly considered incestuous. Some men and women also claim to avoid sexual relations with second cousins, the blood tie being so close, they say, that it would verge on incest. But that is a matter of personal preference. Unions between second cousins are rare but known. Many more unions involve third cousins or more distant kin, who cannot specify their linking ancestor but know that they are related by blood.

Aside from sexual restrictions, there are other distinctions between close and distant kin. Relationships within the inner circle are usually described as trusting, in distinct contrast to the rest of the social universe. Close relatives are not suspected of using sorcery against each other. Should they come into conflict, it rarely passes the point of abusive talk. If a man assaults a close relative, he is harshly criticized in all quarters. To strike a parent in anger is unthinkable. There is a special term for the act, *kondenaú* (from the Spanish *condenado,* condemned). People must search memory to name any instance of this, which they consider "a sin against God."

Among the living, distant relatives, affines, and non-kin are suspected of using poison and other forms of sorcery to harm those whom they envy. In an apparent reversal, it is close kin who, after death, can harm the living, descendants whom they envy. These ancestral spirits, *gubída,* are remembered lineals and their siblings (classificatory lineals). Usually it is deceased parents and grandparents who "bother" the living, but in some cases more remote lineals (or classificatory lineals) afflict their descendants.

In discourse, the distinction between close and distant relatives is not always so clear. People often use terms for close kin when they address distant relatives. Depending on context and degree of personal regard, a speaker may choose to use the general cousin term for a distant relative, or the term for a closer collateral or a lineal relative (choosing one appropriate by gender and generation). An elder second cousin might be addressed as *nidúhen,* my cousin; or, if the speaker feels a special affection for her or wishes to stress their ties, *nítu,* my elder sister. Whatever term a speaker selects, the only way to discover the exact nature of the relationship is by periphrastic reference. In a case such as that just cited, one learns the speaker's relationship to the woman by asking, "One father, one mother?" Very often, the speaker specifies a more distant tie: "My grandfather and her grandmother were brother and sister: one mother."

Kin terms are not obligatory in reference or address for all relatives.[2] (See Appendix 1 for terms of reference.) People commonly use personal names when they speak to or about their peers or juniors. As a matter of courtesy, they should address any elder relatives, including siblings, by kin terms. *Naúfuri,* aunt, and *yau,* uncle, are polite forms of address for elder relatives, affines, even non-kin. But the use of these and other terms in address is highly variable and situational. A man who wishes to soothe his spouse, his elder sister, his young daughter — indeed, nearly any female, whatever her age or their relationship — may call her *núguchun,* my mother.

Relations between distant kin do not entail specific and reciprocal obligations. There is a general charge to treat any relative generously, but such an expansive ideal is difficult to realize. Even among close kin, only lineals have specific financial and ritual obligations to each other. Their relations — and particularly those between mothers and children — are notably intense, and also perpetual. Parents and children are obligated to help support and care for each other throughout life. Even death does not remove obligations to lineal kin, whose needs are met through private offerings and collective rituals.

The brunt of these obligations to lineal kin falls upon women, as mothers and daughters. As daughters, they help to support and care for their aging parents. After their parents die, they organize the necessary rituals for them. As expectant mothers, they protect the well-being of their unborn children through a rather elaborate set of observances. After birth, and throughout life, women continue to care for their children.

Mothers and Children

Relations between mothers and their dependent children show a pronounced asymmetry. Women bear ultimate responsibility for their children, and they expect gratitude and obedience in return. Young children are admonished to show gratitude to their mothers (or other female caretaker) by obeying them, and by thanking them after each meal. As adults, they should give tangible evidence of their gratitude by helping to support their mothers.

On a daily basis, women must see that their children are adequately fed and clothed. They are also responsible for care when their children fall ill. Every sort of illness has its medicine, *árani,* and a woman searches for the correct one when her child is sick.

Minor ailments, such as the common colds that are endemic among children during the rainy season, may be treated with purchased patent medicines or with "bush medicine": teas and poultices made from the leaves and roots of local plants such as fever grass, yama bush, and sorosi (see Cosminsky 1976). Young women often consult their own mothers or grandmothers, who have long experience in treating minor complaints. If their ministrations have no effect, they may consult another older woman, a *gáranitu,* medicine woman, who treats gynecological and pediatric ailments. If the *gáranitu* meets with no success, the woman usually takes her child to the nurse at the nearest rural health station. Should the condition be serious, she will take the child immediately to the hospital; but transportation difficulties and expense often make this a last resort.

Women monitor each other in these matters. They compliment those who have healthy, vigorous children with good appetites. When they see a child who seems chronically underweight or listless, and whose mother shows too little concern about the child's condition, they criticize her negligence. While most human faults and errors are merely bad or unfortunate, child neglect, like parental assault or neglect, is one of the few singled out as "sins."

Women show lifelong, active concern about their children's health and general well-being. They commonly help their grown children with domestic services and support during periods of seasonal unemployment or sickness. In the past, most work was seasonal, and when it lapsed, workers returned home and remained there until the next season began (see Taylor 1951: 55; Gonzalez 1969: 43f.). Probably a greater proportion of workers in Belize now have year-round positions than formerly, but many still work seasonally. Those who are single usually return to their mothers' houses for a period of weeks or months before leaving to look for work again.

Marital problems, as well as seasonal unemployment, may compel women to return to their mothers' houses. Temporary separations, lasting

from a matter of days to months or longer, are rather common. A woman
with dependent children who separates from her spouse and finds herself
without support typically stays with her mother for some period of time.
Usually the woman depends on her mother for support until she and her
spouse reconcile their differences. If the separation is permanent, a matter
which is rarely clear at the outset, she may eventually leave her children
with her mother and leave the village to look for work.

When women return to their mothers' houses to live, they may simply
move from one house to another in the same village. The fact that so many
mothers and daughters live in the same community is due to a number of
factors: the high incidence of local endogamy; women's preference for
uxorilocal residence when they form unions with "strangers" from other
communities; and, of course, the dearth of employment opportunities for
women. As Table 6 shows, uxorilocal residence is more common than virilocal residence in two of the villages. (The third village was established so
recently that it has no native adults, making uxorilocal and virilocal
residence there technically impossible. Most of the unions in that village are
endogamous in the sense that the spouses were born elsewhere but in the
same community.)

TABLE 6
Local Endogamy, Exogamy, and Postmarital Residence

Type of Union	Viliage I (number)	Village II (number)	Village III (number)	Total (no.)	(%)
A. Local endogamy	74	49	23	146	85
B. Local exogamy					
1. uxorilocal residence	4	8	0	12	7
2. virilocal residence	1	3	0	4	2
3. neolocal residence	0	1	9	10	6
Subtotal	5	12	9	26	15
Total	79	61	32	172	100

Few women consent to live in their spouses' natal communities, and
those who do often have short-lived unions. In one village of nearly five
hundred, ten men and four women comprised the non-native population.
All but three, two men and one woman, had spouses who had been born in
the community. A year later, the ten men were still in residence, but two of
the four women had left their spouses and returned to their own communities. In one case, the woman left because of non-support, in the other
because of physical abuse.

Young women realize that the probability of financial hardship or mis-
treatment increases when they live at some distance from their mothers.
They depend on their mothers to help them when other sources of support

fail, and also to protect them during marital disputes. As a rule, people show great reluctance to interfere in marital frays. They usually cite the adage "Husband and wife is nobody's business" and leave the couple to settle their differences themselves. The overriding exception to this general rule is older women, who do not hesitate to step in when their daughters are involved. The fact that a woman can find sanctuary in her mother's house is one reason why many women say that they hesitate to live far from their mothers. An angry man who will intrude into another place of refuge, claiming a right to see his spouse, is quite circumspect about his mother-in-law's house. The man whose wife fled the community after he beat her explained that only her mother had the "right" to keep her from him, and her mother lived fifty kilometers away.

A woman does not always need to seek refuge in her mother's house if she lives nearby. In one case, a man who was mistreating his wife stopped abruptly when his mother-in-law, having been alerted by other women, walked into the yard. She sat down on the steps of the house without speaking to him, and kept her station there until he left. Other men and women explained that a man is "ashamed" to treat his spouse roughly in the presence of her mother.

Women usually try to persuade their daughters to leave men who mistreat them or who do not provide adequate support. They may also pressure their daughters to maintain unions that are unsatisfactory for less serious reasons — say infidelity. The practical reason for this counsel and their caution is clear. If a young woman separates, she and her children lose the man's support, and her mother will be expected to maintain the woman and her children financially until she finds work or another spouse. There is no assurance that she will find either locally, and little likelihood that she will establish another union immediately, especially if she has several children.

Relations between mothers and their grown children are usually informal and affectionate, yet they retain some element of asymmetry throughout life. Adults have no obligation to obey their parents, but they are expected to listen to their advice; and parents consider it their duty to counsel their sons and daughters. Men and women tolerate advice from their parents, and perhaps from other older relatives, when they will not abide such "interference" from their peers or juniors. Still, they do not necessarily heed the advice that is offered, leading older women to complain that their counsel often falls on "hard ears." The only way they can gain compliance from their grown children, as from anyone else, is through persuasion.

Ideally, men and women help to support their mothers. Villagers think it shameful for a woman with grown children to have to seek employment, which at her age, of course, is next to impossible to find. No one criticizes her, but others do speak ill of her children, accusing them of ingratitude and stinginess. Sons and daughters are equally obligated to contribute to their mothers' support, and by some accounts sons have a greater obligation, given their advantage in the labor market (cf. Gonzalez 1969: 57). Nevertheless, older women, and many men as well, describe their daughters as more "mindful" of their needs. They say that daughters "remember" them whereas sons are more apt to "forget" them. Some even express a preference for daughters, citing future security as the reason. A woman who remarked that her daughters had "stayed by" her (and not only in a physical sense), compared them to her sons, saying, "One day sons go!" And then, to underscore her point, she added, *Wügüri iráhü íchiga baúgudin, hiñáru iráhü anüga múnadaun*, "A son gives [to people] outside, a daughter brings into the home."

Many people mention remittances as evidence of daughters' "remembrance." Migrant daughters are said to be far more generous and reliable about supporting their mothers at home. According to men and women alike, most of the remittances regularly sent home are from and to females, usually from daughters to their mothers. It is impossible to verify this for specific Black Carib communities because of the manner in which receipts for international postal money orders are kept. But those available on a district-wide basis for the two southern districts, where the Black Carib population is concentrated, do support the reported local tendency. Receipts for a four-week period, the longest span for which they were available, showed that the donor was female in 64 percent of the cases and recipient in 76 percent. Slightly over half of the money orders involved the transfer of funds from one female to another. Most of the rest were cross-sex transactions, and a minority, about 10 percent, involved two males. The average sum sent by female donors was about $39 and by male donors $32.

There was no way to determine how regularly the donors sent money or the exact relationship between donor and recipient. Still, postal receipts do provide supporting evidence of the reported tendency for remittances to be sent by women to women.[3] They also suggest that daughters do not maintain closer ties with their mothers simply because they tend to live nearby. Even migrant women "remember" their mothers.

No doubt a number of factors enhance the close and enduring ties between mothers and daughters. As children, sons are often suffered to neglect home duties, while daughters are more consistently and swiftly punished for negligence. As adults, women have greater need of their mothers' help, and they reciprocate for the help they receive. And while men's marital responsibilities compete with their obligations to their mothers, women's do not. Women freely admit that a man's primary financial obligation is to support his spouse and children, although they do not think that this responsibility removes his duty to his mother.

A son's marital relationship also tends to limit the contact he has with his mother. One woman, who pays lengthy visits to her two daughters in the towns where they live, rarely visits her son, and then only briefly. She does not make extended visits to her son and his spouse, she explains, because she does not "feel so at home" in their house as she does in her daughters'. As for her son, he rarely visits her. Practically speaking, his mother can offer him very little; he has a permanent job, and his wife provides domestic services. He contributes far less to his mother's support than his sisters do.

This man's sisters, like other young women, depend on their mother for help that is vital to their well-being but is less significant to most men's. It is virtually impossible for any woman with dependent children to be entirely self-supporting, both because of her disadvantaged position in the labor market and because she bears ultimate responsibility for the care and support of her children. If her spouse dies, is disabled, or leaves her, she finds herself in serious financial straits. Even if she can find work, it will scarcely pay a living wage. If she has dependent children, as most young women do, she needs someone to care for them while she works.

Nearly every woman finds herself in these circumstances — with dependent children and without a supporting spouse — more than once in her life. Usually she depends on her mother for temporary support at first, and later for child care while she works. In these circumstances older women very often act as redistributors. A woman who receives money, food, and other goods from her grown children uses some of it to help those in need. As adults, siblings exchange very little directly, even when they live together, and far less if they live apart. But they exchange a great deal indirectly, through their mother.

Like parents and children, siblings have a lifelong obligation to share and to help each other financially whenever necessary. But their relations as adults depend very much on their having a mother (or surrogate mother) in common who acts as a redistributor. Since men do not assume this role with their grown children, paternal half-siblings exchange virtually nothing as adults, and they may scarcely associate as children since they are usually reared by different women. While the blood tie between them is considered as strong as that between maternal half-siblings, the interpersonal bond is not. The strongest ties are those established in childhood, with full and maternal half-siblings who "grew together" in the same household. People often comment that maternal half-siblings are indistinguishable from full siblings in most respects. In contrast, paternal half-siblings are said to be notoriously undependable and ungenerous in financial matters, whether these involve a small loan of cash or a contribution to a ritual event.

"Growing together," being reared by the same woman or women, strengthens ties between the more distantly related as well as between siblings. First cousins, and especially the children of (full or maternal half-)

sisters often live together in their maternal grandmother's house during some part of childhood. Although they are classified as siblings, whether or not they live together as children, the experience leads to closer ties between them. Co-residence during childhood also creates fictive sibling relationships. In the occasional case in which a woman rears two children who are not related, they typically refer to each other as siblings throughout life.

The usual reason why children who are not full siblings, or siblings at all, grow up together is that their parents have separated. Marital separation also affects the nature and frequency of children's contact with their fathers — and, by extension, the nature of their personal relations later in life. Father-child relationships cannot be understood apart from the system of mating.

Marital Relationships

Black Caribs distinguish three sorts of marital unions: legal, extralegal, and secondary. Marriage is a legal relationship established by ceremony, usually in a Roman Catholic church. At marriage, the woman takes her husband's surname and the couple refer to each other (in English) as husband and wife. Extralegal unions are also common and entirely acceptable, although they lack the prestige of marriage. The woman keeps her own surname in this type of union. She refers to her spouse as her "gentleman" and he to her as his "lady." These are the same terms that Creoles use for partners in such unions.

A few men support and alternately reside with two women, one of whom has a secondary status from the community's perspective (but not necessarily from the man's). The woman with the relationship of longer standing is the man's wife or lady, and the other is usually called his "sweetheart." In some cases the women live in the same community, but always in different houses and yards. Men approve of such unions, pointing out that a man with two women enjoys great prestige among his fellows. Women take a different view. They complain that these triangular relationships nearly always lead to conflict between the two women, especially if they have young children and depend heavily on their common spouse for support (cf. Gonzalez 1969: 73). Since few men can provide steady and sufficient support for two households, these unions are uncommon. The vast majority of village men claim to have only one spouse.

In their own language, Black Caribs do not distinguish between legal and extralegal spouses. Nor do they distinguish children born of the unions (or outside any union) as legitimate or illegitimate.[4] What is important is not the nature of the parents' relationship but the acknowledgment of paternity. Unacknowledged children are exceptional.

By cultural definition, marital relationships entail some degree of co-residence. Sexual partners who never reside together are called "friends." They are not considered spouses, not even if the woman bears a child by the man. Only when a man and woman have lived together can they refer to each others' relatives as affines.

A man and woman commonly begin their relationship as "friends," later live together if they are compatible, and perhaps eventually marry. All unions, however, do not conform to this pattern. Extralegal unions may endure for decades without ever being legalized, and some men and women marry at a young age, in their early twenties, without having previously lived together. Since there is no house-building rule (unlike many areas of the West Indies, where a couple live together only if they own a house), a man and woman can marry at a young age, before they have saved enough money to build a house.[5] Most couples, married or not, prefer to establish households separate from their parents, and the majority do so. If they lack the several hundred dollars to build a (lumber) house, they can easily rent one. Over 90 percent of the couples in the three villages surveyed lived apart from their parents. Of the remainder, only 1 percent lived with the man's parent(s), while 7 percent lived with the woman's parent(s). Slightly over half (57 percent) of all couples were married.

Most unmarried men and women say that they hope to marry eventually. For women, marriage offers the promise (but not always the realization) of greater financial security. A man only marries a woman whom he loves, they say, and he is not so likely to leave her for another one. Marriage also conveys prestige. Among themselves, women tease someone who has never married and who has no current spouse, saying that "no man wants her." As for men, people explain that until a man "takes responsibility" for a woman and her children by marrying her, he is not "respected" by other men and women in the community. They imply that he retains his status as a junior, no matter his age, until he marries.

Legality aside, little distinguishes relations between legal and extralegal spouses (including secondary ones). Their customary rights and obligations are the same, with the exception of mourning (see Chapter 9). The legal status of their union does not affect the woman's basic obligation to provide domestic services and care, and the man's primary obligation to support her and their children. Women speak of sexual fidelity as a mutual obligation, while many men suggest otherwise. What most men and women agree upon is that a woman who strays, especially a married woman, deserves rebuke; they tend to regard male infidelity as nearly inevitable. If a man discovers that his spouse is unfaithful, he does not usually confront her lover; he simply leaves her.[6] If a woman discovers that she has a rival, she generally confronts her publicly but does not leave the man, unless he begins to neglect her financially in favor of the other woman. What women usually will not abide from a spouse is non-support or physical abuse. These are uniformly considered legitimate grounds for separation.

Perhaps as many unions end because of mutual incompatibility or because one of the partners prefers to establish a new union. These separations provoke a flurry of criticism, but they occur commonly enough. Decisions to establish and to end marital relationships are essentially individual decisions, and subject to minimal regulation. No amount of social pressure can force a couple to maintain an unsatisfactory relationship. Others' criticism, however spirited, has rather little effect; and men and women do not always heed their mothers' advice to maintain unions that they themselves find unsatisfactory.

For the most part, young men and women establish unions on the basis of physical and emotional attraction — in their own words, on "love." (With age, however, men and women tend to de-emphasize the romantic in favor of the practical: thus, compatibility is more important than attraction.) Marital relationships seem to be more unstable during early adulthood, when financial pressures are the greatest, and many are punctuated by temporary separations and reconciliations. Others, however, may end in informal but permanent estrangement. (Legal separation and divorce are expensive, exceptional, and unnecessary.) In these cases, spouses customarily take their personal property with them, and the children nearly always remain with their mother. Occasionally a man may place one or more of his children with his mother or sister, usually because he intends to continue supporting them and refuses to give the money to his former spouse. But separations are not always a matter of mutual agreement, and if a man refuses to separate peacefully, the woman usually resorts to sorcery rather than the law for help. She obtains *árani,* medicine, to protect her from her former spouse and to keep him away from her.

Although marital relationships may lapse, relationships with other affines do not. Once established, they are permanent (cf. Whitten 1974: 154). Whether men and women disregard or cultivate these ties is largely a matter of personal choice. Women do have the customary duty of providing domestic help for their sons' spouses after childbirth. Otherwise, affines have no specific obligations toward each other.

The use of affinal terms is not required in reference or address. Speakers commonly use the courtesy terms *yau,* uncle, and *naúfuri,* my aunt, when addressing parents-in-law. There are specific terms of reference for parents-, children-, and siblings-in-law. Those for siblings-in-law are applied to a broad range of people, including the spouses of full and half-siblings and of first cousins, as well as the full and half-siblings and first cousins of one's own spouse. Actually, recognition of affines is even broader than this. Many people speak of "cousins-in-law," meaning the spouse of a cousin (of any degree) or the cousin of a spouse.

Because recognition of affines is permanent and broad, and because men and women commonly have more than one spouse during their lives, affinal networks tend to be very large. They include the current and former spouses of relatives as well as the known relatives of spouses, past and current. Many kin networks — made up of all known affines and blood relatives — are so large and so dispersed, throughout Belize and abroad, that they are not easily or precisely calculable. Given this breadth, village women scarcely interact in daily life with anyone outside their kin network; and when they travel to other Black Carib settlements, they usually find some relatives and affines there as well. Men, in contrast, typically work in non-Carib enterprises, where they associate with "strangers," Black Carib and non-Carib alike, on a daily basis.

The system of affinity, and particularly the fact that so many unions lapse, has several consequences. Many people have half-siblings because men and women commonly have children by more than one spouse. In two of the villages surveyed, slightly less than half of the women past the age of childbearing had borne living children by one male, and the remainder by two or more men.[7] Nearly all middle-aged and older men questioned claim children by more than one woman. Their claims are difficult to verify because men, more often than women, mate outside their natal village. Since almost all children remain with their mothers in the event of separation, they have more contact with maternal relatives and less with paternal ones. Marital separation explains, to a degree, the maternal bias of so many genealogies (cf. Solien 1960: 151). It also directly affects the nature and frequency of a man's contact with his children.

Fathers and Children

Ideally, a man ought to support all of his children, whether he lives with them or not, and regardless of their mother's marital status. But if he has children by more than one woman, as so many men do, he finds it difficult to support all of them. Not only are wages rather low, but the man's current spouse will certainly object to his giving money to another woman. (No matter that she bitterly criticizes her own former spouse for not supporting the children she bore him. Women ignore this logical inconsistency, attending first and foremost to the welfare of their children and themselves.) Few men, however, have the means to provide *constant* support to *all* of their children throughout their dependency. As a general rule, a man supports the children of the woman with whom he lives: his current spouse, his mother, or another female relative.

When children of lapsed unions stay with their mothers, their stepfathers support them. In some cases their relationships do not differ, at least outwardly, from those of men and their natural children. A stepchild may take the man's surname, address him as "Pa," refer to him as *núguchin,* my father, and even refer to his children by other women as siblings. One twelve-year-old girl explained this by saying about her stepfather of eight years, "He is my father because he feeds me."

It is difficult to estimate the proportion of children who are supported and reared by men other than their natural fathers. At any given point in time, a high proportion of children live with both of their natural parents: in the three villages, about 60 percent of all dependent children (see Table 7). Some of their parents' unions will end, however, in temporary or permanent separation. In those cases the children will remain with their mothers, or they will be fostered by kinswomen and partially supported by the men of that household. This was the case, by and large, with the children living apart from their natural fathers. Most had a surrogate father, often addressed as Pa, living in the same household. This was their stepfather or, in the case of fostered children, the spouse, son, or son-in-law of their foster mother.[8]

TABLE 7
Residence of Dependent Children (0–16 Years)

Residence	Number	Percent
A. Children living with parent(s)		
1. with both parents	497	60
2. with mother and stepfather	41	5
3. with mother only	101	12
Subtotal	639	77
B. Fostered children		
1. with maternal kin		
a. mother's mother	100	12
b. mother's sister	13	2
c. other	26	3
Subtotal	139	17
2. with paternal kin		
a. father's mother	29	3
b. father's sister	8	1
c. other	16	2
Subtotal	53	6
Total	831	100

Strictly defined, fosterage is the separation of children from both of their natural parents, with care provided by other adults. The usual caretakers are female kin. But many of these women have spouses who also help foster the child, by contributing to the child's support. The critical difference between men and women as foster parents is that *men tend to foster affines' chil-*

dren: the children of their spouses or spouses' relatives. *Women nearly always foster children of blood relatives:* their grandchildren, nieces and nephews, or the children of more remote relatives.

Census data and life histories together suggest that very few children reside with and are reared *exclusively* by *both* of their natural parents, yet nearly all children do reside with both parents for some period of time. This is not so disruptive in fact as it may seem in theory. The twelve-year-old girl mentioned above is a case in point. She lived with both of her parents until the age of two, when the couple separated permanently. She spent the next two years in the same community, living with her maternal grandmother while her mother worked elsewhere in the district. In the interim her mother married; the girl has lived with her mother and stepfather since then. From the child's own perspective, her home life has been very stable, centering on her relationship with her mother and mother's mother. She has lived all of her life in the same village and, in fact, in the same yard, where her grandmother and her mother both have houses. Technically, the girl's mother and grandmother maintain separate households, but the girl sleeps nearly as often in her grandmother's house as in her mother's. In this case, as in most extended families, household boundaries overlap and are highly permeable. This is particularly true of the households of older women, who, like this girl's maternal grandmother, have many lineal relatives as occasional residents.

Notes to Chapter 7

1. *Rása* derives from the Spanish *raza,* meaning race, clan, or breed.
2. Both Gonzalez and Taylor note that variance exists in Black Carib kinship terminology (see Solien 1960; Taylor 1951: 75ff.; 1965b). I also found variation in usage. The most commonly used terms are listed in Appendix 1.
3. The data in Chapter 3 on postal money orders show the same general pattern. Creoles were presumably the main donors and recipients. (Belize City and Belize District are predominantly Creole.)
4. When speaking Carib, people do not distinguish between legal and extralegal spouses. They use the terms *númari,* my companion, and *nawáiai* or *nawáiaun,* my old man or my old woman, for both. Following their own example, I use the term "spouse" to refer to partners of legal or extralegal unions. The terms "husband" and "wife" refer only to legally married spouses. Since the legal status of the parents' union has no effect on a child's status, the conventional sign for a marital tie (=) is used in charts to indicate both types of union. See Slater (1977) for an extended discussion of legitimacy in Caribbean kinship.

5. For a brief discussion of the house-building rule, see Dirks and Kerns (1976: 49f.).

6. This, in theory and sometimes in fact, is the male response to female infidelity. But many men and women say that a man should not leave his spouse on account of rumor, but only if she is found *in flagrante delicto,* which of course is remarkably uncommon.

7. There were 80 women forty-five years of age and older in the two villages. I have excluded 20 of them who were barren (9), bore only one child (8), or claimed one father for all of their children but were widely suspected of having "washpan babies" — children by extramarital liaisons (3). Of the remaining 60 women who had borne two or more children, 29 (48 percent) each claimed one man as the father of her children, 27 (45 percent) claimed two men, and 4 (7 percent) claimed from three to five men as fathers of her children.

8. Most children grow up in households with a man in residence, although he is not necessarily their natural father or present on a daily basis. See Mertz (1976) for the psychological effects of father-absence on Black Carib children.

Chapter 8

HOUSEHOLDS AND EXTENDED FAMILIES

Households and nonresidential extended families are the basic social groups of the Black Carib. Women, as mothers, are structurally central to most households and to extended families. The focal female in an extended family is an older woman, and in most households either a young woman (with dependent children) or an older woman (whose children are grown). She provides a common focus of affection and exchange, and usually acts as the redistributor of food, other goods, and money within these groups. Further, her actions influence both their continuity and composition. If the focal woman leaves the household permanently (as happens when a couple separates and the woman does not own the house), or if she dies, the household usually breaks up, often immediately.[1] With the death of this woman, an extended family segments. Changes in the composition of households, as will be shown, follow in large part from the actions she takes.

The life stage of the focal woman provides a key to understanding both the relationship between extended families and households and variance among the latter: specifically, variation in the range of kin who live together, in residential turnover or stability, and in the "survivorship" of household groups. While some households endure for many years, others are quite short-lived. The composition of some is highly stable and scarcely changes from one year to the next, yet others show a rapid turnover in residents. As for their exact composition, Gonzalez (1969: 68) has pointed out that "it is difficult to isolate any one household form as being typical of the society as a whole." Indeed, the range of kin who live together varies so much that constructing a parsimonious typology presents a challenge. But if attention is directed to the life stage of the focal woman, a clear pattern does emerge. The households of most young women have a fairly uniform and fixed composition, approximating a nuclear family form. These households also tend to be rather "brittle" (cf. Gonzalez 1969: 84f.). They dissolve more frequently than the extended family households of older women, which are typically of diverse and shifting composition but which endure for many years. The fluctuating and diverse composition of such households does not indicate "disorganization" or "weak family structure." These households are more complex, and organized in a manner that is difficult to see without understanding their links to others in extended families.

Households

Black Carib households are non-corporate groups. Residents share a food supply and domicile (Gonzalez 1969: 45, 66) but do not own property in common and do not necessarily form a productive unit. Some households maintain cultivated plots; others purchase nearly all of the food they consume. Most households have an income-earning male in residence, but a few depend entirely on nonresidents for support.

On the basis of composition, these households can be categorized in various ways. Of course, the usefulness of any typology depends on the questions one seeks to answer. In her well-known study *Black Carib Household Structure,* Gonzalez shows how male labor migration and the brittle nature of marital bonds affect household form. She distinguishes between two types of households: affinal households, which include a mating couple, and consanguineal households, which do not. In the Black Carib town she surveyed in 1956, the two types were almost evenly represented. Slightly over half of the households (55 percent) were affinal and the remainder consanguineal. When she again collected figures on residence in 1975, she found little change. Fifty-one percent of the households were affinal, 44 percent consanguineal, and 5 percent single-person (Gonzalez, personal communication). In the three villages surveyed for this study in 1975 a larger proportion (62 percent) were affinal households and the remainder consanguineal (27 percent) and single-person (11 percent).

If other questions are asked about Black Carib households — how they relate to extended families and why they vary in composition, residential stability, and survivorship — a different typology proves useful. That is, it reveals a pattern that the consanguineal/affinal typology does not. Most households fall into two general categories: nuclear family households and extended family households. The former includes two sub-types. Simple nuclear family households contain only a couple and their children in common. In modified nuclear family households, the residents are also related to each other as parent and child, spouse, or sibling, but most of these are incomplete nuclear families. That is, they include *only* a parent and children, siblings, or spouses.[2] Others are modified nuclear families not by omission but addition. These households contain a couple, any of their children in common, *and* some of the woman's children by former unions.

Most extended family households build on the nuclear family core, either simple or modified, by adding residents who are not related to the focal woman as child or spouse. In other cases, the focal woman lives only with non-nuclear relatives: for example, her grandchildren or a niece or nephew. Finally, a few households contain only one person: an older woman, either widowed or separated, or a man. Most of the men are separated or widowers, but a few are confirmed bachelors. Table 8 shows the frequency of the three household types: nuclear family (45 percent), extended family (44 percent), and single-person (11 percent).

TABLE 8
Frequency of Household Types

Type	Number	Percent
Nuclear family households		
simple nuclear	57	23
modified nuclear	53	22
Subtotal	110	45
Extended family households		
extended simple nuclear	46	19
extended modified nuclear	38	16
extended non-nuclear	21	9
Subtotal	105	44
Single-person households		
female	15	6
male	12	5
Subtotal	27	11
Total	242	100

Most households (89 percent) in the three villages fall into the nuclear family or extended family categories. The latter generally include very young or elderly residents under the care of the focal woman. Some 90 percent of them are extended by the fosterage of children (usually grandchildren of the focal woman); most of the remainder have a very elderly man or woman in residence. Nearly all of the households (95 percent) are extended by blood relatives of the focal woman. Specifically, 30 percent include non-nuclear consanguines of both the woman and her spouse (their grandchildren); 65 percent, consanguines of the woman; and 5 percent, blood relatives of the woman's spouse.

In terms of frequency, nuclear family and extended family households are almost evenly represented. They are not evenly distributed, however, by the life stage of the focal woman. As Table 9 shows, the focal female in most nuclear family households is a young woman, and in most extended family households an older woman.[3]

TABLE 9

Life Stage of Focal Female in Nuclear Family and Extended Family Households

Type	Young woman		Older woman		Total	
	number	percent	number	percent	number	percent
Nuclear family households						
simple nuclear	48	54.6	9	7.4	57	27.1
modified nuclear	23	26.1	27	22.1	50	23.8
Subtotal	71	80.7	36	29.5	107	50.9
Extended family households						
extended simple nuclear	11	12.5	35	28.7	46	21.9
extended modified nuclear	4	4.5	34	27.9	38	18.1
extended non-nuclear	2	2.3	17	13.9	19	9.1
Subtotal	17	19.3	86	70.5	103	49.1
Total	88	100	122	100	210	100

The nuclear family households of young women have a uniform and stable composition, but they dissolve more frequently than the extended family households of older women. In one community over the course of a year nearly 20 percent of the former type (4 of the 21 households) disintegrated when the couple separated. Only one extended family household (representing less than 3 percent of the 35 households of this type) broke up during the same period, following the death of the focal woman. Two older women separated from their husbands, but their households did not dissolve. The two men left their wives' houses and joined other households.

Several factors bear on the survivorship of households. The nuclear family households of young women depend on one wage-earner, the woman's spouse, for most of their support. Without it, the household cannot sustain itself. Non-support is a major reason why young women leave their spouses. In addition, very few of these women own the houses they live in. In some cases, their spouses are the owners. In others, the couple occupies a house that belongs to one of their relatives. In either situation, when these women separate from their spouses they usually take their children and join other households. Their estranged spouses generally do the same.

The extended family households of older women differ in a number of respects. They commonly draw their support from several sources. Older women depend on their grown children for some financial help, whether or not they live with them; and nearly half of these women also have wage-earning spouses. In addition, a greater proportion of them own houses.[4] In one community, for example, 42 percent of the houses are owned by women and the remainder by men. Nearly two-thirds of the female owners are forty-five or older. Marital separation does not have the same consequences for their households as for those of most younger women.

The extended family households of older women also show more rapid turnover in residents and greater variation in the range of kin who live in them. A number of specific events can alter household composition. Births, deaths, migration, the formation of marital relationships, marital separation, domestic disputes, and fosterage result in the addition or loss of household residents. The extended family households of older women are most susceptible to such residential change. When a young woman separates from her spouse, she usually "goes home to mother," taking her children with her. A young man may do the same (but rarely with any of his children). If he is single, he typically returns to his mother's house when he loses his employment. Children are generally sent to their grandmothers to be fostered, and so forth.

Residential change does not simply "happen" to the household of an older woman. She may consent or decline to foster children, depending on her relationship with their mother, the state of her health, and a host of other factors. If she welcomes her sons and daughters home, she also encourages them to leave and look for work.[5] She may permit a son's or daughter's spouse to join the household. But by many accounts her "interference" also often leads to the couple's eventual separation. (Men in particular cite this as the main reason they prefer to set up separate households with their spouses.) Finally, domestic disputes do not typically lead to changes in household residence *unless* the disagreement involves the older woman. Interpersonal problems between siblings, for example, may persist without one or the other leaving the household. But when one of the adversaries is the focal woman, the other party often elects to leave — sometimes, but not always, at her request.

In one such case, a woman who had reared her daughter's son from his infancy, when her daughter died, "railed up" at her grandson one day for spending too much time and money with "worthless" companions. He had been working for several months at a nearby plantation, but instead of dutifully giving most of his earnings to her he had recently begun to spend more money on his male friends, usually to buy rum. He was eighteen years old, an age when many young men begin to chafe under the watchful eyes of their elders and to seek approval from male peers rather than kin. (As traditional wisdom has it, men at this age begin to "give [to people] outside.") Her grandson, angry at this rebuke, did not argue the point. He simply moved into his paternal grandmother's house, at her invitation, and began to give her a portion of his wages. The young man was criticized in many quarters for his ingratitude to the woman who had reared him, and the paternal grandmother for her "greed."

In these two particular households, and as a general rule, each resident's primary tie is to the focal woman. Ties with most other residents are secondary, derivative of the primary bond. In other words, siblings (full and maternal half-siblings) live together *because* they are children of one mother, and regardless of whether they have the same father. Men live with their children *if* they live with the mothers of their children. Some young cousins live with each other *because* they are under the care of their grandmother.

The households in Figures 1–4 show the various links of residents through the focal woman. All of the examples are extended family households of older women.[6] The marital status of the women varies: one is separated and another widowed; the other two women live with spouses (legal and extralegal). Two of the women own houses; two do not. Three of the households have male wage-earners (or a pensioner) in residence; one does not. The first two households are of the extended modified nuclear type, the third and fourth respectively of extended simple nuclear and non-nuclear types. Shaded figures in the diagrams represent household residents. For simplicity, only the focal women are named (by pseudonym), and their children are shown only if they or their offspring live in the households.

Household 1

Rufina Alvarez is fifty-five years old. Her husband died fifteen years ago. Two of her children and several grandchildren currently live with Mrs. Alvarez. Her nineteen-year-old son, who works at a nearby plantation, returns to her house every weekend. He and one of his older sisters, who works in Belize City, provide most of their mother's support. Mrs. Alvarez has fostered her daughter's two children for several years, ever since the young woman separated from her spouse and went to Belize City to look for work. Another daughter, more recently separated, moved with her two children to her mother's house after her spouse left her.

Household 2

Balbina Lewis is sixty-one years old. Her husband died fourteen years ago, and several years later she began to live with another man. They have never married and have no children in common. She lives with this man and with two of her daughters' children in his house. One of her daughters lives in the United States. The other recently married a man who is the father of her younger child but not of the elder one, whom Mrs. Lewis fosters. Both daughters help their mother financially. She receives very little from a married son who lives in another community. Her spouse, who is in his mid-sixties, works at a plantation and provides much of the household's income.

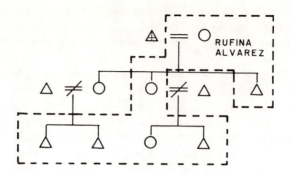

Figure 1. Household 1

Key of symbols in kinship diagrams:

male, △; female, ○; parent/child link, |; sibling link, ⌐¬; marital relation, =; decedent, ⧊, ⊕; extended family member, ▲, ●; broken marital or extraresidential relation, ≠; member of household, ENCIRCLED CHARACTER.

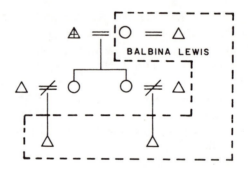

Figure 2. Household 2

Household 3

Marcella Ogaldez is sixty-three years old. Her husband, a retired teacher, receives a monthly pension, the primary source of support for the household. Several of their sons and daughters who work in other districts send remittances now and then. A daughter whose children they foster is the only one who regularly sends money. Another daughter bore a child some years ago but never lived with the father. She remains at home with her parents. Mr. Ogaldez had his house built twenty years ago, when he was teaching in another area of the country. After he retired, he and his wife returned to their natal community to take up permanent residence.

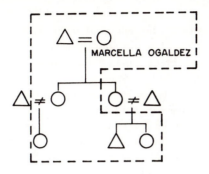

Figure 3. Household 3

Household 4

Geralda Cruz is fifty-seven years old. She has several grown children by a man whom she lived with for many years but never married. A few years after he died, she began to live with another man, and she eventually married him. They have no children in common and recently separated. Her estranged husband has rented a small house in the same community. Mrs. Cruz owns the house where she still lives with five of her daughters' children. Her two daughters and one of her sons migrated to the United States several years ago. She now obtains all of her support from these children, and most of it from the two daughters whose children she fosters.

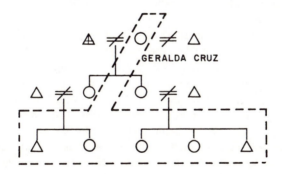

Figure 4. Household 4

One final point, a caveat, bears mention here. Households do not follow a fixed developmental cycle (cf. R. T. Smith 1956; 1978: 342). Most are established as nuclear family households, of either simple or modified type. That is, a man, a woman, and children — of the woman *or* of the couple — form the household. (Very few young couples without children live together, and they almost never occupy a separate house. There was only one case of the latter in the three villages, but a foster child lived with the couple.) Many of the nuclear family households that survive do eventually change to the extended family type. But this may occur very soon after the household is established, since fosterage accounts for most extension. In one such instance, a twenty-five-year-old woman agreed to foster her sister's daughter soon after moving into a house with her new husband and their child. Extended family households can just as readily "revert" to a nuclear family or single-person form with the loss of non-nuclear kin. This is illustrated by the case of a widowed sixty-year-old woman who fostered several grandchildren for a year or so after the parents separated. Eventually the couple settled their differences and took the children to live with them in another district.

However variable in composition, the households of most older women endure for many years. They provide a stable link between other, sometimes short-lived households in extended families.

Extended Families

An extended family is a non-corporate and nonresidential group, composed of the inner core of an older woman's kin network. It generally includes her sons and daughters (as well as any men and women she fostered as children), her grandchildren, current spouses of her sons and daughters, and her own spouse, unless she is widowed or separated.[7] Some extended families also include various other relatives of the older woman who are under her care.

Family members usually live in several different households and communities. The only occasion when they gather (and rarely all of them) is when they sponsor a major ritual event: those that the focal woman organizes or those held on her behalf after she dies (see Chapters 9 and 10). Aside from ritual sponsorship, extended families also act as vehicles of mutual support, providing care and help to family members in need. In both aspects they serve a single end, meeting the needs of close kin either deceased or living.

Various "transactions" define the boundaries of extended families. Spouses are selected from outside the family. (That is, they are non-kin or relatives beyond the first-cousin range.) Although they are incorporated into the family to varying degrees, most remain peripheral members — linked by marital rather than blood ties, with stronger loyalties to another group, and liable to leave because of marital separation. Accusations of sorcery are never made against family members *except* these affines. Fosterage and household residency also define the boundaries of extended families. Residents of a household nearly always belong to the same family group (cf. Gonzalez 1969: 85), and most children are fostered within their mother's or father's extended family. Finally, one family usually shoulders most of the financial burden for any particular ritual event.

Older women, as mothers, occupy the focal position in extended families. An extended family emerges as a woman's children reach adulthood and begin to reproduce, work, and contribute to her support. She provides a shared focus of affection and exchange, a source of care during times of need, and representation in ritual life. Grown siblings exchange more indirectly, through their mothers, than they do directly. They are bound not so much by reciprocal rights and obligations to each other as by their shared relationship to their mother. After her death the family segments.

Segmentation may occur slowly before the woman dies, if she lives past the age of seventy or so. While a very elderly woman continues to receive support from her children, they no longer depend on her as they once did, in part because their own children are grown. Ill health may prevent an elderly woman from fostering children or from taking active part in ritual life. Her daughters, mature women in their forties or fifties, assume these roles in their own extended families. Some elderly women live with one of their daughters; others live by themselves but take meals with their daughters and spend much of the day visiting them.

An extended family does not automatically form or segment as a woman ages. Her efforts are required to transform a network of kin into a noncorporate but organized group. Not all women approach this task with the same degree of determination and vigor. Some have more success than others in their effort to obtain support from their grown children and to help them in turn. Any older woman who feels herself neglected will not conceal her displeasure from her children or from others. She reminds her sons and daughters not only of their obligations to her but also of the help that she gives them. To different degrees, however, older women reinforce their words with action. Thus, a negligent young son may receive visits on payday from his mother — or, if she is indisposed, from his sister, acting as her mother's emissary (cf. Gonzalez 1969: 59). In some cases this requires traveling several hundred miles round trip by freight truck, a time-consuming and tiring journey.

Women agree that in this matter their sons generally need more prodding than their daughters. But young women clearly depend on their mothers' help to a greater degree than their brothers do. Most young women bear children, and they also bear ultimate responsibility for the care of those children. These are givens, but male support is not. As the following case suggests, women's obligations to their children reinforce ties with their mothers.

A young woman, whose father died when she was eight, was sent to live with her father's sister in another community. She remained with her paternal aunt for the next ten years, but often visited her mother. As is quite common in such cases, both her paternal aunt and her mother refer to her as a daughter. The young woman is now working in the United States, and she sends monthly remittances to her mother, who fosters her two young children (by a lapsed union). She also occasionally sends much smaller sums of money to her paternal aunt, as well as gifts at Christmas. These do not, however, approach the value of what she gives to her mother. The young woman is included in two extended families, her mother's (by birth) and her paternal aunt's (by fosterage). But she exchanges more with her mother, who cares for her children, than with her father's sister. The paternal aunt feels slighted and has complained quite openly about her foster child's "ingratitude." She points out that she helped her sister-in-law by taking her child, but she has never enjoyed any appreciable help in return, either from the young woman or her mother. When the young woman's mother recently found evidence that someone was using sorcery against her, she immediately suspected this sister-in-law, saying that she was "jealous."

Some of the strain in this case springs from the fact that women do not normally "help" affines who foster their children.[8] Most women who foster children do receive some support from the mothers, but of course they are usually consanguines. Referring to Table 7 in the last chapter, of the 192 children fostered in the three villages, 139, or 72 percent, were living with women related by blood to their mothers. One hundred of them, or over 50 percent, lived with their maternal grandmothers.[9] Fosterage is an important vehicle for exchanges between women who are blood relatives, especially mothers and daughters.

An older woman and her daughters form the stable core of an extended family and directly help each other with services, goods (especially food and clothing), and money. Men, their spouses and the sons of the focal woman, contribute money, but a daughter's spouse does so indirectly. That is, some of his earnings usually pass to his mother-in-law's hands through his spouse, her daughter. If this man falls sick or is disabled, his spouse normally seeks help from her mother. Many men are indirectly supported by their affines in such circumstances, receiving more from them than from their own blood relatives. Of course, in many cases they have indirectly contributed more to their mothers-in-law than they have directly given to their own mothers. (This may be one reason why older women often encourage their daughters to maintain unions that are financially satisfactory, even if they leave something to be desired in other respects.)

The relations between daughters-in-law and mothers-in-law differ in that these women usually exchange very little. Indeed, many see themselves as competitors for the support of the spouse/son. The man's sisters tend to share this view, since his negligence of filial duty adds to their own burden. One man, complaining of the animosity between his wife and sisters, commented that relations between sisters-in-law tend to be lukewarm, even actively hostile. "Sometimes," he said, "the bad feelings go right up to the old lady" (the man's mother). In his case, there was no love lost between his wife and mother. Both avoided forcing the issue of his primary allegiance and obligations, but privately each criticized the other for her "greed." They maintained a façade of cordiality whenever they met.

There are some exceptions to this rule. A young woman whose marital union is stable and whose mother is dead or lives in a distant community may develop warm relations with her mother-in-law and even come to regard her as a mother. In local parlance, she may act very "attentive" to her mother-in-law, responsive to her needs. Men, however, more often claim this sort of relationship with their mothers-in-law than women do. Of. course, this is only one step beyond a man's usual relations with his spouse's mother.

The distance between a man's mother and sisters and his spouse very often has a physical dimension as well as an emotional one. They almost never live together in the same house or yard, and rarely in adjacent yards. Extended families are localized to varying degrees, and it is women — mothers and daughters — who tend to live close to each other. In some cases, an older woman and one or more of her grown children occupy adjacent houses in one yard and share a kitchen (but not a common food supply on a daily basis). Gonzalez (1969: 69) refers to such localized clusters as "compounds." In Black Carib villages in Belize, most compounds are composed of an older woman and one or more of her grown daughters.

Whether or not her children live nearby, this woman's household is focal to the extended family. In some cases family members are dispersed all over the country and abroad, and only the older woman lives permanently in the home community. More commonly, a number of her children live in the same community, if not in her house or an adjacent one. Wherever they live, her sons and daughters and her daughters' children typically refer to her house as "our house." Her sons' children are less apt to speak of it in this way because they usually spend more time with their maternal grandmother. In theory, when the woman dies her house will belong to all of her descendants; while she is alive, her children and many of her daughters' children will live with her for some period of time. They can consider it "our house" in both senses.

Unlike some of the households they encompass, extended families show pronounced stability. Most of the events that alter household composition or threaten its survival do not have the same effect on extended families. Fosterage usually occurs within an extended family and does not affect its composition. Referring again to Table 7 in the last chapter, the figures show that the vast majority of children (150, or 78 percent) are fostered within the extended families of their maternal or paternal grandmothers. Most of them (113, or 59 percent) live with their mother's mother or mother's sister, while the remainder (37, or 19 percent), live with their father's mother or father's sister. Migration and domestic disputes, like fosterage, affect the composition of households but not of extended families. Families grow larger with births and the formation of marital unions. Losses are due to deaths and marital separation. Since births outnumber deaths, extended families tend to grow larger over time.

Extended families are usually larger than households or compounds, which average six and a dozen residents respectively. The largest include nearly fifty people, but they average between fifteen and thirty. Most have a three-generation range, but some as many as five. Extended families vary in other details as well: the degree of localization in one house, compound, or community; the incorporation of collateral relatives of the older woman; and the number of family members who directly support her.

However they differ in detail, extended families share a uniform, concentric structure. The core of an extended family is the focal woman and her daughters, who have undivided loyalties and nearly exclusive commitment to their own family group. Men — especially married sons and the spouses of these women — find themselves caught between two extended families. This is a chronic cause of resentment and source of conflict between men and women (especially spouses and brothers and sisters) and between women (as affines). The fact that men "give [to people] outside" creates dissatisfaction among their sisters and mothers. Likewise, the fact that daughters "bring into the home" of their mothers arouses the resentment of men, the daughters' spouses.

Several brief examples and one detailed case study of extended families follow. They illustrate structural similarities, especially in the pattern of exchange, and variation in the size, generational range, and dispersion of these families. Some of this variation can be explained in terms of the focal woman's reproductive history and her place in the life cycle. An extended family tends to increase in size and generational range, and to grow more dispersed as a woman's offspring mature, reproduce, and migrate. The following sequence of examples clarifies this. The first involves a woman in her late thirties and the fourth, a woman in her sixties. One of the women bore only one child; another has six surviving children. In the diagrams (Figures 5–9), shaded figures represent family members. Stars indicate those people who directly "help" the focal woman. Daughters' spouses are not starred, but they provide much of the money that the women give their mothers. Households are circled. Only the focal women are named (again, by pseudonym).

Extended Family 1

Felicia Lewis is thirty-eight years old. She has only one surviving sibling, a brother who has lived in the United States for the past ten years. Until her mother's death several years ago, she received news and occasional gifts from him through her mother. They have lost contact since then. Together with her three children, Felicia still lives in the house where she was born and where she lived most of her life with her mother. She receives no financial help from her former spouses. Her seventeen-year-old son, who works at a nearby plantation and spends his weekends at home, provides most of her support. Her elder daughter is pregnant by a young man who works at the same plantation. He supports her, and she in turn gives most of the money to her mother. During the week she sleeps upstairs in her mother's house and takes her meals there. On weekends her spouse comes home, and she stays with him in the rooms downstairs and prepares their meals separately. The people who live in Felicia Lewis's house comprise an "incipient" extended family.

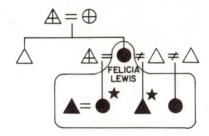

KEY:

Member of extended family:	▲ ●	Broken marital or extraresidential relation: ≠
Direct contributor:	★	
Marital relation:	=	Decedent: ⚠ ⊕

Members: 5

Generations: 2

Contributors: 2

Localization: 1 house

Figure 5. Extended Family (incipient) 1

Extended Family 2

Lucia Ramirez is forty-seven years old. She has several brothers and sisters, one of whom, her youngest brother, she reared after their mother died many years ago. As a young woman she lived briefly with a man from another community and bore a son by him. Her son, now twenty-nine, works as a teacher in another district. He sends her money occasionally for the support of his son, whom she fosters. The child's mother now lives in the United States but only sends him clothing now and then. When she and Lucia Ramirez's son separated she agreed to send her son to Lucia. Her own mother was dead, she had no sisters, and she wished to emigrate to the United States.

Lucia Ramirez married thirteen years ago and has two sons by her husband. He works at a plantation in the district and provides most of the household income. Mrs. Ramirez also receives some help from her youngest brother, to whom she is "like a mother." She fosters one of his sons by a lapsed union. The child's mother is in the United States. Mrs. Ramirez and her brother live in adjacent houses. She owns her house, which she had built several years ago, using money that her eldest son gave her for that purpose. Although she and her sister-in-law spend their days in direct view of each other, they rarely exchange even greetings.

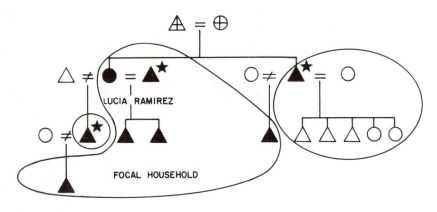

Members: 8

Generations: 3

Contributors: 3

Localization: 3 households in
                2 districts

Figure 6. Extended Family 2

Extended Family 3

Daniela Nunez is fifty-two years old, the eldest of four brothers and five sisters. She was living with her widowed mother when the woman died eight years ago. A year later Daniela replaced her mother's thatch house with a new lumber one, using money she had just won in the national lottery. She lives there now with her spouse and several of her children and grandchildren.

Daniela has had four spouses but has never married. She has lived with her current spouse for eleven years. They do not have any children in common. Her two youngest children and her grandchildren, all of them dependents, address this man as *yau,* uncle, and sometimes also refer to him as their stepfather. He works as a fisherman and provides fish and some income for the household. Daniela receives more money from one of her grown daughters, who sends monthly remittances from the United States. Another single daughter, who works in Belize City, sends her money as well. Daniela fosters children for both of these daughters. Her married daughter offers help when she can, but she depends on Daniela to pay for her son's secondary education. Daniela criticizes her son-in-law for his "stinginess," adding that she hopes her grandson will "remember" her (help her financially) when he is "able." She does not expect very much help from her married son, who lives in another district and rarely visits her. "He has his own responsibilities now," Daniela says. She pointedly adds that she rarely helps him either.

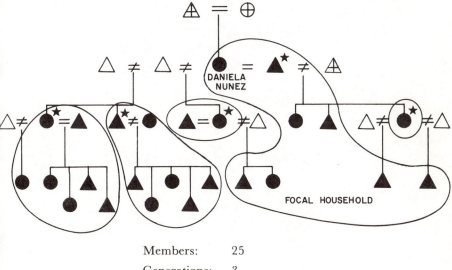

Members:	25
Generations:	3
Contributors:	5
Localization:	5 households in 3 districts and the United States

Figure 7. Extended Family 3

Extended Family 4

Ramona Moreira is sixty-one years old. She bore her only child when she was sixteen, but her union with the child's father lasted only a matter of months. A few years later she began to live with the man whom she eventually married. Her parents died many years ago. She has several siblings, but only one brother and a sister currently live in the community. The sister has seven children and "gave" one of them to Mrs. Moreira, who reared the girl. Today the young woman spends more time in her company than with her natural mother, although she names both women as her mothers. The young woman's husband refers to both Mrs. Moreira and her sister as his mothers-in-law, and to their husbands as fathers-in-law.

Mrs. Moreira's natural daughter lived in a compound with her after she married and until she was widowed, about fifteen years ago. Some years later she began to live with another man in the same community. They still live in his house and have never married. The daughter's children re-

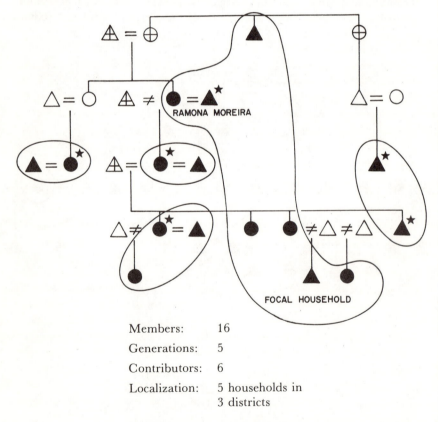

Members:	16
Generations:	5
Contributors:	6
Localization:	5 households in 3 districts

Figure 8. Extended Family 4

mained with Mrs. Moreira, whom they regard as their mother. Their natural mother, they say, is like an elder sister. None of them gives much to her, but they do help their grandmother.

Mrs. Moreira's husband still works regularly and provides most of the household income. She also receives some help from a maternal first cousin's son, her classificatory nephew, whom she fostered for a number of years. This young man and her grandson regard each other as brothers, having grown up together in Mrs. Moreira's house. They currently work and live together at a plantation in the north. Both of them are single and occasionally send money to their "mother."

Mrs. Moreira has one permanent dependent in her care: her mother's brother, a childless and disabled widower. He sleeps in an adjacent house but takes most of his meals with her or with her sister, who lives in the next yard. Mrs. Moreira's grandchildren tease the old man unmercifully and complain that he takes advantage of her largesse. Explaining why she helps him, she says simply, "He is my mother's brother." She and her sister are the eldest females among the old man's next of kin, and classificatory lineals.

The position of this old man and others who depend solely on collateral relatives for support is not an enviable one. They have little to offer in exchange for financial help, and obligations to lineal kin and spouses always take precedence over their needs. Few elderly men find themselves in this position. Most manage to earn some income through fishing. A number of them also receive some support from their own children or, indirectly, from stepchildren (grown sons and daughters of their current spouses).

Unlike men, women depend on kin for financial help from an earlier age, and most of them do receive some support from their grown children. "To be happy when you are old like I am," said one gray-haired woman, "you must have children, especially daughters." Over the course of a year this woman received food, money, clothing, and other gifts from her children.[10] Most of it came directly from her daughters. In return she provided food, shelter, money, and child care. The following account summarizes the events of that year and shows how households in various locales were each directly linked, largely through women's exchanges, to the focal household of the extended family. At the beginning of the year, four of these households were in the same community and two in other districts. At the end of the year, there were three in the same community, two in other districts, and one in the United States.

The members of this extended family — nearly thirty people — are shown in Figure 9. Only the focal woman and her children are named (by pseudonym). Shaded figures are family members. The three grandchildren who are unshaded are her sons' offspring by lapsed extraresidential relation-

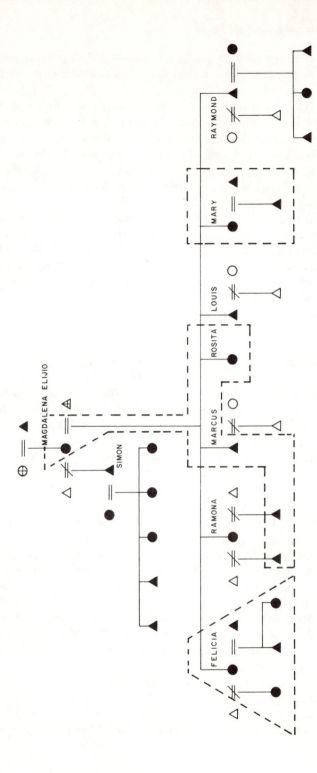

Figure 9. The Extended Family of Magdalena Elijio

ships. She recognizes them as grandchildren but has very little contact with the one child who lives in her village and virtually none with the two who live elsewhere. She does not regard their mothers as daughters-in-law because her sons never lived with these women.

The Extended Family of Magdalena Elijio

Magdalena Elijio is fifty-six years old, a tall, corpulent woman who carries herself with unstudied grace and takes life as it comes. Like so many other women, she is known by her nickname, Maka, or by teknonym, *lúguchun* Simon, Simon's mother. Simon is her oldest child, and she has seven others, four sons and four daughters in all. Before she married nearly thirty years ago, she had a brief liaison with Simon's father, but she never lived with him. When Simon was two years old, Maka began to live with the man she eventually married, after she had borne a son and a daughter by him. All of her children, including her first, took her husband's surname, Elijio.

Shortly after Maka married, her husband had a brief affair with another woman in the community. This woman bore a son by him, who also took the name Elijio. Maka's children recognize the son as a half-brother, but they regard Simon, with whom they were reared by the same mother, as "one of us."

Maka's husband died eleven years ago, and her mother the following year. Her elderly father has taken his midday meals with her since his wife's death, but he still sleeps in his own house. When his health began to fail a few years ago he stopped fishing. He divides his days now between visiting and working on fishing nets and hammocks, earning a little income from their sale. Maka and his other daughter provide most of his food and see to his daily needs.

Throughout the year, several of Maka's children and grandchildren lived in her house. Others lived nearby, including a married daughter whose house stands beside her mother's. At the beginning of the year Maka and twelve others formed three households and lived in two houses in her yard. The women of these households shared the use of her kitchen but usually prepared food separately. (The three households that formed the compound are circled in Figure 9.)

Maka, two of her grown children, Marcus and Rosita, and two grandchildren lived upstairs in Maka's house. She was fostering the grandchildren—one of them three years old, the other five—for her daughter Ramona, a public health nurse posted in another district. Ramona sent her money each month for support. Maka's son Marcus had recently lost his job at a sawmill and had come home to "rest" before striking out to look for work elsewhere. Rosita, seventeen years old and Maka's youngest daughter, had worked on and off for a few months at the nearby banana plantation, taking work whenever it was available. Both Rosita and her brother had given some of their pay to Maka while they were employed. Rosita gave most of hers to her mother, who provided all of her food at home. Marcus, living at a distance then, had given Maka some money during his visits home.

Maka's daughter Mary and her (extralegal) spouse lived downstairs with their two-year-old child. They had begun to live together six months before, when he moved from his own village to work at the banana plantation. Before that he had been employed seasonally by a citrus company. Mary had met him three years before, when she found her first employment with the same company. In their six months together in her mother's house, Mary did what any dutiful daughter does: she helped her mother with whatever she could "spare" from the money her spouse gave her. Her mother in turn did what every mother should do: she bought food for those of her children and grandchildren who needed it. These included her eldest daughter, Felicia, and her children. Felicia lived with her children and husband in a small house in Maka's yard. Felicia's husband was sick and temporarily out of work, for about a month altogether. During that time his wife's relatives (including, indirectly, Mary's spouse) supported his household. He received very little help from his own blood relatives.

Mary's spouse was quick to resent the situation, and particularly his role as provider for another household. He could not fault Mary for helping her mother, nor could he blame his mother-in-law for responding to her children's needs. But his own part in this chain of giving and taking angered him. Eventually he and Mary had a serious quarrel and he left the community to return to his mother's house. Mary and her children moved upstairs with Maka.

Soon after, Maka's son Marcus contacted some relatives who were working in the United States and made plans to emigrate there. His mother gave him some of the money he needed for transportation, a small sum she had saved from Ramona's remittances. Marcus borrowed the balance from a few friends and from his relatives in the United States and left the country. Felicia's husband returned to work shortly after Marcus left.

During this time Maka's two eldest sons, Simon and Raymond, were also employed at the banana plantation. They visited their mother occasionally but offered her little help. Simon had been having financial difficulties for some time, paying for a lumber house that he had recently had built. When he visited Maka he might hand her a few coins, enough perhaps to buy the day's supply of flour but no more. He also occasionally sent his mother some food that his wife bought in bulk at another settlement: a few pounds of flour one week, a small bag of plantains the next. Simon's wife usually took these herself to Maka.

The other son, Raymond, lived with his wife and children in his mother-in-law's house. He rarely gave any money to his mother, a persistent source of irritation to his sisters. Maka herself said simply that since he preferred to help his mother-in-law, he had better seek help from her when he needed it, and not from Maka. As for Raymond's wife, the sisters criticized her glaring lack of generosity toward their mother. Unlike Simon's wife, who was a "good" daughter-in-law, Raymond's wife never brought anything to Maka and was suspected of discouraging her husband from doing so. *Hángitu,* "She's stingy," was the perennial complaint of the sisters. Although Raymond's wife never came to see Maka for expressly social purposes, as Simon's wife sometimes did, her children often played in Maka's yard with their first cousins — Felicia's, Mary's, and Ramona's children. Simon's children played there as well. Sometimes their mother left them there for the day when she needed to collect firewood or do some other task away from the village. Since her own mother spent much of her time in another village where her other daughter lived, Simon's wife depended on her mother-in-law for occasional help with child care. Raymond's wife never left her children with Maka. Her own mother was always available to care for them.

Several months after he left the country for the United States, Marcus began sending money occasionally to his mother. During this time she also received some support from her youngest son, Louis, who had passed the examinations for the police force. He had been assigned to a station in the western district. Since Louis, like many young men working away from home, sometimes neglected to send money to his mother, Maka or Rosita occasionally made a trip to collect it, timing their arrival to coincide with payday. Sometimes Ramona would visit her brother and collect some money for her mother. She was posted nearby, at a rural health station in the same district. At about the same time Felicia was hired on a temporary basis at the banana plantation as a packer. She was absent for two or three days at a time and left her children in Maka's care.

Mary and her estranged spouse eventually made their peace and began to live together again in the ground-level rooms in Maka's house. In light of his past experience, the young man soon decided that they would do better entirely on their own rather than in Maka's house. He found a small house standing vacant on the other side of the village and arranged to buy it, paying half of the sum the owner asked and promising the balance within three months. In the meantime they stayed in Maka's house.

Rosita was unemployed during this time and could see no job prospects in the local area. She decided to write to Marcus, asking him to help her emigrate to the United States. Marcus agreed to lend her money for part of her fare and her mother provided the rest, using money that her son had recently sent her from the United States. Within a week of receiving Marcus's reply, Rosita left the country. She had no hope of entering the United States legally and decided to risk the "back door" (illegal entry across the Mexican border).

The employment situation was very poor for men as well as women when Rosita left. A worsening drought had brought shipments at the banana plantation to a halt, and all of the female packers and some of the male field laborers had been laid off. Mary's spouse and Felicia were among them, but Felicia's husband was one of the few men retained. Mary's spouse, discouraged by this turn of events, spent all of his time and the little money he had in reserve drinking with his circle of young male friends, who had also been discharged. He refused to fish, saying that it would bring no money. Mary's family would eat up any profits, he said, as well as most of the fish. He had the choice of waiting out the drought or looking for work in another district, without any guarantee that he would find it. He decided to wait. Mary halfheartedly defended him to her mother and Felicia, who had begun to mutter between themselves about this new drain on their always slender resources. Their stern economy did not permit them to support an ablebodied man, especially an affine, for any period of time.

For a month or so Maka gave Mary money for food on a day-to-day basis. The tension in the compound mounted as time passed, until one day the young man gathered his possessions and left the village. He said that he was going to visit his mother, but weeks went by without any word from him. Mary received no reply to a letter that she sent. His silence convinced her that he had no intention of returning. She heard rumors from his friends that he was planning to go to the northern district to look for work and also that he had a new (female) "friend" in his own village. She abandoned further efforts to contact him. To help her with her financial problems, Maka offered to buy the house where Mary and the young man had intended to live. She planned to move it to her own yard so that Louis would have separate quarters when he visited and her father could sleep there whenever he chose. As it happened, Louis came home about a month later, having taken a leave of absence from the police force. He had been feeling ill for some time, and the medicine that a physician gave him had not helped his condition.

Rosita, who had quickly found work as a domestic in the United States, had already sent some money to Maka, including some she had collected from Marcus. Simon, who had been one of the few men retained at the plantation, also helped his mother occasionally with money and food during this time.

At Christmas, Ramona came home for a few weeks, bringing food and clothing for her mother and her children, and a new table and some linens for Maka. From the United States Rosita sent a large parcel of clothing that she and Marcus had purchased. She included several dresses in her sisters' sizes and a shirt and hat for Louis. Maka divided the clothing. She gave most of it to Mary and Ramona and only one dress to Felicia. Felicia, unhappy with the division, complained to her mother, but Maka defended herself, saying that Ramona always helped her and Mary needed the clothing. Besides, the two sisters were single. About Felicia she said simply, "She has a man."

A month later, Mary's estranged spouse came back to the village. He stayed with an aunt for a few days, then one morning went to Maka's house. When Felicia saw him enter the yard she confronted him angrily and told him to leave. He protested that he had come to see his child. Felicia countered by saying that she knew he was interested in "courting" Mary again. She said that she wasn't going to see her younger sister bear another child for him to neglect and her mother to support. By this time Maka had come out into the yard with Mary. "Go live with him if you want," she said to her daughter, "but you won't live in my house." As Felicia and the young man continued to argue, a small crowd of onlookers gathered at the edge of the yard. Finally, one of them ran to alert the young man's aunt. She came quickly and persuaded him to leave peacefully with her. Mary saw him later that day, at the aunt's house, after the woman had delivered a message to Mary from him.

Several days later Mary left the village with him. The young man had prospects of a job elsewhere in the district, and he asked Mary to go with him. She left her child with Maka, promising to return for him as soon as they were settled. Maka agreed to these arrangements, but with obvious reluctance and little optimism. In her opinion, the young man had proven himself unreliable too many times in the past. She was anxious about her daughter but also hesitant to "interfere." Her fear was that the union would fail after Mary had borne more children by him. This would be to Maka's disadvantage as well as Mary's. But perhaps, she reasoned, Mary should try to be "patient" with him. It had been her usual counsel when her daughters had marital problems.

Now her major concern was Louis, who still complained of severe headaches, fatigue, and loss of appetite. Maka had suspected from the beginning that the doctor's medicine and her own herbal remedies could not cure him, and she finally decided to consult a shaman on his behalf. This would require time and expense. She did not trust the shaman in her own village and insisted on consulting a different woman, a shaman of greater reputation who lived in another community. Maka would eventually learn from the shaman that Louis was afflicted by a jealous ancestor who demanded ritual attention, the elaborate feast known as *dügü*. She would spend a year collecting the necessary funds and making preparations for it. When the needs of the dead had been satisfied, she hoped, Louis would regain his health and return to work once again. In the meantime, he remained in her care.

Over the course of a year, the composition of Maka's household fluctuated as she responded to her children's problems and needs: their marital difficulties, illness, unemployment and the need to migrate. She provided temporary support—food and shelter—for several of her daughters and their children. She cared for one son who fell sick and offered two of her children money for transportation to the United States. She fostered three grandchildren, provided child care when Felicia worked at the plantation, and took care of her one permanent dependent, her elderly father. She received money, food, clothing, and other goods from her children.

The extended family of Magdalena Elijio is not a "typical" one in every detail. No single family can represent all others. Extended families vary in size, generational range, level of interaction and exchange, and the residential proximity of members. Indeed, each family itself varies in these respects over time. The "vagaries" of individual biography—especially the reproductive history, marital status, and personal qualities of an older woman—influence the particular composition of her family.[11] A woman with very few children is more likely to "recruit" a younger collateral relative into her family than a woman with many sons and daughters. A woman who has a childless, elderly collateral relative may decide to take responsibility for that person, depending on her own resources, her place among next of kin, their personal relations, and other factors. Some women remind their children, persistently and successfully, of their filial obligations. Others depend on a spouse or a specific child for most of their support.

What is entirely typical about Mrs. Elijio's family is its female-centered structure, the pattern of exchange and interpersonal tensions, and the comprehensive care that it can provide. Like other extended families it ordinarily directs help to the living and occasionally, through ritual, to the dead. The next chapter deals with the rituals given to *gubída*, or "family dead" (deceased lineals), and the following one with the role of older women as organizers, and their extended families as sponsors, of these rituals.

Notes to Chapter 8

1. Cf. R. T. Smith's (1973: 125) discussion of lower-class Afro-Guyanese households, and his observation that "household groups normally dissolve upon the death of the focal female." He notes elsewhere that "once the mother dies, the system [of men indirectly contributing to their sisters' support] breaks down and men do not give economic support directly to their sisters" (R. T. Smith 1960: 71).

2. Most of these parent-child households contain mothers and their children (dependent or grown), and only a few of them a man and one or more of his grown children. The wife/mother is temporarily absent from these latter, living with some of her children elsewhere while they attend secondary school. Only 1 percent of the households are all-male, composed of two or three close consanguines.

3. This distribution is statistically significant (.001 level, chi-square). "Older women" refers to those forty-five years of age and older, as well as to one woman in her late thirties and a few in their early forties. (I have included the latter because most of their children are grown and contribute to their support.) The average age of these women is fifty-six.

4. Widows living in houses built by their deceased spouses are included among these house owners because they have primary rights of occupancy. Other women have acquired houses by financing the construction themselves, using money that they or their grown children have earned or, in several cases, with winnings from the national lottery.

5. Although she does not "drive" them from the house, she does urge them to seek employment after some time. Taylor (1951: 52, 55) apparently refers to this when he writes that a man "returns periodically to his native village, and takes things easy — for as long as his earnings last — in the bosom of his family. . . . It is said that when a returned sailor or seasonal worker is given cassava instead of bread with his evening meal, he knows that his money is done, and that it is time for him to get out and look for another job!" This is a very broad hint, since women who grow cassava do so at no expense but their labor, while they must purchase the flour that they use to make bread.

6. All of these households include grandchildren of the senior woman. Nearly 80 percent of the households of this type (extended family households of older women) are extended by grandchildren, and the remainder by other non-nuclear kin: nieces and nephews, cousins, and other relatives of the focal woman.

7. Very little has been written about Black Carib families. Taylor (1951: 73) and Coelho (1955: 84ff.) discuss the nuclear family as a residential unit, but Gonzalez (1969: 84f.) points out that it is often scattered among several households and may be "extremely brittle and unstable." Taylor (1951: 74) and Coelho (1955: 84) also refer in passing to "the wider consanguineal family," but without clearly defining its composition or structure. Coelho (1955: 179) makes mention of "extended families," and Gonzalez (1969: 85) briefly discusses "the extended unilateral family" as an "analytic category."

8. An exception to this rule is women who migrate with their spouses, leaving their children in the care of the spouses' kinswomen. In these cases, the migrant women do "help" female affines who foster their children.

9. The distribution of fostered children is statistically significant (at the .001 level, chi-square).

10. In two communities, 16 percent of all older women were childless. They had never borne any children (11 percent) or had no surviving offspring (5 percent). Slightly over half of them depended on spouses for support. The remainder were single or widowed, and drew most of their support from siblings, sisters' daughters, or both.

11. See Moore's (1978: 73f.) brief discussion of the "heavy social importance of the accidents of kinship," and Yanagisako (1977: 221), who notes variation in the "social form that female centrality takes . . . not only between research populations, but within them."

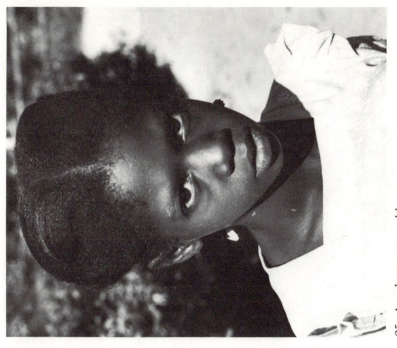

25. An eleven-year-old.

24. A ten-year-old girl.

27. A young woman of thirty-two.

26. An adolescent of fifteen.

28. An older woman (fifty-five).

29. Two women in their fifties, after an end-of-mourning ceremony.

31. An elderly woman (seventy-three).

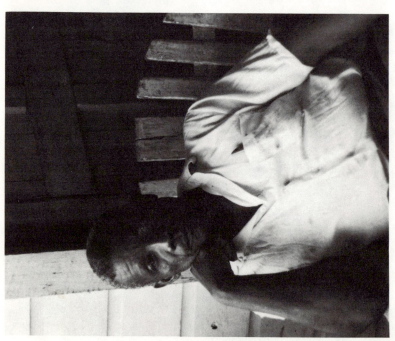

30. An older man of fifty-nine.

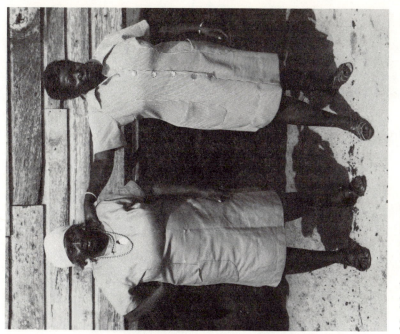

33. Mother and daughter.

32. Brothers.

35. The same infant and his foster mother (maternal grandmother).

34. A fisherman and his step-grandchild.

37. An elderly woman with her daughter's daughter's child.

36. A man with his foster mother (maternal grandmother).

Chapter 9

DEATH AND THE WORK
OF MOURNING

Death and the dead constantly impinge on the world of the living. Certain "signs" presage an impending death: the appearance of a large black butterfly in the house, or the restlessness of infants during the night. Men and women often speak of these signs, dreams of the dead, and unusual noises that they have heard in the night. Although death is a state that the living dread, it is not a subject that they avoid. People typically preface future plans with the phrase "If God spare [my life]," and they also engage in speculative discussions about death and rituals for the dead.

Such a discussion began one morning as a man was relaxing in a hammock under his cousin's house, talking to her while she cleaned some fish to cook for dinner. She was fifty-two years old, a few years his senior, and very active in ritual affairs. Talk shifted to the subject of a recent *amúidahani,* the ritual "bathing" of a dead person's spirit. (According to the belief associated with this ceremony, after burial and the ninth-night wake the spirit begins a long and arduous journey to the afterworld, "the other side." Usually within six months or a year of death, the spirit appears in a dream to a close relative and requests the refreshment of a bath.) The man argued at length that the ritual is unnecessary. He contended that the spirit should not need a bath so soon because the corpse is washed before burial. His cousin merely shrugged, then gave a laconic reply, "Well, you will have one too," as she continued scraping the fish.

Elements of Ritual

Ritual is so common as to be almost an aspect of daily life in Black Carib villages. In one village over a twelve-month period, some sort of collective, death-related observance was held on 102 of the 365 days, and on many days there was more than one. This number does not include the Roman

Catholic feast days or various calendrical holidays celebrated in Black Carib communities.[1]

Rituals for the dead share one stated purpose. They meet the needs of the dead and thereby protect the living from harm — illness, other misfortune, even death — at the hands of a neglected and resentful spirit. Everyone understands this purpose but some question it. The only universally accepted tenet seems to be that death is the greatest misfortune of all, the single affliction for which no medicine, *árani,* exists.[2] Many people, especially the young, express skepticism and ambivalence about the putative powers and needs of the dead (cf. Gonzalez 1969: 57). They also criticize the expense of the death rites, which they consider excessive. They can express disbelief with impunity, at least from the human sphere. No one attempts to enforce conformity in *beliefs* about the dead (but ritual obligations are quite another matter; see Chapter 10). Believers usually comment simply, "Someday the *gubída* [family dead] will catch you [cause you harm]. Then you *must* believe." Like professed skeptics, many believers also complain about the high cost of ritual.

The diversity of opinion about spirits and their needs contrasts with the nearly universal acceptance of church dogma. Most Black Caribs receive formal instruction in the basics of Roman Catholic doctrine as schoolchildren, and atheism is nearly unknown. But knowledge of other spiritual matters is informally transmitted and based on personal experience, which varies from one person to the next. Some men and women remain skeptics throughout life. They argue that the dead require only burial, a novena, and formal mourning, and they scoff at the notion that the dead have any power to harm the living. Others insist that ninth-night wakes are also necessary, if only as a conventional sign of respect and gratitude to the deceased. Still others have experiences which convince them that the dead, long after they are buried, can intrude into the affairs of their descendants. Some of these experiences are sudden and dramatic, as when a skeptic is suddenly possessed during *dügü,* the most elaborate of the rituals for the dead. In other cases, conversion occurs gradually. "I saw many things I could not explain," said one older woman, speaking about the cures effected by shamans and ritual. "Finally I had to believe."

Non-Caribs might distinguish between "traditional" or "indigenous" death rites, such as *amúidahani,* and "Christian" ceremonies, such as burials and novenas. From the Black Carib perspective, however, this distinction is spurious. The rituals form a whole, all intended to satisfy the dead, protect the living, and express the "gratitude" of living kin to the deceased. Shamans, who conduct some of the rites, are pious, usually practicing Roman Catholics, as are the older women who organize most rituals. They attend church and tithe regularly, and many belong to religious sodalities (while few men or young women attend church on a regular basis).

Black Caribs, young and old alike, certainly know that some of their beliefs and rituals are unique. Indeed, they consider that these, with their language, music, and dance (all important elements of ritual), distinguish them from "other races," as they put it. But few think of these beliefs and rituals as non-Christian, as many non-Caribs do. They see no conflict between Roman Catholic dogma and their own beliefs, and in fact often explain the latter in terms of their understanding of orthodox theology. Thus, one woman compared spirits of the dead and their powers to angels, who also can protect or harm mortals. Another explained ritual offerings to spirits of lineal kin by analogy to prayers said for "the souls of the departed" in church. Offerings, like prayers, provide tangible evidence that the living care about the well-being of the dead. Both offerings and prayers center on remembrance.

From a historical perspective as well, "Christian" and "indigenous" (Arawak, Carib, African) elements are nearly inseparable. Black Caribs have been directly acquainted with Roman Catholicism for over 250 years, since their emergence as a distinct cultural group. On that basis alone, Christian elements are nearly as "traditional" to Black Carib ritual as those derived from Amerindian and African sources. About the last two, Taylor (1951: 143) concludes that "the tracing of discrete elements to Arawak, Carib, or to this or that African tribal source, appears to be a well-nigh hopeless task at this stage."

Whatever the derivation of these rituals or particular elements, all conform to a similar pattern. An exhaustive list of common features would require a treatise in itself and is unnecessary here. Even a summary of their shared elements shows their basic unity.

One deceased, remembered person is the focus of ritual attention. The ceremonies have a solemn purpose but typically a festive ambience, and Black Caribs refer to a number of them as "fiestas." Song and dance are integral to most of their celebrations, including these. All of the rituals require cooperative work and the distribution of food to a far wider range of people than is usual in daily life. The sharing of food and strong drink both with the living and (through offerings) with the dead is a central ritual act. It provides the quintessential expression of trust and kinship, and it tangibly demonstrates generosity to the living and gratitude to the dead.[3] Prayers are commonly addressed to the deceased person, as well as to God and the Virgin Mary. Most of the rituals take place at dawn, dusk, or from dusk until dawn. As crisis ceremonies, they occur in response to a death or to sickness thought to be caused by the spirit of a deceased man or woman, or on demand of the spirit (in which case they are regarded as preventive rather than curative medicine). They are held in Black Carib communities, either in a house and yard, church, or *dabúyeiba,* temple. As such, they are intracultural events.[4] Older women take prominent part in these rituals and assist any religious specialist whose help is required.

Rituals for the dead do not, strictly speaking, form a cycle. Only a few are absolutely obligatory, scheduled events which inevitably follow the death of any adult. These include the wake and burial, novena, and ninth-night wake. In some cases, the period of formal mourning by close female kin culminates in *tágurun lúdu,* the end-of-mourning ceremony. The other rites—the Requiem Mass and "feasting" that follows it, *amúidahani, chugú,* and *dügü*—must be requested by a spirit, usually through a dream to a close relative. Most deceased adults are thought to request a Requiem Mass and *amúidahani,* but rather few demand *chugú* or *dügü,* which require a great deal of preparation, considerable expense, and the help of a shaman.[5] These last two rituals are generally "given" to those long dead, the others to the recently deceased. But their timing varies, and the sequence of rituals is not absolutely fixed.

For the purpose of clarity, the usual ritual sequence is shown in Table 10, with Carib and common English names. "Scale" refers both to approximate cost and to number of attendants, not to any difference in importance. All of them are considered important. The minor rituals may attract only a dozen or two participants, most of them older women. Minor events do not require a large expenditure of money or labor, relative to the major rites, and they last only a matter of hours. The major ones, especially ninth-night wakes and *dügü,* are lengthier and attendance much greater. They may draw as many as several hundred people.

These rituals center on mourning, the remembrance of the dead, but most are occasions when the living and the dead enjoy themselves. They are also work. The minor rites require the cooperative efforts of several women; the more elaborate ones demand the labor of a whole cadre.

The Work of Mourning

Death, like sickness, is not a matter for private suffering, borne alone or in silence. Death draws the living together. As soon as news of a death (either that of a current or a former resident) circulates through the community, a throng of people gathers at the house belonging to the deceased or to the next of kin. Details of the death pass quickly by word of mouth. Close kinswomen of the deceased begin to wail, in a customary display of grief, as soon as they hear of the death. Preparations for the wake proceed almost immediately, and primarily involve women, both close relatives of the deceased and other women who volunteer their help to them.

A number of tasks must be accomplished before burial the next day. The body of the dead woman or man must be washed and dressed for burial,

TABLE 10
Sequence of Death Rites

Name	Timing	Location	Scale
Wake and burial, *belúria* and *ábunahani*	obligatory, within 48 hours after death	house and yard, church and burial ground	major
Novena and ninth-night wake, *arísaruni* and *belúria*	obligatory, usually within two or three weeks after death	house and yard	major
End-of-mourning ceremony, *tágurun lúdu*	obligatory, six months or one year after death of a spouse or parent	church, beach, house	minor
Bathing the spirit, *amúidahani*	obligatory if requested, usually within a year of death, sometimes after several years	house and yard	minor
Requiem Mass and feasting, *helé-meserun hiláña* and *eféduhani laugi lemési*	obligatory if requested, usually a year or two after death	church, house	minor
Feeding the dead, *chugú*	obligatory if requested, rarely less than ten years or more than fifty years after death	house	major
Feasting the dead, *dügü*	obligatory if requested, rarely less than ten years or more than fifty years after death	temple	major

usually by old women.[6] In some cases, the funeral garb has been prepared in advance by the deceased. Later in life many women and men give careful thought to their eventual burial and prepare suitable clothing: for a man, a dark suit and white shirt; for a woman, a long white dress. If these were not prepared beforehand, they must be hastily sewn or, in a town, possibly purchased.

While a few men work in the yard, constructing a wooden coffin, women begin to prepare refreshments in the kitchen and over open fires in the yard. On short notice they need to assemble a sufficient amount of coconuts, flour, and other ingredients to make bread, and rice or corn to be roasted and then boiled for *gáfe,* a black coffee-like drink that they sweeten heavily with sugar. The women will distribute this food throughout the night to kin and friends of the deceased who attend the wake. Depending on the supply, they may serve nearly every person in the community who comes to view the body and remains for a few hours or, ideally, the entire night.

Wakes are sedate affairs early in the night. The men gamble or converse, a few women sing hymns, and others sit together talking quietly or help distribute food and rum. In proportion to the amount of rum passed around, conversation grows more animated and the crowd more convivial later in the night. Eventually someone induces a few of the men to provide music for dancing, substituting wooden crates for drums, the usual and preferred instrument. Some of the older women are sure to protest the impropriety of festive music and dance, but only halfheartedly and usually in vain. Soon enough they may take a turn dancing themselves.

Rum is a major expense of a wake as well as of the other death rites, it being almost maxim that, as one man put it, "Where there is death, there must be rum." Close kin of the deceased drink liberally during the wake and before the burial, to give them "courage," they say, and to help them "bear the grief." Rum must be provided to the men building the coffin (along with a small sum of money), to the women who help with food preparation, and to as many of the men and women attending the wake as possible. A large crowd is always desirable, and only a generous supply of rum can insure it. Those who prepare the corpse for burial use rum lavishly to wash their hands when they have finished handling the body. The men who dig the grave will receive some rum as payment for their work, and close relatives of the deceased will brace themselves with rum for the trial of burial.

Throughout the night and the next morning, before the burial, some relatives of the deceased — especially close kin, and usually more women than men — arrive from other communities. As the women arrive, each begins to wail. Wailing is song-like and starkly beautiful, a highly stylized but very moving expression of sorrow. When a woman wails, she eulogizes the deceased and expresses her gratitude for the support and care that person gave her. She speaks tearfully and at length, always in Carib, about the virtues of the dead man or woman. If she is skillful, she will move some of her listeners to tears as she reminisces about the deceased and mourns her loss. A thirty-five-year-old woman, grieving over the body of her maternal grandmother, who had reared her from infancy when she was orphaned, recalled all that her grandmother had given her: affection, financial help, companionship, protection. This is what she said as she wailed during the early-morning hours of the wake:

Mama, are you going away from me today? What support will I have now? Ai, I'll never stop crying after you, Mama. Ai, my grandmother, my mother — Arise! Ai. . . . Every time I wonder what [food] to give my children I'll remember you. Ai, my grandmother, this is undoubtedly your day. . . . Who do you leave me to, Mama? Many people here don't like me. Now that you're gone they'll finish me off. I won't stay here — I'm going to go live with Felicita's mother.[7] Ai, what can I say? Arise now, Mama! Arise from death. . . . Mama, Mama, tell me a story like you used to do. Make me laugh like you used to do, until I almost fainted with laughter. . . . Ai, ai, is this the way it's going to be?

When this woman asked "What support will I have now?" she questioned the means of her own survival. When she cried "Every time I wonder what [food] to give my children, I'll remember you," she meant that her grandmother had always helped her when she was in desperate straits, unable even to buy food for her young children. When she wailed "Many people here don't like me [and] now that you're gone they'll finish me off," this woman expressed a common sentiment: that her protection and security diminished sharply with the death of her "mother." When she wept "Make me laugh like you used to do," she mourned the loss of a lifelong, loved companion.

Few listeners were left unmoved by these poignant words and the woman's unrestrained show of sorrow. Many were later to say *Gayáhuaditu,* "She can cry well," praising her display of gratitude to her dead grandmother. Wailing is a ritual skill that women cultivate, and this woman was thought to wail especially well. People criticize a woman who cries quietly or spiritlessly, calling her ungrateful. Men rarely wail. They customarily approach the open coffin and address a few words of appreciation and farewell to the deceased, speaking stolidly if somewhat tearfully.

There are other moments when the bitter finality of death also grips survivors: as they have their last view of the body, just before the top of the coffin is nailed on in preparation for brief prayers in church and the burial; and again at graveside, when the physical separation is final. The widow, sisters, and daughters of the deceased, who contain their grief in church and while they walk in the funeral procession to the burial ground, customarily abandon themselves to displays of intense sorrow at graveside. Other men and women must physically support them, helping them away from the burial site after the prayers end.

Usually a few men attend to the final covering of the grave, a task that they begin as the adults and children attending the burial ritually throw in handfuls of earth — the purpose of the latter, some say, being to keep the spirit from "coming after" them. The men pile the sand into an oblong mound over the grave and lay palm leaves over it. Markers are rarely more substantial than a simple wooden cross, which the natural elements quickly destroy. The location of the grave soon fades from memory, and within a few years close relatives are often hard put to identify the precise burial site. Even in the months immediately after death, they rarely visit the grave. The burial ground, in a tangled thicket on the margin of the village, is a place that spirits frequent and that the living avoid.

A novena for the deceased usually begins on the first or second Friday after burial. Following Roman Catholic tradition, these prayers assure the repose of the soul and, according to local belief, the detachment of the deceased from the world of the living. The ninth-night wake, held at the conclusion of these prayers, has the same purpose. For the novena, about a dozen older women (who are not necessarily, nor even usually, close relatives of the deceased) gather shortly before dusk each day at the house where the ninth-night wake will be held. A male teacher, recognized for his fluency in Spanish, usually acts as *arísaruti,* the leader of the hour-long session of prayers and songs. Occasionally a woman leads the novena, but few are literate in Spanish, the preferred language for reading the prayers. Many people say that Spanish is more "effective" than English for novenas. Carib is used only in a song or two.

Before the novena begins, a few of the women fashion an altar, which will remain in place until the ninth-night wake, when the prayers end. They cover a table with a white cloth and construct a canopy of white fabric above it. On the table they place candles and a picture of Christ. On the day of the ninth-night wake, the women will devote more time and effort to the altar, embellishing it with bright crepe-paper streamers hung from the canopy. When they add bouquets of hibiscus and other flowers to the table, the previously somber altar takes on a festive look, more in keeping with the tenor of the upcoming event. A ninth-night wake is often compared to a farewell party — in this case, one given by the living to the recently deceased, who "resurrects" the third day after burial and wanders about until given a proper farewell. A ninth-night wake certainly has its somber moments, but these do not dampen the spirit of merrymaking which prevails for most of the night.

Many of the women who attend the novena also lend their help on the Saturday of the ninth-night wake. Early in the morning they begin grating coconut and expressing the liquid for bread-making. Some mix the flour, coconut milk, and yeast, and then knead it, a task that will take most of the morning, given the quantity at hand. Other women prepare dried coconut husks and firewood to be used for baking later in the afternoon. These preparations require a cooperative effort, involving much labor and a large amount of food: 100 pounds of flour and dozens of coconuts may be used for the bread alone. Most of the women bring utensils needed for the day's work, especially mixing bowls and baking pots. A few women occupy themselves with the preparation of coffee and smaller amounts of other foods that are typically served at a ninth-night wake: *bíme kakúle,* a dish similar to rice pudding but sweeter and drier; and *súpu lau wadábu,* conch soup. These are delicacies, not daily fare.

The women cook throughout most of the day, although work slackens at noon, when the heat grows intense; it picks up again later in the afternoon. Occasionally during the day the women are provided with a bit of rum. When they finish baking, each customarily takes several pieces of bread home with her, and perhaps a few coins, recompense for her help. One or two men usually chop a type of pine wood, *gúdi,* that will burn brightly in the yard throughout the night, illuminating it. Late in the afternoon they erect a makeshift shelter beside the house, using a sail from a dugout canoe as the canopy.

After dusk, people begin to gather in the yard, including many children early in the evening. Most of these people live in the community, but among them are relatives of the deceased who have come from other settlements for this occasion. Their number includes some who, because of short notice, were unable to attend the wake and burial.

At about 8:00 P.M. prayers begin inside the house, usually with a dozen or so older women in attendance. Outside in the yard people converse, and a few men play cards and gamble at a table set underneath the sail. After the prayers end, the ambience outside grows more festive as men and women, few at first but their numbers steadily growing, begin to sing and to dance *punta* and other traditional dances. Their singing and dancing continue until morning, save for breaks at midnight and about 5:00 A.M., when some of the women again gather inside the house for prayers.

The few men (usually immediate relatives of the deceased) who sometimes attend the prayers at midnight and at dawn form a distinct minority. Most men remain outside throughout the night. When the midnight prayers end, the women serve bread, coffee, sweet rice, and conch soup to those who have taken part in the novena. They distribute bread, coffee, and any surplus of the conch soup and sweet rice to men and women outside, and they may serve rum to them several times during the night. How often the women serve depends on the number of attendants and the amount of food and drink on hand. Ideally, some bread and rum remain to be distributed to a sizable crowd in the pre-dawn hours before the final prayers.

During the night many people come and go. Children are shepherded off to sleep, usually before midnight, by their mothers or older sisters, who may return at a later hour. Some of the men wander off in pairs or small groups to informal, private drinking parties elsewhere. In terms of sheer size, the crowd at a ninth-night wake is largest around midnight. As many as 250 people may be present, dancing, talking, listening to *Ananci* stories, and enjoying themselves.[8] Rather few of them will stay the entire night. Among those who do are the older women who prepared and served the food and who attended the novena. A few have brought hammocks, which they tie under the house, or sheets to spread on the floor inside the house, to rest on. Most are on hand for the final prayers, which begin at about 5:00 A.M.

As soon as the prayers end, the altar is torn down abruptly, signaling the conclusion of the ninth-night wake. This is another of those melancholy moments that, like burial, is freighted with the bitter fact of death. The women present who are close relatives of the deceased, or who were particularly close friends, wail briefly one final time. Then it is all over. Some of the women face the tasks at hand and begin cleaning up the house and yard, both littered with the sundry debris of a good time. In the yard, a few irrepressible merrymakers begin to sing and dance again. They will not vacate the yard until mid-morning.

Close kinswomen of the deceased do not take part in any of the singing and dancing. Customarily they must mourn for a period of six to twelve months after the death, depending on their relationship to the deceased. Women mourn their parents and legal husbands for a year. They usually mourn extralegal spouses and grandparents for six months, although one woman chose to mourn her maternal grandmother, who had reared her, for one year because "she was my mother." Some mourn their siblings for six months or a year and their parents' siblings for six months. Many say that this is not obligatory, but a voluntary expression of personal regard for the deceased *or* for the survivors. In some cases women choose to mourn a death as an expression of sympathy and solidarity with a surviving kinswoman. This was how one older woman explained her decision to mourn her sister's son for six months. Women do not agree about whether they ought to mourn any of their grown children who die, although apparently they did so in the past (see Taylor 1951: 98). Some, who are otherwise quite strict about these matters, consider this unnecessary and entirely a matter of personal choice. Depending on the number of kin they outlive and the number they choose to mourn, women may spend a significant portion of their adult lives in mourning.[9]

Men and children do not mourn formally. Men certainly express grief at the death of a close relative, but they have no obligation to curtail their activities. They can continue to work and to socialize as usual. Any woman who did so would be criticized in all quarters for being "ungrateful" and "hardhearted."

When Black Carib women mourn they follow several "rules" that limit both what they do and what they wear. They frankly view these restrictions as a sacrifice. Mourning women may attend social events, but only as onlookers. They must refrain from drinking alcoholic beverages and from social dancing, both staple ingredients of nearly any festive occasion.

Women in mourning may dance at *dügü,* but the dance performed for that ceremony — a sort of sedate shuffle — bears little resemblance to the pelvic exuberance of *punta,* the chief dance of merrymaking. During the period of mourning, women should also refrain from quarreling. Very elderly women warn of dire personal consequences for any who ignore these restrictions. They claim that quarreling and drinking become habitual to the woman who indulges in them during mourning.

So far as clothing is concerned, mourning women rarely dress entirely in black, which is known as "full mourning dress." The climate discourages this as daily attire. Usually they wear what they call "second mourning dress" — a print of black and white, dark blue and white, or other somber colors that they would not select otherwise, preferring brighter hues. They do not wear earrings, unless they own black ones, nor any other jewelry during this period. Personal adornment is not in keeping with the intent of mourning.

A widow observes a number of other restrictions as well. After her husband dies, she ceases work for two months. (A woman who survives an extralegal spouse does not have this obligation but may choose to curtail work.) She does no washing or cooking. For about two weeks she should stay inside the house, and for several months she is not supposed to leave it after dark. During this time the bereaved woman needs the help of other women, who take care of her domestic chores, provide companionship, and sleep with her at night. If the woman were left alone, the spirit of the dead man might "bother" her. The presence of others offers protection, discouraging nocturnal visits by the spirit. Usually some of the widow's sisters and daughters, or her mother if she is still living, stay with her.

For women mourning a parent or a spouse, an end-of-mourning ceremony, *tágurun lúdu,* marks the conclusion of these observances.[10] For an extralegal spouse, the ceremony is held six months after burial, for a parent or husband, one year. The day before the ceremony the mourning women, and perhaps a few helpers, bake the bread that they will serve the following day with coffee and rum. They wake before dawn on the day of *tágurun lúdu* to make final preparations. At about 6:00 or 6:30 A.M. the mourning women, dressed entirely or predominantly in black, attend prayers in the church. Like any other service held there, this one is open to anyone who cares to attend, although it mostly draws older women.

After the prayers end, women cluster on the beach to watch the mourning women bathe ritually. Each of the latter has a female partner, typically an aunt or an elder cousin, whom she has chosen to accompany her into the sea. Fully dressed and with their arms linked, each pair walks into the surf and out beyond the breakers. There the escorts of the mourning women submerge them, then help them up, repeating this twice again. Then they leave the water quickly, chilled by their early-morning bath, and walk to the house. As each of the mourning women stands in the doorway, other women grasp the back of the black dress and tear it from her body. The woman removes her underclothing and then walks to another room to dress, screened from view by the women who have gathered around the doorway and stairs.

In a back room, the women, their mourning at an end, put on new dresses and headwraps, all brightly colored, as well as earrings and perhaps some other jewelry. Their wardrobes of old mourning dresses, freshly laundered and folded, are stacked together, to be given away to other women who need them. One of the older women present gives the others rum as they dress, "to warm them" after their cold bath. In the corner of the room they have placed a plate of food and a small bottle of rum, an offering to the spirit of the deceased. Above it hangs a suit of the dead man's or woman's clothing. The offering remains there for a few hours, beside a burning candle, then is removed.

In the main room a few women have begun to serve bread and coffee to the throng of older women — twenty or thirty — who have gathered there. Soon they begin to sing *abaímahani,* songs of remembrance that women sing on many ritual occasions, without instrumental accompaniment or dance.[11] During the course of the singing, one woman distributes rum to the others present. Later, feeling the full effects of several drinks, the women begin to dance *punta* and the atmosphere grows increasingly festive. Outside, the inevitable crowd of spectators gathers, mainly young adults and children, who hover on the periphery at such ritual events. They linger for some time, talking together and paying scant attention to the activity inside the house. A few of the men wait in unabashed hope that some of the rum will pass their way. Inside, the singing and dancing continue until late morning or even early afternoon, depending on the supply of rum and the enthusiasm of the dancers.

In some cases, daughters of the deceased person live in other settlements. If so, they will usually return to their natal community and their mother's house for *tágurun lúdu.* But if they are employed and unable to do so, they will simply resume wearing ordinary dress at the end of the mourning period. No ceremony attends this. *Tágurun lúdu* and all of the other death rites (with the occasional exception of a wake and burial) have traditionally taken place only in Black Carib communities.

Several months or years after a death, a close relative commonly has a dream in which the deceased man or woman requests a bath. Most of the dead make this request, but not always immediately. In one case, the request came ten years after death. *Amúidahani* is the ceremony that meets the spirit's need for the refreshment of a bath. On the day before *amúidahani* some of the close kinswomen of the deceased make the necessary preparations. They bake the bread that will be served the next day, together with coffee and rum. They also prepare two pieces of cassava bread, baking it so slightly that it remains white. They place this cassava bread into a container with four buckets of clear water from a well and then leave it overnight, to dissolve. Early the next morning they strain the mixture, discarding the residual cassava in the sea but retaining the liquid.[12]

Amúidahani takes place in a yard, usually by the house where the deceased lived. A number of close relatives of the deceased, and often some invited guests, gather before dawn by a shallow pit the size of a grave, dug in the sand some hours before. The invited guests include a few of the women who "showed interest" in the previous ceremonies for the deceased by taking active part in them. Depending on their number, as many as twenty women and men may assemble in the pre-dawn darkness while the rest of the village sleeps.

The ceremony itself is simple and brief. Each of the people present, beginning with the closest relative of the deceased — parent or grown child — throws a bucket of water into the pit. They do so in pairs, one person standing at the head of the pit and holding a bucket of the strained cassava water, *sibida,* and the other standing at the foot with a bucket of ordinary water. Throwing the water into the pit, each person addresses the spirit by the appropriate kin term and says, *Iníha dúna lun bágawan,* "Here is water for your bath." After everyone has taken a turn the pit is covered.[13] No trace of it remains in the sand aside from a slight dampness, which soon disappears under the heat of the morning sun.

During *amúidahani,* a candle burns beside an offering of food and rum inside the house. As in the end-of-mourning ceremony, the food is set on a plate, and a suit of clothing belonging to the deceased hangs above it. When the pit has been covered outside, the women begin to distribute food and drink to the guests — bread and coffee first and later rum, after the singing has begun. The women sing *abaímahani* for several hours, with frequent pauses for liquid refreshment. Reluctant to abandon their singing and feeling the urge to dance, they eventually prevail upon a couple of men to provide the drumming that accompanies *punta* and other traditional dances. The festivities usually continue for a few hours longer, until the refreshments, if not the dancers, are exhausted.

Amúidahani is sometimes curative. Occasionally, some close relative of the deceased has been suffering from a minor illness — say recurrent and severe headaches. If the spirit is believed to be the source of these, the symptoms should disappear after *amúidahani.* Likewise, a Requiem Mass may cure some minor illness, or at the least act as preventive medicine. As in the case of the rituals that precede it, the living try to comply as quickly as possible with the spirit's need for attention. They prefer to avoid the various misfortunes, ranging from mild illness to permanent disability or death, that a spirit, resentful of neglect, is thought capable of inflicting on a living relative.

Like *amúidahani,* a Requiem Mass is scheduled in response to a request from the spirit of a deceased man or woman, who usually makes it in a dream to a close relative. If the priest prefers to conduct the Mass in town instead of traveling to the village for that purpose, one or several of the spirit's close kinswomen go there for the ceremony. Upon their return, there are brief prayers in the village church, usually led by a teacher and attended by older women and perhaps a few very old men. After the prayers, all adjourn to the house of the woman who sponsored the Mass, where the "feasting" begins. Bread and coffee are distributed; then the women sing *abaímahani* songs for several hours, dismissing the earlier solemnity of the prayers and slaking their thirst with rum. As in the case of *amúidahani* and *tágurun lúdu,* an offering of food and rum has been set beside a burning candle in a back room, together with a suit of clothing belonging to the deceased. Afterwards, the clothing is given away to "someone in need of it," usually a very elderly man or woman. Although future offerings may be made to the spirit, the clothing is not necessary for them.

Chugú and *dügü* differ from the preceding rituals in a number of respects. They require the services of a shaman, who helps the living communicate with the spirit who demands these rituals. In both cases, large offerings are made to this ancestor, and smaller ones are contributed by other women for their own ancestors. *Chugú* and *dügü* each have a general format, but no two of them are exactly the same. Details of performance vary according to the wishes of the ancestor who requests the ceremony, and also according to the financial capability of the sponsors (cf. Coelho 1955: 192; Taylor 1951: 132). What usually precipitates these elaborate offerings to spirits of the long dead is a series of misfortunes that befall one or several close relatives — especially sickness that resists the healing efforts of doctors and other curers. The afflicted person is usually an adult, but occasionally an adolescent; according to informants and observation alike, the afflicted is more often female than male. The only way to determine whether an ancestor has caused the illness is to consult a *búyei,* shaman. She makes her diagnosis in an invocation ceremony known as *araíraguni,* bringing down the spirits.

Spirits of the dead can be contacted only with the aid of *hiuruha,* spirit helpers of the shaman. *Araíraguni* is usually a small ceremony, involving no more than a dozen to fifteen people who gather in the *gúle,* sanctuary, of a temple. The afflicted person(s) may or may not be present, but one or more representatives must be. Typically this is the mother, grandmother, grown sister, or daughter of the afflicted. During *araíraguni,* the deceased grandfather of the sick person may complain that his descendants have neglected him.[14] Perhaps they have repeatedly ignored his requests, made to them in dreams, for a small offering in the home: a plate of his favorite foods, a bit of rum, and a candle. He has retaliated by causing one or more of them to sicken. Now he demands *chugú* or perhaps *dügü*, specifying who is to contribute, the amount of their contribution, the various foods to be offered, the manner of the offering's disposal (either burial or disposal at sea), the length of the ceremony, and even the date.

Very often a representative, or one of the several elderly women who usually attend any *araíraguni*, negotiates with the spirit on behalf of the descendants, perhaps pleading for more time in which to prepare. Spirits speak in peculiar voices, in high-pitched, wavering tones that are difficult to understand (except when they specify the sums of money to be contributed by various people, on which point they are remarkably clear!). One of the oldest people present usually clarifies and explains many details of the spirit's demands to the others.

When some agreement has been reached, those present bid the spirit good-bye. The shaman, screened from view and said to be in an altered state of consciousness during the interview, reappears suddenly in their midst. She may fall into the gathering from the screen that she retired behind earlier, or even from outside the building, having apparently been "lifted" from her place inside by the spirits.

This ceremony may be repeated once more upon completion of *chugú* or *dügü*. At this final *araíraguni*, the ancestor who requested the ritual offering will announce satisfaction with it or demand further offerings, or even require that the entire rite be repeated. The last seems to occur very rarely, but the mere threat of it tends to insure compliance with the spirit's wishes. It also adds a real element of suspense to the final *araíraguni*, after *chugú* or *dügü*, at which the descendants learn whether their offering was acceptable.

Chugú and *dügü* differ in cost, length, and attendance. *Chugú* is a one-day affair, essentially an elaborate offering accompanied by frequent prayers (led by the shaman and addressed at various points to God, Christ, the Virgin Mary, and individual ancestors), and by the singing of *abaímahani*. The food is usually offered in the house of the afflicted person, the offering displayed on tables in the morning and left there all day, until its final disposal. Other women in the community also bring plates of food, small offerings for their own ancestors. They leave the food beside the main offering until late afternoon, when they retrieve it and take it home. Some reportedly eat the food, but most claim to discard it or to give it to a very elderly person, who will not suffer ill effects by eating food that spirits have "tasted." *Chugú* involves no drums, dancing, or possession—standard features of *dügü*—and far less preparation and expense. (A shaman responded to a request for *chugú* from her dead father within three days, just after winning a large sum of money in the national lottery.) Even when *chugú* requires more advance preparation, it is largely a community affair, drawing few people, if any, from a distance.

The line between *chugú* and *dügü* is not absolute (cf. Taylor 1951: 115). Sometimes a spirit demands that *chugú* be followed by a night of *dügü*, or *ában lumáragari*, one session, as it is termed. This is a night of dancing in the temple, including the danced rite of placation, *amálihani*, led by the shaman.[15]

Dügü has long been the paramount ceremony for the dead, the most lengthy, costly, and elaborate.[16] The earliest account of it dates from the last century, when Thomas Young (1847: 131ff.) witnessed *dügü* in Honduras, probably in the late 1830s. He mentions that "some time previous" to *dügü*, messages had been sent to distant "friends and relatives" to inform them of the date of the ceremony. In Young's day, people traveled to Honduras from as far away as Belize to take part in *dügü*. A century later, Taylor (1951: 115) put the maximal distance of travel at 100 miles. Today, with changes in the transportation and communication system, people may come from as far away as the United States. In some cases, migrants return to attend *dügü* not for an afflicted relative but on their own behalf: they have fallen ill while abroad, and finding no help at the hands of doctors, they have come home for a ritual cure.

The central stated purpose of *dügü* is the appeasement of an ancestor (or, very rarely, more than one, acting in league) who has afflicted one or more descendants. This focal spirit is the guest of honor, so to speak, at *dügü*, which is a feast in every sense of the term — three days and nights (occasionally more) given over to drinking, dining, dancing, and conviviality in the temple. As much as a year's preparation precedes *dügü*. If the spirit demands, a new temple must be built specially for the occasion. The sponsors of *dügü* must purchase a lavish supply of rum and prepare great quantities of cassava bread and *hiu*, cassava beer. A hog (or several) and perhaps even a cow are purchased in the months before the rite and fattened for slaughter. Dozens of chickens must also be procured, some for sacrifice and others to round out the feast for human diners. Other food for the offering — fish and shellfish — is obtained shortly before *dügü* begins. A small group of men and women travel by dugout canoe to the nearby cays that dot the coastal waters. They fish there and spend two nights, traditionally returning at dawn on the third day with their catch: fish, conchs, crabs, and other fruits of the sea. Their return, with a procession to the temple, marks the start of *dügü*.

For the next three days, work continues apace as many women prepare the food that both the ancestors and human participants will consume. At various points throughout this period, the hog and some of the chickens are sacrificially slaughtered and their carcasses displayed. But the central ritual act of *dügü* is the *amálihani* (or *máli*, from the verb *amáliha*, to placate, appease), the dance of placation. *Máli* is usually performed eight times on each of the first two days or "sessions," *lumáragari,* of *dügü,* with dozens of dancers taking part.[17] Three men provide musical accompaniment with drums as the shaman, shaking rattles, leads the dancers. They form a circle and move slowly with a shuffling step, often in a counterclockwise direction but sometimes reversing this mid-dance. Most of them are women, outnumbering the men by as many as ten to one. The song they sing is said to be very ancient; indeed, it contains words whose meaning has been lost. Various verses describe the parts of the chicken that are to be offered ("Here are the entrails"). The song begins and ends with the refrain "Oh my grandmother, we are placating you." Whether the *máli* is for a male or female spirit, the dancers address their song to *nagütü,* my grandmother (cf. Taylor 1951: 121f.).

Each *máli* lasts for less than thirty minutes and is followed by a brief period of rest for the dancers and drummers. But sometimes one of the dancers, or even several, continue on when the music stops, possessed by ancestral spirits who temporarily "use" the bodies of the living to enjoy themselves and perhaps to speak through them to the assemblage. More women than men are usually possessed during *dügü* (but of course most of the dancers are female), and usually by an ancestor, but not always the focal spirit.[18] Many of the dead take part in *dügü,* having been invited by the spirit guest of honor (just as the sponsors of *dügü* invite the living to join them in the feast).

Anyone who dances in *dügü* must bring a small portion of rum as an offering; and on the second day many women bring plates of food as offerings for their own ancestors, to be displayed with the main offering for the focal spirit. Asked to explain these offerings and their presence at *dügü,* they say that descendants of the focal spirit "must" attend, and that they themselves are well advised to do so. If their own ancestors found that they had not bothered to provide an offering of food and rum — that is, had not bothered to attend — they would grow angry, jealous, and consequently dangerous. Believers commonly warn the negligent and skeptics about this, saying *Hagímarubadibu,* "They will envy you."

By making these small offerings, women protect their children and grandchildren from harm at the hands of jealous and resentful ancestors. "I don't worry myself about attending," said one young man. "My mother represents me." This young man and many others remain outside the temple during *dügü,* spectators rather than participants; or they enter the temple briefly, to gain a better view but not to join in the dancing. Few men, aside from drummers and some descendants of the focal ancestor, participate bodily in *dügü;* but many women, who are not descendants, do.

These are the women who provide much of the labor required for *dügü,* and their efforts are rewarded, usually on the second day, with *hedéweihan mútu,* the people's gift. Some of the food collected for *dügü* is reserved for the offering, but the greater part is distributed among the living, either in pre-pared form during meals or raw, as in the people's gift. A large portion of the hog's (and sometimes a cow's) carcass forms the latter. Each of the many women who have helped with preparations receives several pounds of raw meat. The drummers and the fishermen who provided the seafood for the offering also receive some meat. Most of the cassava bread and chickens are consumed by the dancers and drummers during meals eaten in common in the middle of the night, and they drink most of the rum as well. As for the spirits, rather little flesh is offered to them. (They are said to favor the hog's blood more, particularly when prepared as *morcilla* (blood pudding), or, as it is called in Carib, *fíngiligun.* The blood is mixed with some water and boiled, then fried in oil or lard with onion, salt, and black pepper.)

Events on the third day of *dügü* vary. The offering, wrapped in plantain leaves, is usually disposed of privately, often in the pre-dawn darkness. La-ter there may be more *máli* if requested. A special offering, the *águdahani,* burning, is also made on the final day. The shaman prepares *fúnsu,* a frothy drink of beaten eggs and rum (similar to eggnog but without the cream), ig-niting some of the rum in the course of preparation. Each person in the temple takes a small calabash of *fúnsu* to the *gúle,* a small room at the back of the temple. Privately addressing a few words to the ancestors, each drinks the *fúnsu,* then returns to the main room. During the rest of the day, women sing their *abaímahani.* Ideally, enough rum remains to be distrib-uted to them in small portions throughout the day.

One imperative of *dügü* is that all of the food and drink that the sponsors collect must be offered to the dead, shared with attendants, or otherwise distributed among the living. They cannot retain any for themselves. If they are "greedy," stingy with the spirits and their human guests, they will certainly fall ill, victims of their jealous ancestors. In the occasional case in which some cassava bread remains after *dügü,* the shaman may suggest that it be sold and the profits donated to the church or religious sodality. One man, with more than a trace of regret in his voice, explained the imperative of total distribution, saying, "They [the ancestors and the people] want it *all.*"

Older women collect and distribute this food and drink. They take a more active part than young women and men in nearly all aspects of ritual life.

Notes to Chapter 9

1. These included all of the rituals listed in Table 10, except *dügü,* which was not held during that twelve-month period. Of the 102 events, the great-

est number were novenas. All but one of the rituals held were for deceased men and women native to the village. Those who die while living in non-Carib locales are usually buried in their natal towns or villages, where the appropriate rituals are also performed.

2. Suicide is virtually unknown. The men and women whom I questioned found it unthinkable that anyone might choose to die. Taylor (1951: 116) notes the "divergence in beliefs and attitudes" about many supernatural phenomena.

3. Food-sharing is an act of trust for a people who suspect that many a death has resulted from the ingestion of poisoned food or drink. Although many men and women claim to exercise caution about accepting food from anyone other than close kin and friends of long standing, I never saw anyone decline food or drink distributed on ritual occasions.

4. Non-Caribs are not necessarily excluded from these. The few who live in any village (most of them men with Black Carib spouses) routinely attend ninth-night wakes. Non-Caribs who live in other communities occasionally receive invitations, especially to ninth-night wakes, but rarely attend.

5. Coelho (1955: 171) writes that "the dead never fail" to demand *amúidahani, chugú,* and *dügü,* and Taylor (1951: 113) also states that these ceremonies are "always 'sought' sooner or later." My own informants occasionally claimed that a particular relative had never requested *amúidahani,* and I found many instances of deceased parents and grandparents who had never asked for *chugú* or *dügü.* This discrepancy might be explained by a higher frequency of *chugú* and *dügü* in the past, but many claim that these are performed more often today, especially *dügü.* They attribute this increase to prosperity, saying more people can now afford the expense. (In theory, of course, financial capacity does not determine whether *dügü* is held, but see Coelho 1955: 219.) The apparent inconsistency between other accounts and my own may derive from the distinction Black Caribs draw between the ancestor who demands *dügü* and others who "share" it. This was how they explained a case in which the spirit of a long-dead man requested *dügü* of his grandchildren and great-grandchildren. The spirit's siblings, children, and some of his (deceased) grandchildren were said to have taken part in *dügü* with him.

6. I had no opportunity to see the preparation of an adult's body for burial. The adults who died in the village where I lived were all male. The few women whose burials I attended had died elsewhere, and their bodies were transported to the village in coffins. I did help several old women prepare the body of an infant for burial. The preparations were roughly the same as those for an adult, as my informants and as Coelho's (1955: 172) and Taylor's (1951: 97) described them.

7. The teknonym "Felicita's mother" refers to the youngest daughter of the deceased woman, the aunt of the speaker. Niece and aunt had been reared together, were about the same age, and regarded each other as sisters.

8. Taylor (1951: 99) defines these as folk stories which are "typical West

Indian Negro tales." *Ananci,* the protagonist of these tales, is a spider (see Beckwith 1924).

9. I can only offer an estimate based on the experience of several older women I questioned, each of whom had mourned for several years. At that point, they had spent between 10 and 20 percent of their adult lives in mourning.

10. The literal meaning of *tágurun lúdu* is "throwing off the black cloth." The term *lúdu,* for black cloth or mourning clothing, obviously derives from the Spanish word *luto,* mourning.

11. *Abaímahani* are composed by women, who often receive the words from a deceased relative in a dream. Women sing these songs on ritual occasions and sometimes when they visit the sick, since the songs are believed to ease pain and hasten healing. Hadel (1972: 118ff., 170ff.) translates a number of *abaímahani.* Also see Taylor (1951: 117f.), Coelho (1955: 179f.), and Cayetano (1977).

12. No one could explain to me why strained cassava water is used; it is simply "traditional" (cf. Coelho 1955: 177).

13. I literally stumbled across the ceremony at this point. Both *amúidahani* and the disposal of the main offering of *chugú* and *dügü* are very private affairs. Like Taylor and Coelho, I did not witness either and can only provide secondhand accounts (see Coelho 1955: 176; Taylor 1951: 114, 128). I did take part in the feasting that followed the ritual bathing.

14. I found no evidence that either male or female spirits more frequently request rituals, nor did my informants think there was any gender difference in this matter. The *araíraguni* I attended happened to be for a male ancestor.

15. At present, the combination of *chugú* with one night of *dügü* seems to be more common in Belize than the simple *chugú.*

16. For detailed accounts of *dügü,* see Coelho (1955: 193ff.), Taylor (1951: 115ff.), Macklin (1972, 1976), and Wells (1980).

17. Most of the people who take part in *dügü* dress in ordinary clothing. Women must have their heads covered when they dance; men must remove their hats to do so. In some cases, descendants of the focal ancestor wear clothing dyed orange at the spirit's request. The dye is obtained from the pulp that encloses seeds of the annatto tree *(Bixa orellana).* In the past, descendants sometimes smeared this on their faces, hands, and feet (Taylor 1951: 119; cf. Conzemius 1928: 203).

18. Macklin (1972) and Chamberlain (1979) discuss various aspects of possession.

Chapter 10

RITUAL ORGANIZATION

Questioned about women's prominence in ritual, Black Caribs routinely insist that "anyone" (excluding children) may take part. If the question is pressed—particularly "on location," where so many of the dancers are visibly older women—they offer various explanations. Some say simply that these women are "more interested." Others suggest that they have grown more attuned to the supernatural as they age; or that, possessing better memories than men, they more easily master the intricate details of the death rites (cf. Coelho 1955: 143, 183). Older women themselves speak of their "gratitude" and "duty."

The ritual "aptitude" of these women is firmly grounded in social experience. They have learned by doing. They also have greater access to both the labor and the funding that all collective rituals require. Every ritual for the dead has a female organizer who has lent her help to other women in the past. She calls upon them for labor and seeks the financial wherewithal from her extended family. Few women shirk this duty.

Obligation and Ritual

What people personally believe about the needs and powers of the dead does not wholly determine whether they contribute to or take active part in ritual events. The rites are prescribed, and next of kin are responsible for seeing that they are held. The oldest women of a community badger any who have the means but show reluctance to sponsor the various rituals. They remind them of their obligations and describe in vivid detail the dire supernatural consequences of default. If the next of kin hesitate to hold a ninth-night wake, they argue that the spirit will not leave earth, that the spirit will haunt and perhaps harm those who were too stingy to provide the proper ritual. As for the later rituals, especially *chugú* or *dügü,* which are costlier than many of the others, they warn that the neglected spirit may take the life of a descendant.

These pressures are brought to bear only where *collective* and *public* rituals are concerned, where neglect of the dead means stinting the living as well. A man or woman who neglects to make private offerings is simply warned by a shaman and others punctilious about these matters.

To choose one example from many, a shaman dreamed one night that a childless woman who had died two years before wished to have a small offering of food and rum placed in her house. She also wanted her niece to air and clean her house, which had stood vacant and locked since her death. In the dream the spirit brandished a stick and threatened to hit her niece if she did not comply with her wishes. This is a very common motif in dreams about dead parents and other ancestors. The next morning the shaman went to see the dead woman's niece, her sister's daughter, who is about fifty years old and very active in ritual affairs. She told the woman about her dream and advised her to make the private offering as soon as possible. The niece protested that she had borne the responsibility for her aunt's wake, burial, ninth-night wake, and *amúidahani*. Her brothers and sisters had given some money, but she (the eldest female among next of kin), had devoted a great deal of effort, and no little expense herself, to discharge these obligations. Recently she had dreamed that her aunt wished to have a Requiem Mass, and she had arranged that as well. Now, the woman said, her aunt must be satisfied; she suggested that the shaman had misunderstood the dream. The shaman left, muttering about the niece's "hard ears" and saying that she would regret her carelessness when the spirit made one of the other nieces or nephews or their children ill. No one else ever broached the matter with the niece, although the shaman openly complained of it to others.

Non-believers require more warnings than believers, but even the latter sometimes hesitate to sponsor rituals because they require much time and effort to organize, to say nothing of the expense. One older woman, who dreamed that her sister's son wanted a bath, frankly admitted her unwillingness to devote attention to *amúidahani* at that particular time. She acknowledged her responsibility for it. The man's mother was dead, his only sister lived abroad (and could not be expected to return except for a major event, like *dügü*), and his children were adolescents. But she had various pressing domestic matters to attend to and preferred to delay the event. Her mistake, she said, had been to mention her dream to a neighbor. Now she would have to put aside the other work and organize *amúidahani*, not because the spirit could not wait a bit but because she wished to avoid criticism and accusations of neglect.

Among believers and non-believers alike, social pressure often outweighs the threat of supernatural revenge. Most men and women express far more anxiety about criticism from the living than about punishment by the dead. People who evade these duties are commonly charged with ingratitude and stinginess if they have the financial means to sponsor the ritual. If they are too "poor" to do so, they are the objects of pity or ridicule, which is even worse (cf. Coelho 1955: 215). The rewards for fulfillment of ritual obligations are also social. After most events, people say approvingly that the sponsors have (tangibly) shown their gratitude to the dead, and that they have also shown that they are "able" (to afford the expense). The reputations of sponsors may rise or fall depending on their response to ritual obligations.

Participation in Ritual

Unlike a private offering, made by one person in the home, any collective ritual has many participants: minimally a dozen or so, maximally several hundred.[1] Questioned about who organizes, sponsors, and attends rituals for the dead, men and women invariably respond with generalizations: "All of the relatives of the dead person should attend," or "All of the relatives should contribute whatever they can spare," or "Anyone can attend, and you give according to your conscience." In fact, however, attendance varies widely. Whether a particular ritual event is a "good" one or not depends on the amount of food and drink, money, and labor contributed to it, and on the number of people who attend it. The size of "the crowd" indicates whether a ritual is exceptionally lavish, good, middling, or poor. Judgments about it are made both while the event is in progress and after the fact. "Good" rituals draw many people. "Poor" ones attract very few, and their numbers dwindle during the course of the event.

Several factors influence attendance. Among these are timing and publicity, the amount of food and drink prepared and distributed, and the identities of the deceased, the organizer, and the other sponsors. The most reliable predictor of total attendance is the amount of rum available for distribution. Observation, as well as informant opinion, suggests that a plentiful supply of rum and a generous hand in distributing it assure a large crowd. As one woman stated with obvious pique on a ritual occasion, "You must feed these people rum!" Rum is the ritual lodestone, so to speak, that not only attracts many people initially but also insures their presence to the conclusion of the event. The supply of rum does not, however, measurably affect the number of core participants.

Organizationally, rituals center on an organizer and her extended family. She recruits the *core participants* who provide money, food and drink, and labor for the event. In general, the organizer is the eldest female among the deceased's next of kin. This woman, her grown children, and to varying degrees their spouses — an extended family — act as *sponsors*.[2] They contribute most of the funds but, except for the organizer, do not necessarily all attend the event. Other older women provide most of the equipment and labor and, in some cases, small contributions of provisions and money, which they give directly to the organizer. These *workers* are drawn from the personal network of the organizer. They are consanguines of all degrees, affines, and friends whom she has helped at past events.

Beyond this core is a highly variable body of *attendants*. These men and young women contribute only their presence. They sing and dance but give little or nothing in the way of goods or services. Their numbers are usually proportional to the amount of food and drink available. Figure 10 represents ritual organization.

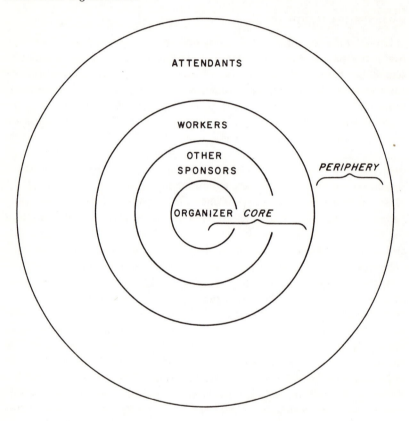

Figure 10. Ritual Organization

Rituals vary widely in the number of attendants. Asked to explain their presence, some say frankly that they regard it as recreation, an occasion for conviviality and pleasure: "This is what we enjoy." They come to enjoy themselves at the sponsors' expense. Rituals for the dead are not fixed tableaux, and the composition of the crowd is always in flux at the major events. There may be a peak of 250 people at any given point, yet during the course of the event nearly everyone in the community attends. This mercurial quality is not so evident at the minor rites, where most of those who take part are older women.

Every event, major and minor alike, has a stable, sedentary core of participants: the organizer, usually some of her grown children, and the older women who contribute their labor. These women explain their presence not in terms of recreation but obligation, either general or specific: obligation to the dead *or* to an organizer. Older women usually specify their relationship with the organizer, saying that they help her because "she is my cousin"—or sister-in-law or *comadre* or simply a friend who has helped them in the past. Women who offer their help are always rewarded with rum, food, and (at the major events, which require so much preparation) perhaps a few coins. But the recompense is small compared to the work, and their assistance is in the nature of a favor extended or returned, not of hired labor.

For the minor rites, a half-dozen people or fewer suffice to provide funds and labor. For the major events, a dozen to several dozen people contribute, and attendants may number in the hundreds. Ultimately, the success of a ritual depends on the efforts of the organizer: her ability to secure funds, recruit workers, and inform others of the event.

Organizers and Their Work

Older women take responsibility for organizing rituals for the dead. In twenty-seven rituals held in one village during a period of fourteen months, the organizer of each was the eldest female among the deceased's next of kin living in that community. The factors of gender, maternal status, kin relationship to the deceased, and age yielded this pattern: all of the organizers were female, all of them had borne children, most were consanguines of the deceased, and their average age was fifty-five. (They ranged in age from thirty-five to eighty-six.) Table 11 shows the kin relationship between the organizer and the deceased man or woman for whom the ritual was held.[3] Nearly two-thirds of the rituals were organized by *lineals* (mothers, daughters, or daughters' daughters) or *maternal classificatory lineals* (aunt or first cousin) of the deceased.

The position of organizer is an informal one. The woman who is "in charge" collects the funds, sets the date, informs others of the event, sees to the purchase of supplies, and oversees preparations before and during the event. In the case of *chugú* and *dügü* the shaman shares supervisory responsibility. Otherwise, one woman undertakes the major responsibility, often with some help from her daughters or perhaps a sister or other female relative. Female affines rarely assist each other in this way. Indeed, in some cases they disagree about who ought to organize a particular event. In one

TABLE 11

Relationship of the Female Organizer of Ritual to the Deceased

Ritual	Consanguineal Relationship					Affinal Relationship	
	M	D	DD	MZ	MZD	Spouse	Other
Wake and burial	2	1	1		1	3	1
Novena and ninth-night wake	3	1	1		1	3	2
Tágurun lúdu						1	
Amúidahani				1			
Requiem Mass and *eféduhani*	2						
Chugú		1	1				
Dügü		1					

such instance, the spouse and mother of a deceased man gave separate ninth-night wakes in the same community. In another, a woman refused to organize *amúidahani* for her deceased spouse, saying it was his mother's responsibility to do so. (Community opinion was divided, and eventually the mother acceded, despite her poor health. With the help of a daughter, she organized the ritual bath for her deceased son.) Very rarely, women who are blood relatives also disagree about organizational responsibility. In one such case, two sisters who lived in different communities organized separate ninth-night wakes for their deceased mother. The prevailing opinion was that both wanted to show that they were grateful to their mother and also that they were "able." One man shrewdly observed that this had not happened when the sisters' father died; they had contributed to the ninth-night wake that their mother organized. But after "the old lady" dies, he observed, siblings often drift apart, and this was simply an extreme example of that drift.[4]

Such cases are instructive but distinctly uncommon. Most of the conflict that arises concerns contributions. Everyone is not equally willing or able to help pay for rituals for close kin. Usually, most of the money comes from the organizer's extended family. She may seek funds but obtain little from other close relatives of the deceased. In one case, a woman organized a ninth-night wake for her first cousin, using her own savings and money she obtained from her spouse and grown children. The deceased woman had only one child, a son, who had paid for most of the burial expenses but who provided very little for the ninth-night wake. He was widely criticized, of course, for having forced others, more distantly related, to bear the expense.

For any ritual, but particularly the costly major ones, financing is the organizer's first and most important task. The amount of money she collects determines the lavishness of the event and, consequently, the number of people who attend it. Memorable events draw extraordinarily large crowds. People recall that there was food and drink to distribute until its conclusion, that nearly everyone in the community attended, and that many visitors came from other communities as well. "There were people like sand," they say, using a feature of the local landscape to signify the human multitude on such occasions. Poorly financed and attended rituals, in contrast, fade quickly from public memory.

A large crowd is desirable for both mystical and social reasons. Spirits of the dead are not satisfied with lackluster, poorly attended rituals. In the case of *chugú* and *dügü* they may demand that the rite be repeated. Well-attended rituals also provide visible evidence that the sponsors are "able" to afford the expense of feeding a large number of people, that they are capable of "supporting the crowd." Attendance is seen as a tangible measure of reputation as well, a gauge of the esteem of others for the organizer, other sponsors, and the deceased. A large crowd, it is said, makes them feel "appreciated."

A teacher, who in his village was the only surviving close relative of his deceased uncle, acted as the sole sponsor of a ninth-night wake for him. (His uncle died in Honduras, and a ninth-night wake was reportedly held there as well.) The teacher's wife organized the event, and he paid for a generous supply of rum. Predictably the event was well attended, and many of those present commended the man for showing his gratitude and for his generosity. The sponsor himself regarded the large crowd as a sign of his own good standing in the community. As he surveyed the throng of people in his house and yard he commented with obvious satisfaction, "I have a lot of friends, you know. I am well liked here." (Most of the older women, however, explained their presence in terms of their personal relationship with his wife.)

The expense of ritual varies, depending on the scale and lavishness of a particular event (see Appendix 2). But even a minor rite is quite costly, given the relatively low wages and high cost of living in Belize (cf. Coelho 1955: 213ff.). The least expensive, *amúidahani,* costs more than half a week's wages of a male manual laborer. The expense of an adequate wake and burial exceeds a male worker's fortnightly pay, even when the coffin is a modest one, made of pine and constructed locally. If a more expensive and professionally made casket is purchased in town, the wake and burial expenses may equal a month's wages. Ninth-night wakes typically cost about the same amount. The cost of *dügü,* the most expensive ritual of all, is usually estimated at about $350, but the more elaborate cost as much as

$600—about four to seven months' wages. Despite the emphasis on having a generous supply of rum, an equivalent sum or much more is spent for food as for drink at these events.

Aside from the supply of food and rum, timing and publicity also affect the attendance of ritual events. Very elderly men and women can remember a time when ninth-night wakes were held exactly nine days after burial, but that custom has long since been superseded by the practice of scheduling these for a Saturday night. The stated reason is that more people can attend an event on a Saturday than one held midweek (cf. Coelho 1955: 175; Taylor 1951: 98). Usually the ninth-night wake is scheduled for the second Saturday after burial, the novena having begun the previous week, but it may be delayed in order to assure a large crowd. When two deaths occur within the same week, one ninth-night wake is usually put off so that "the crowd is not divided" between the two events.

There is more flexibility and even an element of strategy in selecting the date for *dügü*. Often it is scheduled to coincide with a holiday period, when many migrants will be home. At present *dügü* is usually held in the summer months, between July and September, when many seasonal workers and government employees have holidays and visit their natal communities. Lent is the only time of year when death-related ceremonies (aside from wakes and burials) are *not* held. *Chugú* and *dügü* are not scheduled for the stated reason that the shaman's spirit-helpers are absent, at the shrine at Esquipulas, Guatemala.[5] Ninth-night wakes are delayed until after Easter, their festive ambience considered inappropriate during the solemn Lenten period. Village populations also seem to be at an annual low during Lent. Christmas visitors have long since departed, and most seasonal workers are employed during this period. A number of older women may also be absent, having joined the Easter pilgrimage to Esquipulas. "The crowd" would probably be smaller at this particular time of year than at others. Scheduling the minor death rites is less problematic. The number of attendants is smaller, most of them older women who live in the community. Minor events are commonly held during midweek.

Whatever date is selected for *dügü* or any other major ritual event, it must be publicized clearly and widely. This is not always an easy task, given the dispersal of friends and kin throughout the country and the rudimentary nature of the communication system. Most of the information passes by word of mouth and, for the major death rites, must reach other Black Carib settlements and migrants living in other districts. Transmitting the pertinent details about date and place is extremely important, especially since migrant kin are potential contributors.

"Informing the people" is the organizer's responsibility, and she typically begins by personally informing her peers, other older women. This is an expeditious way to proceed, not only because these women will provide most of the necessary labor, but also because women visit other Black Carib villages more frequently than men do. They can be counted on to tell others there of the impending event. The organizer does not always "invite" others, in the strict sense of the word. An invitation is not needed to attend the major rites. Wakes and burials and ninth-night wakes, as well as *chugú* and *dügü*, are community events, open to anyone who wishes to take part, including visitors from outside the community. In the case of *dügü*, however, the organizer may decide to visit other Black Carib communities for the specific purpose of inviting people there to attend. She usually extends the invitations to the senior residents of households but phrases them in terms of "you and your family."[6]

Occasionally an organizer fails to publicize a ritual event adequately or accurately, and her other efforts are for naught. An extreme case occurred when an older woman planned a ninth-night wake for her son. All of her other grown children lived in different districts, and they were to bring the necessary food and drink for the event. The appointed Saturday dawned, but without the arrival of the supplies or the woman's children. All morning a small crowd of women hovered around her house, talking to her and among themselves. As the morning passed, they grew angry. They accused the woman's sons of preferring to spend their money drinking with their friends rather than "helping" their mother and dead brother. The daughters, they said, were "hardhearted and ungrateful." At midday, when there was still no sign of the supplies, nor any message from the errant sponsors, a few of the women decided to solicit small contributions from the organizer's kin who lived in the community and who, they said, might help her "save face." They approached her consanguines and affines alike, and by mid-afternoon had collected enough from a number of reluctant donors to buy a small amount of flour and rum. The bread that they baked was served at midnight with coffee, but without other accompaniment. As for the rum, there was so little that few people attended the event, and most of those who did left early. By 2:00 A.M. only the older women who had helped with preparations remained, and they stayed until dawn and the final prayers. By consensus, the ninth-night wake had been a "poor" one and a humiliation for the organizer.

The next Friday several of the woman's children arrived, armed with all the supplies necessary for the event that they expected to be held the following night. The many people who had maligned the woman's sons and daughters the week before began to speak more charitably about them when they realized that their mother had been at fault. She had vacillated about delaying the ninth-night wake an extra week, and had not clarified the date when her children attended the burial of their brother.

Blunders like this are uncommon. Most older women have some experience in organizing ritual events, and they have the guidance of other women as well, who are "interested" to see that the death rites are carried out correctly and successfully. On any ritual occasion, a number of women act as self-appointed advisors to the organizer. These women are expert in the minutiae of ritual protocol that has never been written down and that they have learned through many years of observant participation.

Older Women and Ritual

Older women whose children are grown and mothers dead take visibly more active part in rituals for the dead than men or young women. In theory, people are obligated to contribute to rituals for their deceased spouses and lineal relatives, and ideally for more distant kin as well. In fact, funding comes largely from within the extended family of the organizer. That rituals should be organized by women — or more specifically that the eldest female among the deceased's next of kin should assume this responsibility — is not stated as a "rule." Yet women who occupy this position but try to evade duty (an uncommon occurrence) are roundly criticized for their negligence.[7] In other words, it seems to be a matter of tacit knowledge that older women organize rituals and otherwise take active part in them.[8]

These women can be said to form a ritual cult, an informal group of people that convenes to perform rituals for the dead (cf. Spring 1978: 171). They organize ritual events and hold them (with the exception of *dügü*) in their houses and yards, the residence of the focal household of their extended families. Older women are the sole attendants at many of the minor rites. At major ritual events they form the core participants, offering their skills and labor for the occasion. Many of them are well versed in the details of ritual performance, having learned them through direct participation. They control a body of valued knowledge that has never been written down in entirety (ethnographic accounts notwithstanding) and that most young women and men grasp only in broad outline.

Older women also have access to other resources that collective rites require. They can call on other women, whom they have helped at past events, for assistance. They can seek funds from their grown children, with whom they maintain relations of mutual support. The expense of most rituals exceeds the capacity of a single individual or household. When, as occasionally happens, a man takes major responsibility (like the man who sponsored a ninth-night wake for his deceased uncle), he bears nearly all of the expense. When an older woman assumes responsibility she usually receives contributions from several of her sons and daughters. (They contribute according to ability and "conscience," rarely equally.) Many men and women balk at making sizable contributions for rituals aside from those that their mothers organize. They commonly suspect others of keeping the money for their own purposes, and they complain that their contributions tend to go unrecognized. When their own mother organizes an event, others assume that her children have provided most of the funding. Together with their mothers, they receive credit for "doing their best," showing their gratitude and generosity. This is so even if they do not attend the event (as close relatives "should" do). A migrant who makes a financial contribution commands far more respect than one who attends the event empty-handed.

Ritual participation is not entirely a matter of obligation but also of choice. Men and women are obligated to take part in rituals for their lineal relatives, but many older women participate actively in nearly all rituals for the dead. At *dügü* ten times as many women as men may sing and dance in the temple. Older women prepare offerings of food and drink for their own ancestors and carry them to the temple, which structurally resembles an enlarged, traditional house. As daughters of the dead, they "bring into the home" during *dügü*. As mothers of the living, by this act they protect their children and grandchildren from supernatural harm at the ancestors' hands.

Childless women, as a general rule, are visibly less active in ritual affairs. Lacking grown children, they have less ability to fund ritual and less incentive to take part in it. Eleven percent of the older women in one community had never borne children, and over half of them never helped with preparations for any of the twenty-seven rituals. Further, none of them organized any of these events. All but one of the organizers had one or more surviving grown children. The single exception was a woman whose only child had died in infancy and who fostered a kinswoman's young daughter. She organized a ninth-night wake that her husband sponsored for his deceased uncle.

Many older women speak in general terms of their ritual activity as a means of protecting their children and grandchildren. One woman, who fosters several grandchildren for two daughters who work in the United States, claimed that she takes care to make private offerings whenever her ancestors request them through dreams. She also makes ritual offerings whenever *chugú* and *dügü* are held in her community. Pointing out that her daughters have always enjoyed good health, she attributed this to her attentiveness to the dead. If she neglected her ancestors, she said, they might cause her children to fall ill, an unpleasant prospect for a woman like herself, who depends on her children for support and who must provide for them when they are ill. Her daughters' distance provided no protection, she said. There is no escaping the ancestors' needs and demands.

By taking part in rituals organized by others, women return help extended to them in the past and assure themselves of assistance at future events that they organize. But most cite concern for their children's well-being, and by extension their own, as the major reason why they join in *chugú* and *dügü*. Indeed, this concern sometimes leads them to contribute substantially to rites for their children's paternal ancestors, although in theory they have no strong obligation to do so. One case will illustrate this point and several others: the importance of an extended family in ritual sponsorship, the peripheral role of a childless woman in ritual activity, and the conflict that may arise between female affines over organizational responsibility.

A woman whose son was sick consulted a shaman and learned that her son's father, in league with his mother (the son's paternal grandmother), was causing his illness. According to the shaman, they demanded *dügü*. Soon after, the woman went to another community to see the only surviving sibling of her deceased husband, a sister, to inform her of the request for *dügü*. The sister showed scant interest in her nephew's health or her dead brother's and mother's demand. This highly unusual and disconcerting display of negligence was widely criticized. The sister claimed that she was "too busy" to be involved in the preparations and, more to the point, she said that her dead brother's children were the "fittest to pay." She herself was a childless widow. Although many women insisted that she should have undertaken responsibility for the ceremony, it is doubtful that she could have done so. She simply lacked the necessary resources: a number of grown sons and daughters or a spouse to provide the required funds, and a network of female friends and relatives in her deceased brother's community to provide the labor.

Eventually, the eldest son of the deceased man undertook major financial responsibility for the rite, at his mother's urging and with her promise to organize it. She and her grown children and their spouses — an extended family — provided most of the funds. Excluding the expense for cassava bread and chickens, which were offered in small amounts by relatives of all degrees who attended the ceremony, the woman paid for 20 percent of the expenses and her eldest son for 45 percent. The rest of his full siblings directly contributed a total of 20 percent. Altogether, one extended family paid for 85 percent of the expenses of *dügü*. The balance was made up by small sums from other descendants of the deceased paternal grandmother, the first cousins of the organizer's children. Ten households contributed . nearly all of the money spent for food, drink, and other supplies and labor (cf. Coelho 1955: 193).

Asked why she had contributed so much money and effort, the woman replied that the health of her children depended upon their paternal as well as maternal ancestors. If her sister-in-law had been willing to organize the event, she herself would have played a more marginal role. But certainly she would have helped with preparations and contributed some money. The purpose of the rite, after all, was to cure her son.

Few women take active part in ritual until their own mothers cease to do so, either because they die or grow disabled with age. The exception to this is rites that they sponsor for their own lineal relatives. On other occasions their mother's offering suffices. (Theoretically, of course, a woman's children must depend on a paternal kinswoman to represent them with an offering to their paternal ancestors, but this does not seem to be a matter of great concern.) After their mother dies, all of the daughters tend to take part in ritual events. In theory, one could represent her siblings as well as their children to their (maternal or paternal) ancestors. But again, women view ritual activity as a matter of maternal and filial obligation, and as a form of protection for their children and grandchildren. It serves as very visible evidence of their lifelong responsibility for the well-being of their offspring, of their efforts to protect and enhance it. Ritual obviously also provides a vivid object lesson in morality, illustrating the positive consequences of care and the negative effects of neglect of lineal kin. In rituals for the dead, women collectively express their responsibility for lineal kin.

By fulfilling obligations to the dead and meeting their needs, older women say that they protect their descendants and themselves from harm at the hands of ancestral spirits. It is a subject on which they speak frequently and at length. Ritual obligations and the "sin" of neglecting deceased kin are topics of perennial interest to older women, who care for both the living and the dead. They speak as warmly on these subjects as they do when they criticize a woman who is careless with her children, a man who does not adequately support his spouse or offspring, or an adult who is so ungrateful as to neglect an aged parent.

Certainly there are striking parallels between the ancestors' paradoxical position of strength and dependence and their own. Ancestral spirits must depend on their distant, living descendants for nourishment and care; they have the capacity to help them with advice, offered in dreams; they punish neglect. Likewise, older women depend on their sons and daughters, who may live at a distance, for "help." They offer their counsel and various other forms of care; and, like the ancestors, they provide a point of unity for dispersed kin who do not interact in daily life. Older women do not consciously perceive and articulate these parallels. Yet their concern with the ancestors certainly contains an element of self-interest and perhaps some sense of identification as well. They will join those on "the other side" before many years pass.

Notes to Chapter 10

1. There are a number of published and unpublished studies that provide detailed accounts of the performance of death rituals. They do not clearly specify who organizes, sponsors, and attends them, and on some points seem to conflict. Excerpts from these accounts follow. All emphases are mine.

Wake and burial: Taylor (1951: 97) states that the *"immediate family"* is responsible for burial expenses and arrangements. The wake is attended by "only the *family,* the immediately *accessible kin,* and a few friendly *neighbors.* " Coelho (1955: 174f.) writes that *"all the friends and relatives of the dead"* attend. He mentions the presence of old women, men, and "persons of all ages," including children. As for the expenses, *"relatives* and closest *friends of the family"* are expected to help with them.

Novena and ninth-night wake: Taylor (1951: 98) writes that "the *family,* the *kindred,* and *any others* who wish to honor the dead" attend the novena. This seems to be based on informants' statements. Taylor adds that he personally attended a novena one night and saw about "twenty-five people, mostly *old* or elderly." Adams (1957: 381) states specifically that *"only women* participate," and Coelho (1955: 175) simply observes that the prayers are led by "an *old* man or woman." About the ninth-night wake there is little information. Taylor (1951: 100f.) implies that it is a community event, attended by men and women of all ages. Perhaps in reference to the organizer, he mentions that "the *head* of the bereaved *family"* often acts as a "master of ceremonies" for the event.

Tágurun lúdu: There is no information about the end-of-mourning ceremony.

Amúidahani: According to Taylor (1951: 114), it is the *"immediate family"* that ritually bathes the spirit of the deceased. Coelho (1955: 176) writes that "only the surviving *spouse and children* of the deceased person" participate. Both statements are based on informants' accounts.

Requiem Mass and *eféduhani:* There is no information about the "feasting" and singing that follow the performance of a Requiem Mass.

Chugú: Taylor (1951: 114f.) states that *"all direct descendants* together with any surviving siblings of the dead person or persons for whom the rite is given and of their siblings are, children excepted, in duty bound to attend, and to bring such contributions in the form of drink, fish, meat, or other foodstuffs as may be acceptable to the dead." Coelho (1955: 179, 181f.) is more specific about sponsorship than about attendance. He describes *chugú* as a "feast given by the members of an *extended family* to their deified ancestors." About both *chugú* and *dügü* he states that *"all relatives* are informed of the decision so that they will keep the day free to come to the celebration; each is also expected to help defray a part of the expenses, according to his position and means, or contribute in kind." At another point he writes of *chugú:* "In theory, all the members of the extended family should come together" to hold the rite, but "this is hardly ever done in practice." He adds that those who cannot attend send contributions.

Dügü: Taylor (1951: 115) states that, in theory, the same people participate in *dügü* as in *chugú,* but the former is "in general much better attended." At various points he speaks of this ritual as being sponsored by a *"family," "household,"* and *"lineage."* He notes several times that far more women than men participate as dancers (Taylor 1951: 116f., 119ff., 126). Coelho (1955: 193) writes that *dügü* requires the "joint efforts of *many ex-*

tended families" and that "the economic resources of at least *a dozen households* are pooled." Palacio (1973: 6) and Macklin (1976: 3) both refer to a *"family"* as hosts of this rite. Palacio states that "for *close relatives* attendance is obligatory." He observes that the number of consanguines involved in any particular *dügü* tends to increase the further removed the ancestor is from living generations. Gonzalez (1969: 49) writes that "the individual household or family group was never autonomous in matters concerning the supernatural. Generally *segments of a larger kinship group* cooperated in making offerings to various ancestral spirits, calling in members from towns and villages up and down the coast." In another context, she observes that although in theory all lineal descendants of the honored ancestor are supposed to attend the event, only some of them do so. She suggests that individuals choose which rituals to attend, and that their choice is related to their participation in *non-unilineal descent groups,* "a group of persons descended from one common ancestor who ultimately share in the inheritable property of a given individual" (Solien 1959a: 580).

The apparent conflicts in these accounts may derive from the fact that some are normative statements about who "ought" to sponsor and attend these rituals while others are based on observations. Coelho's account of *chugú* and *dügü* comes entirely from informants' statements since neither of these rituals was held during his fieldwork. Taylor observed several *dügü* but was not so interested in who sponsored and took part in them as in the performance itself. His general statement about attendance at *chugú* and *dügü* parallels what my own informants told me.

Terminological differences may also explain some of the variance in these accounts. The terms "lineage," "household," "immediate family," "extended family," and simply "family" have been used interchangeably and loosely, and generally left undefined.

2. Cf. Coelho (1955: 88f.), who implies that men contribute to rituals sponsored by their spouses' blood relatives.

3. In the three cases in which the female organizers were "other" affines (see Table 11), they and their husbands were cited as being "in charge" jointly. In two cases, the husband was the brother of the deceased, the only surviving adult lineal relative, and the primary sponsor; in the third case, the husband was the nephew of the deceased, the only surviving close relative in the community, and the sole sponsor.

4. The two sisters were older women with grown children. Their extended families each sponsored a ninth-night wake for the deceased woman.

5. Kelsey and Osborne (1943) describe the shrine. It draws pilgrims from all over Central America, as well as from Mexico (Chiñas 1973: 77).

6. According to informants, the organizer might say, *Narúduha-ñabibu háma sun bidúheñu lídaun nubárasegun,* "I am inviting you and your relatives to my affair."

7. If the eldest female among next of kin is very elderly and in ill health, one of her daughters may take major responsibility for organizing the

ritual. (In one case, the elderly woman still played an advisory role.) No one accuses such elderly women of negligence.

8. Men and young women simply assume that older women do so, and that they have greater knowledge than anyone else about ritual matters. When I raised questions about various rituals, they routinely directed me to "the old heads who know about these things." Asked for names, they specified various knowledgeable older women.

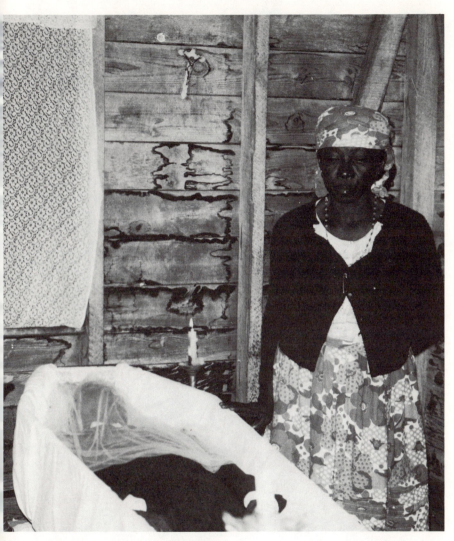

38. An older woman mourning her father.

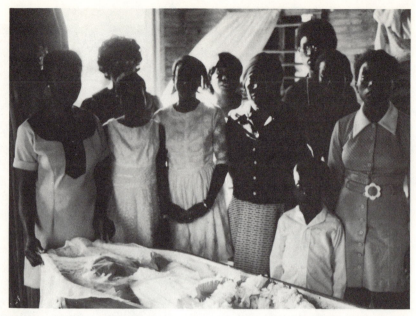

39. Family members mourn their mother and grandmother.

40. Older women preparing for the ninth-night wake.

41. Baking wheat bread for the ceremony.

42. A procession of older women to the temple.

43. A small temple.

44. A shaman.

Chapter 11

NECESSITY AS MOTHER
OF CONVENTION

Female responsibility to lineal kin serves as an organizing principle of Black Carib kinship and ritual, and as the focus of female unity and collective action. Maternal obligations are primary, broadly defined, and lifelong. As mothers, women share common concerns and a valued identity, one that commands respect (not only from their children). Motherhood connotes strength, the capacity and duty to protect others.[1] Women act together to achieve this end.

Many episodes in daily life, in moments of conflict, and on ritual occasions as well attest to the cultural value of motherhood. A man, brushing away his small daughter's tears, addresses her as *núguchun,* "my mother," as he holds her close and tries to comfort her. Another man, whose wife has fled from him, gives up his heated pursuit when he learns that she has found sanctuary in her mother's house. Only her mother, he says, has the "right" to protect her from him. A young woman, wailing over the body of her maternal grandmother, who reared her, cries, "What support will I have now? Ai, I'll never stop crying after you, Mama." It is axiomatic that mothers provide their children with food, protection, counsel, and other help. Hence, again and again when I met women they routinely asked, "Is your mother alive?" or, as they usually put it, "Do you have your mother?"

The Bonds of Motherhood

Structurally, most households and all extended families center on mother-child ties. Those between older women and their grown daughters have a special strength, visibly shown in patterns of residence and exchange. These women form an interest group of sorts, based on their common responsibilities and shared needs as mothers. To be a mother requires not only lifelong personal effort but the help of other women as well. A young woman must see to the daily care of her children, teach them proper conduct, punish misbehavior, find medicine when they fall ill, and, if need be, seek employment in order to feed and clothe them. She typically turns to her mother for help in any facet of child care. Likewise, an older woman offers her grown children counsel, provides food and shelter in time of unemployment or marital separation, represents them in ritual to protect them from supernatural harm, and seeks ritual cures if others fail. She obtains money from her grown children to fund the rituals she organizes. She must turn to other women for assistance with food preparation and ritual performance.

Parenthood has profoundly different cultural meaning and social consequences for Black Carib men and women. Maternal obligations are more broadly defined and strictly enforced (largely by women). They provide the basis for collective action by women. On ritual occasions, older women cooperate to meet their obligations to children and other lineal kin, living and dead. They also act together to enforce the many other conventional duties of motherhood. When, for example, a young woman neglected certain postpartum observances, her mother advised her to follow them. The daughter did so, but soon said openly that she could no longer bother with such "superstitions." One of the oldest women in the community, respected for her medicinal knowledge, then approached the young woman and reminded her of the importance of these "rules." Other older women offered the same counsel. They remarked that this was their duty: "She doesn't know. She must learn."

Sexual misconduct is still another form of maternal negligence, and opposed as such by older women. A single young woman who does not confine herself to one "friend" raises questions about which man has fathered the child she bears. She risks denying the child paternal support and a full set of kin. A woman who engages in an extramarital affair is an irresponsible mother because her conduct imperils her children's means of support. If her spouse discovers her infidelity he may justifiably leave her, shifting his support to the household he joins. (Of course, this increases the burden of responsibility for the woman's mother.)

A whole set of beliefs elaborating the theme of maternal obligation and female self-restraint warn that irresponsible conduct by women endangers others. A woman who is pregnant or has recently given birth may harm her child's health by consorting with a man other than the father of that child. A menstruating woman (a potential mother, a woman capable of bearing children) jeopardizes others if she neglects certain "precautions," or restrictions. An older woman who tries to avoid organizing a required ritual puts her children and other lineal kin at risk: the angry spirit may cause one or more of them to fall ill.

Women find it more difficult to enforce paternal obligations, and men rarely make any attempt to do so. That men show little interest in, or capacity for, cooperative effort with each other is consistent with the nature of their daily work and responsibility to kin. Their primary obligation is to support the women and children with whom they live (ideally their own children, but in reality sometimes the children of other men). They meet this obligation through individual effort, in the wage economy or through own-account work. Occasional attempts by men to form agricultural cooperatives, usually with government encouragement and assistance, have all quickly failed.[2] Beaucage (1966: 190), discussing male and female commercial groups among Black Caribs in Honduras, contrasts the stability of women's groups with *"la fragilité de groupements masculins."*

Missing Links

Historical evidence suggests that in the distant past, collective action by men also had a fleeting quality and an external focus. According to eighteenth-century accounts, men organized only to raid a common enemy, especially the British. Their unity was based on opposition, and its force was externally directed. The loss of political autonomy, and the entry of men into the labor market of Central America, presumably eroded their need or capacity for collective action.

While records from the eighteenth century cast light on relations among Black Carib men, women rarely emerge from the shadows. Accounts from the seventeenth and nineteenth centuries, however, do attest to their active role in ritual and to the strength of ties with lineal kin.

That Africans lived with the Carib before 1650 is certain. Father Breton, a French missionary who spent twelve years (from 1641 to 1653) with the Carib in Dominica, recorded special terms they used for *"les enfants engendrez des Sauvages & des Negresses,"* children born of Carib men and Negro women.[3] African components of Black Carib culture can be assumed, although not directly documented with historical records.[4] As for Amerindian elements, Father Breton noted a number of customary practices of the Carib that have survived to the present day among the Black Carib: the use of teknonyms, observance of postpartum dietary and sexual restrictions by men and women, and menstrual restrictions.[5] By his account, marital separation was quite common, the men being "free to leave their wives." Women held primary responsibility for their children: "When the father dies or leaves his wife, all the children stay with the mother and she takes care of them, while the husband does not bother about them any more." And again: "If their husbands leave them, the wives keep all the children, and do not give the husband any unless forced to do so, for when the children grow up they become a source of support and subsistence."[6] Sons, of course, generally left their natal villages at marriage, while daughters remained near their mothers and sisters. Female lineal kin formed the stable core of each village.[7]

Given his missionizing intent, Father Breton wrote at some length about the "superstitions" of the Carib. His comments suggest that Carib ritual was ancestor-focused: "They believe there are male and female among the gods, who are many. They often consult them, whether for the success of their wars or for the end of their sicknesses. . . . These gods have numerous offspring and these children have children. These all come to drink the offerings. . . . Even though [the Caribs] find [the offering] as they left it, they say that it is not the same."[8] (That these offerings were for ancestors is also implied in the Carib word for God, recorded by William Young [1801: 292f.] at the end of the eighteenth century: "*naketi,* i.e., *Grandmere.*"[9] Today the Black Carib address their song of offering to *nagütü,* my grandmother. They speak of the song as very ancient, with certain words whose meaning they no longer know.)

Both men and women, according to Father Breton, could become shamans, or *bóye (búyei).*[10] When the Carib prepared for a raid, or when someone fell ill, a shaman was summoned to call down the spirits and present an offering of food and drink. This was done at night, inside a "hut." "Once I attempted to enter with a fire brand in order to prevent this abomination," wrote Father Breton, "but the women stopped me." Women themselves took part in the various "feasts," singing and dancing with a "shuffling" step, sometimes in a circle. With the men, they drank liberally on these occasions (to excess, in Father Breton's view). Women showed great interest and skill in curing. Father Breton referred more than once to the "remedies which the women apply to the sick."[11]

Nearly two centuries later, Thomas Young visited Black Carib settlements in Central America. He took special note of the "Affection for Old People," who were "supported by their sons or other relatives, and . . . treated and spoken of with much respect, the children seeming to vie with each other in testifying their affection" (Young 1847: 125f.). Since men worked seasonally for wages, daughters presumably saw to the daily care and support of their aged parents (as they do today).

Young (1847: 132ff.) also explicitly commented on the "great numbers" of women who sang and danced at *dügü.* The following excerpts from his account show many parallels with present-day performance:

> This feast lasts from three days to a week, and they all contribute, by bringing their offerings of liquor. . . . The feast commences at sunset, when the drums as well as the liquor are put into requisition, and the play and singing commence, and are kept up with all the vigour and

enjoyment so characteristic of the Caribs. . . . Numerous large and beautifully clean cotton hammocks are slung around for the accommodation of the old people (who do the looking-on part), the weary traveller, or the exhausted dancers. It is a maxim, on these events, that good drinking ought to be accompanied by good eating. They therefore take care to have a number of little tables well, and even sumptuously furnished. . . . The Carib women also in great numbers join in the festivities. . . . They dance and sing, the dancing being merely a movement to and fro with their hands and feet, alternately, accompanied by a peculiar intonation of voice. . . . They equip themselves on these occasions as well as their finances will permit, and the variety of hues in their dresses is remarkably pleasing. A large handkerchief of some gay colour and lively pattern is tied round the head, the ends falling on the shoulder. . . . The men are all jauntily equipped, and have an air of easy gaiety about them. . . . It is general custom at their feasts for all the men to get drunk, but they seldom quarrel. Some of them will drink the horrible aguardiente [rum], and still more vile anisoú [anise-flavored rum], during the continuance of the feast, without being much affected. . . . It seems surprising, that be they ever so intoxicated at night, they appear in the morning as if nothing unusual had happened.

Women today dance and sing in the same manner, and their dress is much the same: gathered skirts, blouses, and bright headwraps. The "vile anisoú," a perennial favorite, is now largely consumed by women, men preferring the unadulterated variety of rum. The physical endurance of attendants remains "surprising" to non-Caribs who witness *dügü*, and good humor and "enjoyment" still prevail on this occasion. *Dügü* has its solemn moments — particularly *amálihani*, the danced rite of placation. But for the rest there is the pungent humor, always tart and often ribald, that flavors social life.

The only clear evidence of recent change in ritual points toward a decline in direct participation by men. When Taylor (1951: 117, 126) witnessed *dügü* in Belize over thirty years ago, women "at a conservative estimate" outnumbered men by four to one. Today the proportion of male dancers is smaller. While many men gather to watch *dügü*, rather few enter the temple to dance. Taylor also noted a decline in the singing of *arúmahani* (the male equivalent of women's songs of mourning, *abaímahani*); "whereas *abaímahani* attract scores of women of all ages, it is with difficulty . . . that five old men may be found to stand up and perform a few *arúmahani*."[12] Today one or two old men may join women in their songs of remembrance, but they no longer sing their own together. In the past, many shamans were men. At present, the practicing shamans in Belize are women.[13]

It bears emphasis here that men *have* preserved a very old processional dance, *wanáragua* (in English, "John Canoe"). The precise origins of the dance are unknown, but historical evidence suggests an African ancestry. In the past, slaves in Jamaica, St. Vincent, and other areas of the West Indies performed John Canoe at Christmas.[14] Thomas Young (1847: 135), who saw men dance *wanáragua* in Honduras, described their near-acrobatic feats. "Soon after the music strikes up," he wrote, "a dancer appears, who after throwing his body into all conceivable postures, now jumping up and down grotesquely, then advancing and retreating affectedly, and then after bending himself on one side so as nearly to fall down, he kicks about with great energy, till at length he gives a whirl, a bow, and retires; another taking his place, and so it continues until they are all exhausted."[15]

Wanáragua differs in many respects from the rituals that women organize. Few men take part (usually half a dozen or so). The costumed and masked dancers range in age from adolescents to men in their sixties. They perform *wanáragua* at Christmas, a holiday shared with non-Caribs in Belize. The men do not dance in one fixed place. They move from house to house, and sometimes travel to non-Carib locales to perform. *Wanáragua* explicitly serves worldly purpose: it entertains, and people reciprocate by offering coins and rum to the dancers. Men cite pleasure, profit, and prestige as their motives for taking part: they enjoy dancing; each gains prestige and money by dancing well.

Wanáragua is distinctively male in its emphasis on *individual* prowess, *direct and immediate profit,* and *movement from place to place* (including non-Carib locales). The secular nature of the dance does not fully account for this. On Settlement Day, females take center stage at a secular event, but in a very different manner. Each Black Carib community in Belize sends an adolescent girl to Dangriga, center of the festivities, to take part in a contest there. Wearing traditional dress, the contestants show their proficiency in singing, dancing, and speaking Carib. In the weeks before the contest, older women in each town and village instruct their delegate, sharpening her skills. The girl who wins the competition brings prestige to her home community. Settlement Day is of recent origin, but the contest follows a familiar, perhaps very old format: *females represent others* at this *collective celebration of ancestry* — and not, it is said, for personal gain.

Evidence from the past suggests that men have selectively preserved *wanáragua,* a festive dance — and women, certain rituals for the dead. Women have held fast to these despite declining attendance by men. Their prominence in ritual does not follow simply from the absence of men, although this certainly heightens the visibility of women today. Indeed, accounts from the last century and recent past suggest great continuity in the role of women in ritual. (Thomas Young himself noted the *presence* of men, the *singing and dancing* of women.) The cultural conservatism of older women — especially in matters of ritual and kinship — is proverbial today. Questions about custom often elicit the response, "You must ask the old heads, who know about this" or "It's the old heads who care about such things." The suggested informants are nearly always women in their fifties or older. These women express (and enforce) in the community at large the lessons that all young children learn at their mother's knee — and occasionally at her hand.

Lessons Learned

Women today visibly play a key role in perpetuating a set of rituals that stress responsibility to kin: the obligation to protect younger lineals, to express gratitude to elder lineals. Following cultural command (often expressed as ancestral demand), women offer food to their deceased lineals on many ritual occasions — demonstrating their gratitude, protecting their children and grandchildren.

In ritual, they express the major moral tenets that they teach their children. Mothers reproduce these values in the children on whom they must one day rely for their own food (cf. Maher 1976: 69). They try to instill a sense of responsibility and gratitude in their sons and daughters. From a very early age, children learn to help their mothers and to thank them for food. The tiny child sent off on an errand or taught to return an empty bowl after dinner with a word of thanks begins to master an important lesson. A young woman whose child neglects assigned duties and common courtesy — who refuses to help her or to acknowledge her help — will spare the rod only so long. At each infraction she warns the errant child with words that are almost litany: "So you are ungrateful. . . . *One* day you'll see — I'll get the rope and *lash* you. . . . You'll remember then." And one day she does — suddenly, without final warning, and in clear sight of other children. Even the smallest cannot fail to grasp the meaning of this public spectacle, this vivid object lesson: hurling angry words about ingratitude, a wrathful woman descends upon her child, rope in hand — and no one intercedes. No one, as many people said, has the "right."

Older women also expect gratitude (in the form of financial help) from their grown children. They obviously cannot enforce it directly with physical sanction. But like the young mother who repeatedly warns her child of an imminent lashing, they persistently caution that dereliction of duty brings supernatural punishment, usually in physical form (sickness). Ancestors carry the same message in dreams, where they often brandish a stick as they demand offerings. "Who owes must pay," the common saying runs. The negligent will finally suffer great pain.

Most of the rituals that older women organize serve to show the interdependence of lineal kin, the importance of gratitude to elder lineals. This meaning holds great significance for them. Like the ancestors, many must depend on younger lineal kin for the food they eat. Adherence to tradition represents their livelihood, and transgressions pose a direct threat to their welfare. By upholding convention, older women provide a measure of security for themselves — and, in the eyes of many, for their children and grandchildren as well.

Women act together to achieve this end (just as ancestors may act in league if the living fail to respond to a request made by one of them). Men and women who disregard duty can expect an initial warning from their mothers or other elder kinswomen. If they ignore this, they must contend with other older women in the community, who take it as their duty to offer the same counsel. The young woman who neglected certain postpartum "rules" finally decided to comply with them rather than to face the daily warnings and reproach of other women (cf. Hadel 1972: 76).

Men find it easier than women to elude this "collective conscience." Since most of them work away from home, their daily conduct escapes such careful scrutiny. Their workplace provides a ready refuge if need be, and their wages give them a measure of independence. Both the expectation and enforcement of male responsibility pale in comparison with that of female duty. Mothers permit a degree of irresponsibility in their young sons that they do not tolerate in their daughters. Boys enjoy greater freedom than their sisters do — and with it, greater chance to evade duty. Girls are more often at hand and more subject to discipline. Even as adults, their choice is to bow to custom or to pay a daily price for flaunting it.

The force of tradition bears more heavily and directly on women than on men, but it undeniably offers them greater benefit as well. Their cultural conservatism derives from a complex of incentive and constraint — not from unfamiliarity with other ways of life. It is grounded both in "is" and "ought," in economic and cultural imperative. A woman must care for her children, but she does not have the means to provide for them or herself singlehandedly. The outer world offers her little help, neither ready employment nor legal definition and enforcement of others' obligations to her. Later in life, women lack even the opportunity to find temporary employment. They must depend on others for their daily bread — that is, on the display of gratitude for lifelong care, on reciprocity for past and current help. Many women who freely admit that they once regarded various "rules" as so much superstition give them increasing credence as they age. Convention assumes immediate significance, holds present value. Tradition spells out duty, and older women act together to enforce it.'

Age, Childbearing, and Female Status

The overriding concerns of women toward their children and other kin remain constant throughout their lives. But as they grow older, reaching a position of seniority among lineal kin and passing the age of childbearing, the way in which they deal with these concerns changes. Older women address them in ritual, together and in a public context. The public and collective aspects of their actions deserve emphasis, as does the women's loss of reproductive capacity. These bear on the question of female status, and variation over the life course.

The relation between women's fertility and the central roles they take in ritual is generally inverse: as the former declines and ends, the latter gradually begins. By their mid-forties, women have borne their last children, and at about this age they begin to take more active part in ritual affairs. I have suggested that their participation can be understood in terms of a complex of cultural and material factors that have "predisposing" and "enabling" effects. They both incline and empower older women to take a central role in ritual. But this is only one facet (and the most obvious) of a more general change in women's social relations as they age. That is, their role in ritual is one aspect of, and in part conditioned by, the loosening of certain constraints on social conduct and interaction. They enjoy greater freedom of movement, association, and activity as their fertility declines and they pass the age of childbearing. They are no longer bound by the culturally defined and socially enforced restrictions that they observed during their childbearing years, that their own daughters observe, and that once limited the nature and frequency of their daily contact with people other than close kin.

In cross-cultural perspective, these restrictions seem rather mild. Black Carib women of any age appear to be remarkably autonomous relative to women in many other cultures. This was my initial impression, and one that the sustained observations of fieldwork supported. I found that the social identity of these women does not derive primarily from their relationships with men (as wife, sister, daughter, or the mother of sons) but from motherhood itself. Moreover, all young women are eligible to bear children. (That is, marriage is not a prerequisite for sexual relations or childbearing.) Female sexuality and labor are not treated as the property of men, nor are women subject to the authority or direct control of men in their daily lives.[16] They choose their own spouses and leave unsatisfactory unions at will. They control the products of their labor and can acquire and hold property in their own right (for example, houses). And so forth.

In hindsight, however, I find that cross-cultural contrasts between "women here" and "women there" offer less insight than the intracultural contrasts I observed: those between young women (of childbearing age) and older (postreproductive) women, and between men and young women. Between these categories, differences emerge in "degrees of freedom," or autonomy in movement, association, and activity. Simply put, young women have less than men or older women.

Let me summarize here some of the restrictions that I have described at length in previous chapters, and that apply to women of childbearing age in Black Carib communities. Many of these are perhaps largely symbolic (with multiple meanings, conscious and otherwise). Others, however, clearly serve to limit the nature and frequency of young women's daily contact with people other than spouses and close kin.

Menstruating women are supposed to stay at home and to avoid public gatherings, especially ritual events (not because they are "unclean" but because the scent of their menstrual blood might attract malevolent spirits). Before and after childbirth women also observe a set of formal restrictions that limit activity and movement. (These are more numerous and strictly enforced than those that apply to fathers of unborn or newborn children.) Like the ones that pertain to menstruation, the stated purpose of these restrictions is to protect other people. It is surely not a coincidence that so many specific restrictions surround menstruation, pregnancy, and childbirth. Menstruation indicates fecundity; pregnancy and childbirth demonstrate it. In other words, they provide tangible evidence of a childbearing capacity.

Even without such evidence, it is common knowledge that women of a certain age—those between about fifteen and forty-five—are potentially fertile. Whether or not they are menstruating or pregnant, young women simply do not move about a village so freely as men and older women do. Those who value their reputations do not "drift about" by themselves, indulging in "idle talk" (and perhaps arranging a tryst with a man). Nor do they openly engage in solitary visits with men other than spouses or close kin. When they leave the village for a few hours during the day to collect firewood or coconuts, or when they attend ritual events at night, they generally go in the company of other women. (The stated purpose is to protect themselves from spirits; but a young woman who walks down the beach alone, or who leaves a ritual event by herself, is suspected of an assignation.) The comments of many young women suggest that the weight of other women's opinion—rather than the burden of domestic duties or fear of harmful spirits or concern about male regard—leads them to observe most of these conventions. In many aspects of personal conduct, young women are expected to show greater restraint than men or older women.

Older women, in contrast to the young, are visibly "more social." When they visit others—whether women or men, in the community or elsewhere, alone or in company—no one mutters that they are "drifting about," nor do others automatically assume a sexual motive for their visits. Those who drink liberally on ritual occasions are said to be "enjoying themselves," just as men are when they "spree." If young women drink to excess, however, others criticize their lack of restraint. Nearly always, such criticism of personal conduct carries innuendos about probable sexual misconduct and negligence of duty.

In sum, the capacity to bear children (and potentially to engage in illicit sexual relations) carries a social cost. Those who bear the children also bear most of this cost. The loss of fertility is accompanied by the loss of many constraints: it offers gains to women in the form of greater freedom of movement, association, and activity.

Cross-cultural studies of female status largely overlook such significant differences in the social lives of young and post-reproductive women.[17] Yet many common indicators of female subordination — exclusion from political affairs and ritual, seclusion, harsh penalties for sexual misconduct — apply to women only during their childbearing years, not after. Even in the most homogeneous community and "simple" society, all women are not necessarily bound by the same restrictions. My own research with the Black Carib, and cross-cultural evidence as well, suggests that with the loss of fertility come certain social gains: commonly an increase in autonomy, sometimes in power; and in certain cases the liberty to take part in political and ritual activities from which young women are formally excluded.[18]

Put another way, the female life cycle has aspects of a controlled experiment. Its unique variable, the capacity to bear children, is age-related, and tangibly demarcated by physiological events — menarche and menopause. Many of the cultural restrictions that limit the autonomy and power of women pertain to them only during this life stage. In some cultures people explicitly speak of older women as "like men," and ethnographers remark that they enjoy various "male" prerogatives. The Nuer, for example, say about an old woman, "she has become a man" (Evans-Pritchard 1974: 237).[19] Likewise, "the Mende acknowledge that there are 'sensible' women, and it is clear that social status depends almost as much upon age as upon sex. The Mende themselves explain this by saying that they look upon a woman as a man when a certain age is reached" (Little 1948: 9). Among both the Nuer and the Mende, older women can hold ritual and political positions generally assumed by men, and for which young women are ineligible.

Older women share one primary characteristic with men: they cannot bear children. Perhaps their prerogatives are better understood as those of adults who lack the capacity to bear children, not of men per se. And perhaps the diverse cultural restrictions that apply to young women do not indicate the subordination of women per se, but the relatively more stringent control of childbearing adults. In short, the categories "male" and "female" are global ones, and not wholly adequate for analysis because they mask significant and highly specific variables. One of these, the capacity to bear children, is gender-linked but also age-related. It distinguishes young women from men, but also from older women. With regard to this specific variable, men and older women constitute one analytic category, and childbearing women another. Adults seem to be categorized in this manner in various cultures: hence the proverbial statements that explicitly equate older women with men.

In the literature on female status, in contrast, women are generally treated as one unitary category, and men as another. Quinn (1977: 182f.) points out that female status itself has usually been conceived of as a "unitary construct," to be explained by a "key" variable. She suggests, however, that more is to be gained by viewing "women's status as a composite of many different variables, often causally independent one from another" (cf. Whyte 1978). Age and reproductive capacity are among these "many different variables."[20] By focusing on *variation among women* in any given culture (not only cross-cultural similarities or differences among them, or female-male differences), we can ask why some women have more autonomy and power than others in specific domains. We can try to account for this by learning not only which *conditions* of their lives vary, but also how the *actions* they take differ.

In the Black Carib communities I studied, older women are not bound by most of the culturally defined and socially enforced restrictions that apply to women of childbearing age. Instead, they act as the primary enforcers of those "rules." Beyond the increased autonomy that they enjoy, older women (especially the mothers of grown children) exercise greater power, largely through their collective action and use of a public forum in pursuit of common good.

Common Cause

Older women, who share compelling concerns based on their age, gender, maternity, and position of seniority among lineal kin, join to give them voice and collective force. They organize around an issue of largely female interest: care of lineal kin, living and dead. Ritual reinforces traditional obligations and lines of exchange between lineals. These represent the livelihood of Black Carib women, especially as they grow older.

Elsewhere in the world, women in positions of financial dependence also try to create and sustain a sense of obligation in their children or others. In many cases, however, they must act alone, and without benefit of collective support and sanction. They lack any conventional ("legitimate") means to publicize and enforce their claims. Others can too easily denigrate or ignore their efforts, dismiss them as a form of "emotional blackmail" (Maher 1976: 68). For Black Carib women, ritual elevates and sanctifies the same end. It provides a vehicle to express traditional and perpetual obligations. Whatever its particular message, "ritual is always a statement about continuity" (Myerhoff 1978: 229).

While Black Carib women have certain recognized rights as mothers, they give far greater emphasis to their own obligations and those of others. What older women express in ritual is not the legitimacy of right but the sanctity of duty. Anyone may neglect their rights, and a "right which goes unrecognized by anybody is not worth very much . . . [while an] obligation which goes unrecognized by anybody loses none of the full force of its existence" (Weil 1952: 3). To create a sense of obligation in others, to sustain and enforce it, is to exercise power (cf. Friedl 1967: 108). That older women do so in the name of morality and common good does not lessen its force. That they act together heightens it.

Women spend their lives at this task, from a vantage point as the transmitters of culture and upholders of moral tenet. Young mothers try to instill a sense of responsibility and gratitude in their children, and they punish negligence — in public and with memorable severity. Later in life, they collectively enforce conventional duty. For well over a century, "great numbers" of them have joined to celebrate obligations to kin with song, dance, food, and drink. "Who owes must pay" — but however high the price, all enjoy and recall the moment. Many people who gather to watch any ritual explain their presence with the words "This is what we enjoy." Older women say "This our duty." Ritual attracts, entertains, reminds, instructs.

When women sing and dance and feast, the voice of conscience speaks — not in a nagging whisper but a joyful shout.

Notes to Chapter 11

1. This notion of motherhood parallels that of certain areas of West Africa where "the bearing of children demonstrates that women are strong and active agents in a society," and where men and women "look upon their biological and classificatory mothers as strong and supportive figures" (Hoffer 1974: 173). Anglo-America, in contrast, has a well-documented history of treating the female reproductive role as evidence of weakness (Gordon 1976). Women are seen not as protectors but as needing "protection" (through restriction of their social rights). As Spring (1978: 167) points out, Western assumptions about motherhood have colored some anthropological accounts of women in Africa (and elsewhere).

2. See Taylor (1951: 56), Hadel (1972: 87), and Chibnik (1975: 55).

3. Some of the entries in Father Breton's annotated dictionary are quite lengthy. This one, unfortunately, simply gives the meaning of the three terms he recorded (Breton 1892: 12f.). Curiously, there seems to have been no equivalent term for the children of Carib women and African men.

4. Thousands of Africans had reached the West Indies by the time Father Breton wrote. In the preceding century (1551–1640), over 1,200 Spanish slave ships left the coast of West and West Central Africa (from

Sierra Leone to Angola), many of them bound for the West Indies (Curtin 1969: 104). Gonzalez has documented many parallels between the social life of the Black Carib and other peoples of African descent in the West Indies (see Solien 1959b; cf. Coelho 1955: 264ff.).

5. See Breton and de la Paix (1958: 13), Breton (1958: 19, 20, 24, 25), and Breton (1892: 221, 298, 373). Several of these practices have a different rationale today.

6. See Breton (1892: 282), Breton (1958: 21), and Breton and de la Paix (1958: 15).

7. Helms (1976b, 1981) argues that contemporary household structure, built around "consanguineous female cores," derives from the matrilocal extended families of the seventeenth-century Carib.

8. See Breton and de la Paix (1958: 5), Breton (1958: 4), and Breton (1892: 283). Offerings of cassava were placed on tables when shamans asked for remedies to cure "the sick person on whom the god [ancestral spirit?] has descended" (Breton 1958: 4).

9. Breton (1892: 284) recorded the word *Icheiricou* as the Carib term for *Dieu*. In the ethnographic compilation of his notes, the term is translated as "guardian spirit" (Breton 1958: 3).

10. Breton (1892: 83) defined *bóye* as "medicin . . . ou pour mieux dire, magicien, mõ [moins] medecin, &c." His comments suggest that shamans used strictly supernatural means to cure, while women often applied herbal remedies (Breton 1958: 46). For references to male and female shamans, see Breton (1892: 283), Breton (1958: 3f.), and Breton and de la Paix (1958: 5).

11. See Breton (1958: 2, 11, 44, 46), Breton (1892: 216, 269), and Breton and de la Paix (1958: 24).

12. Both Taylor (1951: 128) and Coelho (1955: 188) mention a decline in the performance of *arúmahani*.

13. According to Gonzalez (1969: 50), in the past shamans were "in most cases" men. Taylor (1951: 110) comments that female shamans "rarely if ever conduct the cult rites." When I asked several older women about this they insisted that in the past, as today, any shaman could do so. They recalled one particular man, however, "a famous *búyei,*" who usually conducted "the big ones," the most lavish events. At the time of my fieldwork, one very old man was identified as a former shaman, long since discredited and ineffectual. One young man was being "sought" by the spirits but had not yet become a shaman. Of the four women identified as shamans, two were practicing ones. The other two had chosen to "retire," one many years ago and the other rather recently.

14. For the history of John Canoe, see Dirks (1976) and Kerns and Dirks (1975). The dance has survived in Jamaica only in vestigial form (Cassidy 1961: 262). Whipple (1976) describes another processional dance, *Pia Manádi,* which Black Carib men still perform on occasion in Belize.

15. The men whom Young (1847) saw apparently were not costumed. Men (and women) do this dance and others, such as *punta,* on festive occa-

sions, but men wear costumes and perform *wanáragua* as a processional dance only at Christmas.

16. This belies Goodenough's (1970: 22) well-known assertion that the "universal tendency to male dominance over women and children . . . gives men a proprietary interest in the sexuality of women and in the labor and services that women and children can provide. Men tend to treat these things as a form of property." See di Leonardo's (1979) critique of Goodenough's argument and his use of ethnographic evidence.

17. More specifically, childbearing capacity is generally overlooked as an age-related variable; and women of childbearing age, a specific category, are implicitly equated with the general category "women" (e.g., Ortner 1974). For a comprehensive review of studies of women's status, see Quinn (1977).

18. The comments of many ethnographers suggest that older women enjoy greater freedom of movement, association, and activity. Among the most explicit are Harrell's (1981: 207) about the rural Taiwanese, Murphy and Murphy's (1974: 1051) on the Mundurucú of Brazil, Linton's (1942: 594) on the Comonche, Chiñas's (1973: 60) about the Isthmus Zapotecs of Mexico, Benet's (1974: 85) on the Abkhasians of the Soviet Union, and Mernissi's (1975: 84) about Morocco.

19. Presumably, the meaning of this is figurative. But according to Skultans (1970: 648), some Welsh women take "the change" (menopause) quite literally: "Finally, women envisage 'the change' as a period of time when certain ill-defined anatomical changes are taking place within their bodies. This was the reason most often cited to me in answer to the question as to why 'the change' was called 'the change.' One seventy-year-old lady told me that at the menopause, women turned into men inside."

20. Wallman (1978: 24, 52) argues that "there is no analytic meaning in such concepts as 'the position of women' or 'the female role' in society X or society Y." She suggests that "our particular epistemology of sex prevents an understanding of the social systems of ourselves and others by *masking variations in the significance of being female*, and . . . this significance in fact varies with . . . class, context, task, rank, race, *age*, profession, kinship, wealth, and economics — with any or all of the other dimensions of a situation of which it can form only a part" (emphasis added).

Appendix 1

KINSHIP TERMINOLOGY

The terms of reference shown below are in first-person singular form. For an explanation of the use and forms of other pronominal prefixes, see Hadel (1975 I: vi).

Consanguineal Terms	Male Speaker	Female Speaker
1. my mother	*núguchun*	*núguchun*
2. my father	*núguchin*	*núguchin*
3. my daughter	*niraü, nisáni*	*niraü, nisáni*
4. my son	*niraü, nisáni*	*niraü, nisáni*
5. my elder sister	*nítu*	*níbugaña*
6. my younger sister	*namúlalua*	*namúlalua*
7. my half-sister	as in 5 and 6	as in 5 and 6
8. my elder brother	*níbugaña*	*náti*
9. my younger brother	*namúlen*	*namúlen*
10. my half-brother	as in 8 and 9	as in 8 and 9
11. my grandmother	*nagütü*	*nagütü*
12. my grandfather	*náruguti*	*náruguti*
13. my grandchild	*nibári*	*nibári*
14. my great-grandparent	*níyuna,* or as in 11 and 12	*níyuna,* or as in 11 and 12
15. my great-grandchild	*nílawa*	*nílawa*
16. my great-great-grandchild	*nágura*	*nágura*
17. my sibling's child	*nínibu,* or as in 3 and 4	*nínibu,* or as in 3 and 4
18. my parent's sister	*naúfuri*	*naúfuri*
19. my parent's brother	*niaúrite*	*niaúrite*
20. my parent's sibling's daughter (first cousin)	as in 5 and 6	as in 5 and 6
21. my parent's sibling's son (first cousin)	as in 8 and 9	as in 8 and 9

22. my grandparent's sister	as in 11	as in 11
23. my grandparent's brother	as in 12	as in 12
24. my cousin, relative	*nidúhen*	*nidúhen*

Affinal Terms	Male Speaker	Female Speaker
1. my spouse	*númari*	*númari*
2. my spouse's mother	*nímenidi*	*nágüri*
3. my spouse's father	*nímedamuru*	*nímedamaru*
4. my daughter's spouse	*nibárimu*	*nibárimu*
5. my son's spouse	*nídiñu*	*nídiñu*
6. my spouse's sister	*nugúñau*	*nígatu*
7. my spouse's brother	*nibámu*	*nugúñau*
8. my sister's spouse	*nibámu*	*nugúñau*
9. my brother's spouse	*nugúñau*	*nígatu*

Appendix 2

RITUAL EXPENSES

The following figures show the cost of various rituals performed during 1975–76 in Belize. Most of these were average or "good" events (in terms of expense and attendance). The cost of *dügü* is atypically high because this particular one was exceptionally lavish. "Strong rum," which is usually purchased for ritual events, is diluted with an equal part of water, doubling the amount for consumption and reducing the alcoholic content (probably to about 80 proof).

Amúidahani

Food			
all ingredients for bread and "coffee" drink		$	6.00
Drink			
1 qt. strong rum			3.60
Labor			
fee for digging pit			1.00
	Total	$	10.60

Wake and Burial

Food			
25 lbs. flour		$	5.00
10 lbs. sugar			1.00
corn for "coffee" drink			1.00
misc.			1.00
	Subtotal	$	8.00
Drink			
½ gal. strong rum		$	7.25
Labor			
payment for preparing corpse for burial:			
cash		$	3.00
+ 1 qt. rum			3.60
payment to gravediggers:			
1 qt. rum			3.60

payment to carpenter for coffin			10.00
	Subtotal	$	20.20
Other Supplies			
misc. (candles, clothing for corpse, etc.)		$	15.00
	Total	$	50.45

Ninth-night Wake

Food
1 sack (96 lbs.) flour		$	18.00
25 lbs. sugar			2.50
lard			4.50
48 coconuts			3.00
yeast and spices			1.25
rice			2.00
4 lbs. corn for "coffee" drink			.75
	Subtotal	$	32.00

Drink
1 gal. strong rum		$	14.50

Labor
payment to fisherman (for conchs used in soup):			
cash		$	2.00
+ 1 pt. rum			1.80
payment to *arísaruti* (leader of novena):			
cash			2.00
+ 1 pt. rum			1.80
payment to women who decorate altar:			
1 pt. rum			1.80
payment to cooks:			
1 qt. rum			3.60
	Subtotal	$	13.00

Other Supplies
candles		$	3.25
misc.			3.00
	Subtotal	$	6.25
	Total	$	65.75

Requiem Mass and Eféduhani

Food
10 lbs. flour		$	2.00
5 lbs. sugar			.50
corn for "coffee" drink			.50
misc.			1.50
	Subtotal	$	4.50

Drink
1 qt. strong rum		$	3.60

Labor
  fee for Mass $ 2.50
Transportation
  round-trip fare for at least one adult from
  village to town to attend Requiem Mass $ 4.00

                                Total $ 14.60

Dügü

Food
  1 cow $ 50.00
  40 pans cassava bread, @ $7 ea.   280.00
  3 pigs, @ $20 ea.   60.00
  150 chickens, @ $3.50 ea.   525.00
  1 sack flour   18.00
  plantains   7.50
  rice   10.00
  70 lbs. sugar   7.00
  coffee   12.00

                            Subtotal $ 969.50

Drink
  15 gal. strong rum, @ $14.50 ea. $ 217.50
Labor
  shaman $ 40.00
  3 drummers   31.00
  5 men who built temple:
    1 gal. rum   14.50
  cooks:
    cash and rum   15.00

                            Subtotal $ 100.50

Other Supplies
  matches $ 1.50
  cigarettes   11.00

                            Subtotal $ 12.50
                            Total $1,300.00

REFERENCES

Adams, Richard N.
　　1957　*Cultural Surveys of Panama — Nicaragua — Guatemala — El Salvador —*
　　　　Honduras. Scientific Publications no. 33. Washington, D.C.: Pan
　　　　American Sanitary Bureau.
Alexander, Jack
　　1977　"The Role of the Male in the Middle-class Jamaican Family: A
　　　　Comparative Perspective." *Journal of Comparative Family Studies*
　　　　8(3): 369–89.
Amoss, Pamela, and Stevan Harrell
　　1981　"Introduction." In *Other Ways of Growing Old,* ed. Amoss and Har-
　　　　rell, pp. 1–24. Stanford: Stanford University Press.
Anonymous
　　1773　*Authentic Papers Relative to the Expedition against the Charibbs and the*
　　　　Sale of Lands in the Island of St. Vincent. London.
Anonymous [Wentworth, Trelawney]
　　1834　*The West India Sketch Book,* vol. 1. London: Whittaker and Co.
Arens, W.
　　1979　*The Man-Eating Myth: Anthropology and Anthropophagy.* New York:
　　　　Oxford University Press.
Ashcraft, Norman
　　1973　*Colonialism and Underdevelopment: Processes of Political Economic*
　　　　Change in British Honduras. New York: Columbia University
　　　　Teachers College Press.
Ashcraft, Norman, and Cedric Grant
　　1968　"The Development and Organization of Education in British
　　　　Honduras." *Comparative Education Review* 12(2): 171–79.
Beaucage, Pierre
　　1966　"Les Caraïbes noirs: trois siècles de changement social." *Anthro-*
　　　　pologica 8(2): 175–95.
　　1970　"Economic Anthropology of the Black Carib of Honduras." Ph.D.
　　　　dissertation, University of London.
Beckwith, Martha W.
　　1924　*Jamaica Anansi Stories.* New York: American Folk-Lore Society.
Benet, Sula
　　1974　*Abkhasians: Long-living People of the Caucasus.* New York: Holt,
　　　　Rinehart, & Winston.

Benezit, E.
   1976   *Dictionnaire critique et documentaire des peintres, sculpteurs, dessinateurs, et graveurs,* 10 vols. New ed. Paris: Librairie Grund.
Blake, Judith
   1961   *Family Structure in Jamaica.* New York: Free Press.
Bogue, Donald
   1971   *Demographic Techniques of Fertility Analysis.* Chicago: Community and Family Study Center.
Bolland, O. Nigel
   1977   *The Formation of a Colonial Society: Belize, from Conquest to Crown Colony.* Baltimore: Johns Hopkins University Press.
Bott, Elizabeth
   1957   *Family and Social Network.* London: Tavistock.
Bouton, Jacques
   1958   "Concerning the Savages Called Caribs." (From *Relation de l'établissement de Français depuis l'an 1635 en l'isle de Martinique,* 1640). Tr. Marshall McKusick and Pierre Verin. Human Relations Area Files, ST 13.
Brady, Eugene
   1895   "Our Trip to Belize, British Honduras." *Woodstock Letters* 24: 274–86.
Brana-Shute, Gary
   1976   "Drinking Shops and Social Structure: Some Ideas on West Indian Male Behavior." *Urban Anthropology* 5(1): 53–68.
   1979   *On the Corner: Male Life in a Paramaribo Creole Neighborhood.* Assen, The Netherlands: Van Gorcum.
Brana-Shute, Rosemary
   1976   "Women, Clubs, and Politics: The Case of a Lower-class Neighborhood in Paramaribo, Surinam." *Urban Anthropology* 5(2): 157–85.
Breton, Raymond
   1892   *Dictionnaire Caraibe-Français (Edition facsimilé).* Human Relations Area Files, ST 13.
   1958   "Observations of the Island Carib: A Compilation of Ethnographic Notes from Breton's Carib-French Dictionary (1665)." Tr. Marshall McKusick and Pierre Verin. Human Relations Area Files, ST 13.
Breton, Raymond, and Armand de la Paix
   1958   *An Account of the Island of Guadeloupe.* Tr. Thomas Turner. Human Relations Area Files, ST 13.
Brigham, William T.
   1887   *Guatemala, the Land of the Quetzal.* New York: Charles Scribner's Sons.
Bristowe, Lindsay, and Philip Wright
   1890   *The Handbook of British Honduras.* Edinburgh: Blackwood and Sons.

Buhler, Richard, S.J.
　1976　*A History of the Catholic Church in Belize*. Occasional Publications no. 4. Belize: Belize Institute of Social Research and Action.
Bujra, Janet
　1979　"Introductory: Female Solidarity and the Sexual Division of Labor." In *Women United, Women Divided: Comparative Studies of Ten Contemporary Cultures*, ed. Patricia Caplan and Janet Bujra, pp. 13–45. Bloomington: Indiana University Press.
Bullard, M. Kenyon
　1974　"Hide and Secrete: Women's Sexual Magic in Belize." *Journal of Sex Research* 10(4): 259–65.
Burdon, John A.
　1934　*Archives of British Honduras*, vol. 2. London: Sifton Praed & Co.
　1935　*Archives of British Honduras*, vol. 3. London: Sifton Praed & Co.
Carey Jones, N. S.
　1953　*The Pattern of a Dependent Economy: A Study of the National Income of British Honduras*. London: Cambridge University Press.
Cassidy, Frank
　1961　*Jamaica Talk*. London: Macmillan and Co.
Cayetano, Eldred Roy
　1977　"Garífuna Songs of Mourning." *Belizean Studies* 5(2): 17–22.
Census Research Programme (CRP)
　1975　*1970 Population Census of the Commonwealth Caribbean*, vol. 4, pt. 16, "Economic Activity, Occupation, and Industry." Kingston: University of the West Indies.
Central Bureau of Statistics (CBS)
　1948　*West Indian Census*, vol. 1, pt. E, "British Honduras." Kingston.
Chamberlain, Cynthia
　1979　"Ritual Possession Trance and Ancestor Illness among the *Garífuna* of Honduras: An Analysis of the *Gubída* Cult." M.A. thesis, Louisiana State University.
Charles, Cecil
　1890　*Honduras: Land of Great Depths*. New York: Rand McNally.
Chibnik, Michael
　1975　"Economic Strategies of Small Farmers in Stann Creek District, British Honduras." Ph.D. dissertation, Columbia University.
Chiñas, Beverly
　1973　*The Isthmus Zapotecs: Women's Roles in Cultural Context*. New York: Holt, Rinehart & Winston.
Clarke, Edith
　1966　*My Mother Who Fathered Me*. Second ed. London: Allen & Unwin.
Coelho, Ruy
　1949　"The Significance of the Couvade among the Black Carib." *Man* 49: no. 64.
　1955　"The Black Carib of Honduras: A Study in Acculturation." Ph.D. dissertation, Northwestern University.

Cohen, Yehudi
  1955   "Character Formation and Social Structure in a Jamaican Com-
          munity." *Psychiatry* 18(3): 275–96.
  1956   "Structure and Function: Family Organization and Socialization
          in a Jamaican Community." *American Anthropologist* 58(4): 664–86.
  1971   "Four Categories of Interpersonal Relationships in the Family
          and Community in a Jamaican Village." In *Peoples and Cultures of
          the Caribbean,* ed. Michael Horowitz, pp. 412–35. Garden City,
          N.Y.: Natural History Press.
Coke, Thomas
  1789   "Some Account of the Late Missionaries to the West Indies in
          Two Letters to the Rev. J. Wesley." In *Journal and Addresses* [of
          Thomas Coke], Schomberg Collection of Negro Literature and
          History, New York Public Library.
Collver, Andrew, and Eleanor Langlois
  1962   "The Female Labor Force in Metropolitan Areas: An Interna-
          tional Comparison." *Economic Development and Cultural Change*
          10(4): 367–85.
Colonial Office
  1861   "Blue Book of Statistics for the Colony of British Honduras."
          C.O. 128/42. Public Records Office at Kew, England.
Columbus, Christopher
  1968   *The Journal of Christopher Columbus.* Tr. Cecil Jane. London: An-
          thony Bland.
Comfort, Alex
  1956   *The Biology of Senescence.* London: Routledge & Kegan Paul.
Comitas, Lambros
  1977   *The Complete Caribbeana, 1900–1975: A Bibliographic Guide to the
          Scholarly Literature,* 3 vols. Millwood, N.Y.: KTO Press.
Conzemius, Eduard
  1928   "Ethnographical Notes on the Black Carib *(Garif).*" *American An-
          thropologist* 30(2): 183–205.
  1930   "Sur les Garif ou Caraibes noirs de l'Amérique Centrale." *Journal
          of the Royal Anthropological Institute* 25: 859–77.
Cosminsky, Sheila
  n.d.   "Birth Rituals and Symbolism: A Quiché Maya-Black Carib
          Comparison." Unpublished ms.
  1976   "Medicinal Plants of the Black Carib." *Actes du XLII⁴ Congrès Inter-
          national des Américanistes* 6: 535–52.
Cowgill, Donald, and Lowell Holmes
  1972   "Summary and Conclusions: The Theory in Review." In *Aging
          and Modernization,* ed. Donald Cowgill and Lowell Holmes, pp.
          305–23. New York: Appleton-Century-Croft.
Crowe, Frederick
  1850   *The Gospel in Central America.* London: Charles Gilpin.

Cumming, Elaine, and David Schneider
   1961   "Sibling Solidarity: A Property of American Kinship." *American Anthropologist* 63: 498–507.
Curtin, Phillip
   1969   *The Atlantic Slave Trade: A Census.* Madison: University of Wisconsin Press.
Davenport, William
   1961   "The Family System of Jamaica." *Social and Economic Studies* 10(4): 420–54.
Davidson, George
   1787   "The Copy of a Letter from a Gentleman in the Island of St. Vincent . . . Containing a Short History of the Caribbs." In *The Case of the Caribbs in St. Vincent,* pp. 6–21. London.
Davidson, William V.
   1974   *Historical Geography of the Bay Islands, Honduras.* Birmingham, Ala.: Southern University Press.
   1976a "Black Carib *(Garífuna)* Habitats in Central America." In *Frontier Adaptations in Lower Central America,* ed. Mary W. Helms and Franklin O. Loveland, pp. 85–94. Philadelphia: Institute for the Study of Human Issues.
   1976b "Dispersal of the *Garífuna* in the Western Caribbean." *Actes du XLIIᵉ Congrès International des Américanistes* 6: 467–74.
Davis, Richard
   1973   "Muang Matrifocality." *Journal of the Siam Society* 61: 53–62.
Department of Statistics
   1961   *West Indies Population Census: Census of British Honduras.* 2 vols. Kingston: Jamaica Tabulation Centre.
di Leonardo, Micaela
   1979   "Methodology and the Misinterpretation of Women's Status in Kinship Studies: A Case Study of Goodenough and the Definition of Marriage." *American Ethnologist* 6(4): 627–37.
Dillon, A. Barrow
   1923   *Geography of British Honduras.* London: Waterlow and Sons.
Dirks, Robert
   1972   "Networks, Groups, and Adaptation in an Afro-Caribbean Community." *Man* 7(4): 565–85.
   1976   "John Canoe: Ethnohistorical and Comparative Analysis of Carib Dance." *Actes du XLIIᵉ Congrès International des Américanistes* 6: 513–23.
Dirks, Robert, and Virginia Kerns
   1976   "Mating Patterns and Adaptive Change in Rum Bay, 1823–1970." *Social and Economic Studies* 25(1): 34–54.
Dobson, Narda
   1973   *History of Belize.* London: Longman.
Du Tertre, Jean-Baptiste
   1958   "Concerning the Natives of the Antilles." (From *Histoire générale des*

isles . . . dans l'Amérique, 1667.) Tr. Marshall McKusick and Pierre Verin. Human Relations Area Files, ST 13.

Duval, Benjamin
1879   *A Narrative of Life and Travels in Mexico and British Honduras.* Boston: W. F. Brown and Company.

Dwyer, Daisy Hilse
1978   "Ideologies of Sexual Inequality and Strategies for Change in Male-Female Relations." *American Ethnologist* 5(2): 227-40.

Edwards, Bryan
1794   *The History, Civil and Commercial, of the British West Indies,* vols. 1 and 2. Second ed. London: John Stockdale.
1801   *The History, Civil and Commercial, of the British West Indies,* vol. 3. Second ed. London: John Stockdale.
1819   *The History, Civil and Commercial, of the British West Indies,* 5 vols. Fifth ed. London: John Stockdale.

Erikson, Erik
1964   "Inner and Outer Space: Reflections on Womanhood." *Daedulus* 93(2): 582-606.

Evans-Pritchard, E. E.
1974   *Nuer Religion.* New York: Oxford University Press.

Exquemelin, Alexandre
1951   *Buccaneers of America.* Reprint of 1684 ed. London: Allen & Unwin.

Firth, Raymond, and Judith Djamour
1956   "Kinship in South Borough." In *Two Studies of Kinship in London,* ed. Raymond Firth, pp. 33-63. London: Athlone Press.

Firth, Raymond, Jane Hubert, and Anthony Forge
1969   *Families and Their Relatives: Kinship in a Middle-class Sector of London.* London: Routledge & Kegan Paul.

Floyd, Troy
1967   *The Anglo-Spanish Struggle for Mosquitia.* Albuquerque: University of New Mexico Press.

Fowler, Henry
1879   *A Narrative of a Journey across the Unexplored Portion of British Honduras with a Short Sketch of the History and Resources of the Colony.* Belize: Government Press.

Fox, Robin
1967   *Kinship and Marriage.* Harmondsworth: Penguin.

Friedl, Ernestine
1967   "The Position of Women—Appearance and Reality." *Anthropological Quarterly* 40(3): 97-108.

Froebel, Julius
1859   *Seven Years' Travel in Central America, Northern Mexico, and the Far West of the United States.* London: R. Bentley.

Galindo, Juan
1833   "Notice of the Caribs in Central America." *Journal of the Royal Geographic Society* 3: 290-91.

Geertz, Hildred
1961 *The Javanese Family: A Study of Kinship and Socialization.* New York: Free Press.
Gibbs, Archibald R.
1883 *British Honduras: An Historical and Descriptive Account of the Colony from Its Settlement, 1670.* London: S. Low, Marston, Searle, & Rivington.
Gonzalez, Nancie
1965 "Reply to Taylor." *American Anthropologist* 67(6): 1526–27.
1969 *Black Carib Household Structure.* Seattle: University of Washington Press.
1970a "Toward a Definition of Matrifocality." In *Afro-American Anthropology,* ed. Norman E. Whitten, Jr., and John F. Szwed, pp. 231–44. New York: Free Press.
1970b "Cakchiqueles and Caribs: The Social Context of Field Work." In *Marginal Natives: Anthropologists at Work,* ed. Morris Freilich, pp. 153–84. New York: Harper and Row.
Goodenough, Ward
1970 *Description and Comparison in Cultural Anthropology.* Chicago: Aldine.
Gordon, Linda
1976 *Woman's Body, Woman's Right: A Social History of Birth Control in America.* New York: Grassman.
Graves, Algernon
1970 *The Royal Academy of Arts: A Complete Dictionary of Contributors and Their Work from Its Foundation in 1769 to 1904,* 4 vols. Reprint of 1905 ed. East Ardsley: S. R. Publishers.
Great Britain
1860 *Calendar of State Papers, Colonial Series, America and West Indies, 1574–1660.* London: Her Majesty's Stationery Office.
1870 "British Honduras." In *British Parliamentary Papers,* "Reports on the State of Her Majesty's Colonial Possessions," vol. 49, pt. 1, pp. 17–35. London: Her Majesty's Stationery Office.
1880 *Calendar of State Papers, Colonial Series, America and West Indies, 1661–68.* London: Her Majesty's Stationery Office.
1889 *Calendar of State Papers, Colonial Series, America and West Indies, 1669–74.* London: Her Majesty's Stationery Office.
1933 *Calendar of State Papers, Colonial Series, America and West Indies, January, 1719 to February, 1720.* London: His Majesty's Stationery Office.
Greenfield, Sidney
1966 *English Rustics in Black Skin.* New Haven: College and University Press.
Gullick, C. J.
1976 *Exiled from St. Vincent.* Malta: Progress Press.

Hadel, Richard E., S.J.
  1972 "Carib Folk Songs and Carib Culture." Ph.D. dissertation, University of Texas, Austin.
  1975 *A Dictionary of Central American Carib,* 3 vols. Belize: Belize Institute of Social Research and Action.
Hafez, E. S. E.
  1978 *Human Reproductive Physiology.* Ann Arbor: Ann Arbor Science Publishers.
Harrell, Stevan
  1981 "Growing Old in Rural Taiwan." In *Other Ways of Growing Old,* ed. Pamela Amoss and Stevan Harrell, pp. 193–210. Stanford: Stanford University Press.
Helms, Mary W.
  1976a "Introduction." In *Frontier Adaptations in Lower Central America,* ed. Mary W. Helms and Franklin O. Loveland, pp. 1–22. Philadelphia: Institute for the Study of Human Issues.
  1976b "Domestic Organization in Eastern Central America: The San Blas Cuna, Miskito, and Black Carib Compared." *Western Canadian Journal of Anthropology* 6(3): 133–63.
  1981 "Black Carib Domestic Organization in Historical Perspective: Traditional Origins of Contemporary Patterns." *Ethnology* 20(1): 77–86.
Henderson, G.
  1809 *An Account of the British Settlement of Honduras.* London: Baldwin.
Henriques, Fernando
  1968 *Family and Colour in Jamaica.* Second ed. London: MacGibbon and Kee.
Herskovits, Melville
  1937 *Life in a Haitian Valley.* New York: Alfred A. Knopf.
  1958 *The Myth of the Negro Past.* Boston: Beacon Press.
Herskovits, Melville, and Frances Herskovits
  1947 *Trinidad Village.* New York: Alfred A. Knopf.
Hoch-Smith, Judith, and Anita Spring, eds.
  1978 *Women in Ritual and Symbolic Roles.* New York: Plenum Press.
Hoffer, Carol
  1974 "Madam Yoko: Ruler of the Kpa Mende Confederation." In *Woman, Culture, and Society,* ed. Michelle Z. Rosaldo and Louise Lamphere, pp. 173–87. Stanford: Stanford University Press.
Horowitz, Michael
  1967 *Morne-Paysan, Peasant Village in Martinique.* New York: Holt, Rinehart & Winston.
Huxley, Aldous
  1934 *Beyond the Mexique Bay.* London: Chatto and Windus.
Jackson, Anthony
  1971 "Kinship, Suicide and Pictographs among the Na-Khi (S.W. China)." *Ethnos* 36: 52–93.

1979   *Na-Khi Religion: An Analytical Appraisal of the Na-Khi Ritual Texts.* The Hague: Mouton.

Keesing, Roger
   1966   "Kwaio Kindreds." *Southwestern Journal of Anthropology* 22(4): 346–55.

Kelsey, Vera, and Lilly de Jonghe Osborne
   1943   *Four Keys to Guatemala.* Revised ed. New York: Funk & Wagnalls.

Kerns, Virginia
   1976   "Black Carib *(Garífuna)* Paternity Rituals." *Actes du XLIIe Congrès International des Américanistes* 6: 513–23.
   1977   "Third-Generation Research on the Black Carib: Bridging the Generation Gap." Paper presented at the annual meeting of the American Anthropological Association, Houston.
   in   "Past and Present Evidence of Inter-ethnic Mating." In *Current*
   press   *Developments in Anthropological Genetics: Population Structure of the Black Caribs,* vol. 3, ed. Michael Crawford. New York: Plenum Press.

Kerns, Virginia, and Robert Dirks
   1975   "John Canoe." *National Studies* 3(6): 1–15.

Labat, Jean-Baptiste
   1970   *The Memoirs of Père Labat.* Tr. and ed. John Eaden. London: Frank Cass.

Labor Department
   1971   *Annual Report of the Labor Department for the Years 1970 and 1971.* Belize: Government Printer.
   1972   *Annual Report of the Labor Department for the Year 1972.* Belize: Government Printer.

Laguerre, Michel
   1978   "Ticouloute and His Kinfolk: The Study of a Haitian Extended Family." In *The Extended Family in Black Societies,* ed. Demitri Shimkin,, Edith Shimkin, and Dennis Frate, pp. 407–45. The Hague: Mouton.

Las Casas, Bartolomé de
   1656   *The Tears of the Indians.* London.
   1971   *History of the Indies.* Tr. and ed. Andrée Collard. New York: Harper and Row.

Leacock, Eleanor
   1978   "Women's Status in Egalitarian Society: Implications for Social Evolution." *Current Anthropology* 19(2): 247–75.

Linton, Ralph
   1942   "Age and Sex Categories." *American Sociological Review* 7(5): 589–603.

Little, Kenneth
   1948   "The Changing Position of Women in the Sierra Leone Protectorate." *Africa* 18: 1–17.

MacCormack, Carol
   1980   "Nature, Culture and Gender: A Critique." In *Nature, Culture, and*

Gender, ed. Carol MacCormack and Marilyn Strathern, pp. 1–24. Cambridge: Cambridge University Press.

Macklin, Catherine
1972 "Aspects of Black Carib Religion." B.A. thesis, Harvard University.
1976 "The Garífuna 'Thanksgiving.'" *Belizean Studies* 4(6): 1–6.

McMahon, A. W., Jr., and P. J. Rhudick
1964 "Reminiscing: Adaptational Significance in the Aged." *Archives of General Psychiatry* 10: 292–98.
1967 "Reminiscing in the Aged: An Adaptational Response." In *Psychodynamic Studies on Aging,* ed. Sidney Levin and Robert Kahana, pp. 64–78. New York: International Universities Press.

Maher, Vanessa
1976 "Kin, Clients, and Accomplices: Relationships among Women in Morocco." In *Sexual Divisions and Society: Process and Change,* ed. Diana Baker and Sheila Allen, pp. 52–75. London: Tavistock.

Marks, Arnaud
1976 *Male and Female in the Afro-Curaçaoan Household.* The Hague: Martinus Nijhoff.

Marshall, Bernard
1973 "The Black Caribs — Native Resistance to British Penetration into the Windward Side of St. Vincent 1763–1773." *Caribbean Quarterly* 9(4): 4–19.

Matthews, Basil
1971 *The Crisis of the West Indian Family.* Reprint of 1953 ed. Westport, Conn.: Greenwood Press.

Maudslay, Anne C., and Alfred P. Maudslay
1899 *A Glimpse of Guatemala.* London: John Murray.

May, Jacques, and Donna McLellan
1972 *The Ecology of Malnutrition in Mexico and Central America.* Studies in Medical Geography vol. 2. New York: Hafner Publishing Co.

Mayer, Adrian
1966 "The Significance of Quasi-Groups in the Study of Complex Societies." In *The Social Anthropology of Complex Societies,* ed. Michael Banton, pp. 97–122. New York: Praeger.

Mernissi, Fatima
1975 *Beyond the Veil: Male-Female Dynamics in a Modern Muslim Society.* Cambridge: Schenkman Publishing Company.

Mertz, R. E.
1976 "The Effect of Father-Absence on the Development of Psychological Differentiation among Black Carib Students in Belize." Ph.D. dissertation, University of Arizona.

Metzgen, Monrad, and Henry Cain
1925 *The Handbook of British Honduras.* London: West India Committee.

Ministry of Education
1972 *Primary Education Rules.* Belmopan, Belize.

Mintz, Sidney
　1966　"The Caribbean as a Socio-cultural Area." *Cahiers d'Histoire Mon-diale* 9(4): 912–37.
　1968　"Caribbean Society." In *International Encyclopedia of the Social Sciences,* ed. David Sills, 2: 306–19. New York: Macmillan and Free Press.
Mogey, John M.
　1956　*Family and Neighborhood.* London: Oxford University Press.
Montgomery, George W.
　1839　*Narrative of a Journey to Guatemala and Central America in 1838.* New York: Wiley & Putnam.
Moore, Sally Falk
　1978　"Old Age in a Life-Term Social Arena: Some Chagga of Kiliman-jaro in 1974." In *Life's Career—Aging,* ed. Barbara Myerhoff and Andrei Simic, pp. 23–76. Beverly Hills: Sage Publications.
Morlan, Albert
　1892　*A Hoosier in Honduras.* Indianapolis: El Dorado Publishing Co.
Morris, Daniel
　1883　*The Colony of British Honduras, Its Resources and Prospects.* London: Edward Stanford.
Munroe, Robert, Ruth Munroe, and John Whiting
　1973　"The Couvade: A Psychological Analysis." *Ethos* 1: 30–74.
Murphy, Yolanda, and Robert Murphy
　1974　*Women of the Forest.* New York: Columbia University Press.
Myerhoff, Barbara
　1978　"Bobbes and Zeydes: Old and New Roles for Elderly Jews." In *Women in Ritual and Symbolic Roles,* ed. Judith Hoch-Smith and Anita Spring, pp. 207–41. New York: Plenum Press.
Okley, Judith
　1975　"Gypsy Women: Models in Conflict." In *Perceiving Women,* ed. Shirley Ardener, pp. 55–86. New York: John Wiley.
Ortner, Sherry
　1974　"Is Female to Male as Nature Is to Culture?" In *Woman, Culture, and Society,* ed. Michelle Z. Rosaldo and Louise Lamphere, pp. 67–87. Stanford: Stanford University Press.
Otterbein, Keith
　1966　*The Andros Islanders.* Social Science Studies no. 14. Lawrence: University of Kansas Publications.
Otterbein, Keith, and Charlotte Otterbein
　1977　"A Stochastic Process Analysis of the Developmental Cycle of the Andros Household." *Ethnology* 16(4): 415–25.
Palacio, Joseph
　1973　"Carib Ancestral Rites: A Brief Analysis." *National Studies* 1(3): 3–8.
Pim, Bedford
　1863　*The Gateway of the Pacific.* London: Lowell Reeve and Co.

Poggie, John, Jr., and Pertti Pelto
   1969   "Matrilateral Asymmetry in the American Kinship System." *Anthropological Quarterly* 42(1): 1-15.
Potter, Sulamith Heins
   1977   *Family Life in a Northern Thai Village: A Study in the Structural Significance of Women.* Berkeley: University of California Press.
Price, Richard
   1973   "Introduction." In *Maroon Societies,* ed. Richard Price, pp. 1-30. Garden City, N.Y.: Anchor Press.
Quinn, Naomi
   1977   "Anthropological Studies of Women's Status." *Annual Review of Anthropology* 6: 181-225.
Roberts, Orlando
   1827   *Narrative of Voyages and Excursions on the East Coast and in the Interior of Central America.* Edinburgh: Constable.
Rodman, Hyman
   1971   *Lower-class Families: The Culture of Poverty in Negro Trinidad.* New York: Oxford University Press.
Romney, D. H., et al.
   1959   *Land in British Honduras.* Colonial Research Publications no. 24. London: Her Majesty's Stationery Office.
Rosaldo, Michelle Z.
   1974   "Women, Culture, and Society: A Theoretical Overview." In *Woman, Culture, and Society,* ed. Michelle Z. Rosaldo and Louise Lamphere, pp. 17-42. Stanford: Stanford University Press.
   1980   "The Use and Abuse of Anthropology: Reflections on Feminism and Cross-Cultural Understanding." *Signs* 5(3): 389-417.
Rouse, Irving
   1948a "The Arawak." In *Handbook of South American Indians,* ed. Julian Steward, 4: 507-39. Washington, D.C.: Government Printing Office.
   1948b "The Carib." In *Handbook of South American Indians,* ed. Julian Steward, 4: 547-65. Washington, D.C.: Government Printing Office.
Sanborn, Helen
   1886   *A Winter in Central America and Mexico.* Boston: Lee and Shepard.
Sanday, Peggy
   1981   *Female Power and Male Dominance.* New York: Cambridge University Press.
Sanford, Margaret
   1971   "Disruption of the Mother-Child Relationship in Conjunction with Matrifocality: A Study of Child-Keeping among the Carib and Creole of British Honduras." Ph.D. dissertation, Catholic University of America.
Sauer, Carl O.
   1966   *The Early Spanish Main.* Berkeley: University of California Press.

Sawatsky, Harry
  1969 *Mennonite Settlement in British Honduras.* Berkeley: Department of Geography, University of California.
Sheldon, William
  1820 "Brief Account of the Caraibs, Who Inhabited the Antilles." *Transactions and Collections of the American Antiquarian Society* 1: 365-433.
Shephard, Charles
  1831 *An Historical Account of the Island of St. Vincent.* London: W. Nichol.
Shimkin, Demitri, Edith Shimkin, and Dennis Frate, eds.
  1978 *The Extended Family in Black Societies.* The Hague: Mouton.
Skultans, Vieda
  1970 "The Symbolic Significance of Menstruation and Menopause." *Man* 5(4): 639-51.
Slater, Mariam K.
  1977 *The Caribbean Family: Legitimacy in the Caribbean.* New York: St. Martin's Press.
Smith, Michael G.
  1962a *Kinship and Community in Carriacou.* New Haven: Yale University Press.
  1962b *West Indian Family Structure.* Seattle: University of Washington Press.
Smith, Raymond T.
  1956 *The Negro Family in British Guiana.* London: Routledge & Kegan Paul.
  1960 "The Family in the Caribbean." In *Caribbean Studies: A Symposium,* ed. Vera Rubin, pp. 67-79. Second ed. Seattle: University of Washington Press.
  1971 "Culture and Social Structure in the Caribbean: Some Recent Work on Family and Kinship Studies." In *Black Society in the New World,* ed. Richard Frucht, pp. 251-72. New York: Random House.
  1973 "The Matrifocal Family." In *The Character of Kinship,* ed. Jack Goody, pp. 121-44. London: Cambridge University Press.
  1978 "The Family and the Modern World System: Some Observations from the Caribbean." *Journal of Family History* 3: 337-60.
Solien, Nancie
  1959a "The Nonunilineal Descent Group in the Caribbean and Central America." *American Anthropologist* 61(4): 578-83.
  1959b "West Indian Characteristics of the Black Carib." *Southwestern Journal of Anthropology* 15(4): 300-307.
  1960 "Changes in Black Carib Kinship Terminology." *Southwestern Journal of Anthropology* 16(2): 144-59.
Spring, Anita
  1978 "Epidemiology of Spirit Possession among the Luvale of Zambia." In *Women in Ritual and Symbolic Roles,* ed. Judith Hoch-Smith and Anita Spring, pp. 165-90. New York: Plenum Press.

Squier, E. G.
  1855 *Notes on Central America.* New York: Harper.
  1870 *Honduras; Descriptive, Historical, and Statistical.* New York: Trübner
         & Co.
Stack, Carol
  1974 *All Our Kin: Strategies for Survival in a Black Community.* New York:
         Harper and Row.
Staples, Robert
  1972 "The Matricentric Family System: A Cross-Cultural Examina-
         tion." *Journal of Marriage and the Family* 34(1): 156–65.
Stephens, John Lloyd
  1841 *Incidents of Travel in Central America, Chiapas, and Yucatan,* vol. 1.
         New York: Harper and Brothers.
Stuart, Bertie A. Cohen
  1979 *Women in the Caribbean: A Bibliography.* Leiden: Department of
         Caribbean Studies, Royal Institute of Linguistics and
         Anthropology.
Swett, Charles
  1867 *A Trip to British Honduras and to San Pedro, Republic of Honduras.*
         New Orleans: Price Current.
Tanner, Nancy
  1974 "Matrifocality in Indonesia and Africa and among Black
         Americans." In *Woman, Culture, and Society,* ed. Michelle Z.
         Rosaldo and Louise Lamphere, pp. 129–56. Stanford: Stanford
         University Press.
Taylor, Douglas
  1946 "Kinship and Social Structure of the Island Carib." *Southwestern
         Journal of Anthropology* 2(6): 180–213.
  1949 "The Interpretation of Some Documentary Evidence on Carib
         Culture." *Southwestern Journal of Anthropology* 5(4): 379–92.
  1951 *The Black Carib of British Honduras.* Viking Fund Publications in
         Anthropology no. 17. New York: Wenner-Gren.
  1961 "New Languages for Old in the West Indies." *Comparative Studies in
         Society and History* 3: 277–88.
  1965a "A Biased View: A Rebuttal to Solien." *American Anthropologist*
         67(6): 1524–26.
  1965b "Tradition in Black Carib Kinship Terminology." *International
         Journal of American Linguistics.* 31(3): 286–91.
Thieme, Ulrich
  1953- *Allgemeines Lexikon der bildenden Künstler von der Antike bis Gegenwart,*
    62 37 vols. Leipzig: E. A. Seemann.
United Nations
  1978 *Statistical Yearbook, 1977.* New York: United Nations Publishing
         Service.
Uring, Nathaniel
  1727 *A History of the Voyages and Travels of Captain Nathaniel Uring.* Second
         ed. London: Clarke.

Valois, Alfred de
  1861 *Méxique, Havane et Guatemala: notes de voyage.* Paris: Collection Het-
         zel, E. Dentu.
Wallace, Anthony F. C.
  1971 "Handsome Lake and the Decline of the Iroquois Matriarchate."
         In *Kinship and Culture,* ed. Francis Hsu, pp. 367–76. Chicago:
         Aldine.
Wallman, Sandra
  1978 "Epistemologies of Sex." In *Female Hierarchies,* ed. Lionel Tiger and
         Heather Fowler, pp. 21–59. Chicago: Beresford Book Service.
Weil, Simone
  1952 *The Need for Roots.* Tr. Arthur Wills. New York: Putnam.
Weiner, Annette
  1976 *Women of Value, Men of Renown: New Perspectives in Trobriand Ex-
         change.* Austin: University of Texas Press.
Wells, Marilyn
  1980 "Circling with the Ancestors: Hugulendii Symbolism in Ethnic
         Group Maintenance." *Belizean Studies* 8(6): 1–9.
Whipple, Emory
  1976 "Pia Manadi." *Belizean Studies* 4(4): 1–18.
Whitten, Norman E., Jr.
  1974 *Black Frontiersmen.* New York: Halsted (Wiley).
Whitten, Norman E., Jr., and John F. Szwed
  1970 "Introduction." In *Afro-American Anthropology,* ed. Norman E.
         Whitten, Jr., and John F. Szwed, pp. 23–60. New York: Free
         Press.
Whitten, Norman E., Jr., and Alvin Wolfe
  1973 "Network Analysis." In *Handbook of Social and Cultural Anthropology,*
         ed. John Honigmann, pp. 717–46. Chicago: Rand McNally.
Whyte, Martin
  1978 *The Status of Women in Preindustrial Societies.* Princeton: Princeton
         University Press.
Wilmott, Peter, and Michael Young
  1960 *Family and Class in a London Suburb.* London: Routledge & Kegan
         Paul.
Wilson, Peter
  1971 "Caribbean Crews: Peer Groups and Male Society." *Caribbean
         Studies* 10(4): 18–34.
  1973 *Crab Antics: The Social Anthropology of English-speaking Negro Societies
         of the Caribbean.* New Haven: Yale University Press.
Yanagisako, Sylvia J.
  1977 "Woman-Centered Kin Networks in Urban Bilateral Kinship."
         American Ethnologist 4(2): 207–26.
Young, Michael
  1954 "Kinship and Family in East London." *Man* 54: no. 210.

Young, Michael, and Peter Wilmott
  1957   *Family and Kinship in East London.* London: Routledge & Kegan
          Paul.
Young, Thomas
  1847   *Narrative of a Residence on the Mosquito Shore.* London: Smith, Elder
          and Co.
Young, William
  1795   *An Account of the Black Charaibs in the Island of St. Vincent's.* London.
  1801   "A Tour through the Several Islands of Barbadoes, St. Vincent,
          Antigua, Tobago, and Grenada in the Years 1791 and 1792." In
          Bryan Edwards, *The History, Civil and Commercial, of the British West
          Indies,* 3: 259–301. Second ed. London: John Stockdale.

INDEX